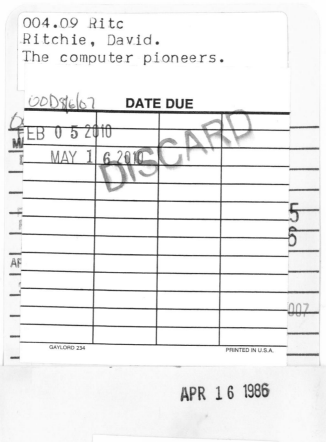

# BY DAVID RITCHIE

# THE COMPUTER PIONEERS

# THE MAKING OF THE MODERN COMPUTER

Simon and Schuster
New York

Published by Simon and Schuster
A Division of Simon & Schuster, Inc.
Simon & Schuster Building
Rockefeller Center
1230 Avenue of the Americas
New York, New York 10020

SIMON AND SCHUSTER and colophon are registered trademarks of
Simon & Schuster, Inc.

Designed by Bonni Leon
Manufactured in the United States of America

1   3   5   7   9   10   8   6   4   2

Library of Congress Cataloging in Publication Data

Ritchie, David, date.
The computer pioneers.

Bibliography: p.
Includes index.
1. Computers—History.   I. Title.
QA76.17.R58   1986        004′.09        85–22237
ISBN 0-671-52397-X

# ACKNOWLEDGMENTS

So many persons helped with the making of this book that it would be impossible to list them all here. Special thanks must go to my literary agent, Carol Mann; the libraries of Virginia Polytechnic Institute and the University of Virginia; and the men and women who agreed to share their memories of computers for this project, including I. J. Good, George Stibitz, Kathleen Wicker, and Thomas Andrews.

*To Dr. Fred Diehl*

# CONTENTS

# PREFACE

When Howard Aiken, one of the preeminent figures in the making of modern computers, was asked to contribute his reminiscences to an oral history of the computer, he pointed to a shelf full of technical papers and doctoral dissertations and said, "*There* is the history of computing!"

In a sense Aiken was right. The story of the computer is, in the final analysis, a history of machines and the concepts they embodied. But there is a human dimension to the history of computing as well, and this book tries to convey something of that human element: the colorful personalities, the collaborations and conflicts that shaped the development of the modern computer.

With this human dimension added, the computer's history is much easier to understand, for the evolution of computers was determined as much by who said what to whom over lunch as by the solution of $f(x) = y$. Some of the men and women you are about to meet are the Newtons, Edisons, and Faradays of our time. I hope I have done justice to them and to their work.

Besides introducing the reader to some of the personalities involved in modern computer history, this book tries to correct some widely repeated misconceptions and errors of fact. Total accuracy is of course difficult to achieve. As those famous chroniclers of computer history, N. Metropolis and J. Worlton, point out, "A history is by its nature an approximation to the reality that was." Some histories of computers have been more approximate than others, however, and in consequence numerous errors—some of them minor, but many gross—have found their way into print. Once there, they have proven extremely hard to eradicate. To paraphrase Mark Twain, the difference between a cat and a historian's error is that the cat has only nine lives.

In my effort to correct as many of those errors as possible, I was aided greatly by the writings and the kind cooperation of many men and women who were intimately involved in the making of the machines described here. It is sad to have to report, however, that some computer pioneers refused to be interviewed for this work because they had grown disgusted with the inexcusable blunders in certain earlier books; they were unwilling to risk getting misquoted and misrepresented in another "goddamned history," as one well-known computer expert put it. "I've been burned too often," said another. "I won't cooperate in the making of anything unless it's a scholarly bibliography—not a work of journalism." Such attitudes are understandable but do little or nothing to halt the perpetuation of errors. So the assistance of those who did agree to help with this project is doubly appreciated.

Wherever possible, I have used what historians call primary sources: interviews with or writings by the individuals who figure in this story. This policy helps greatly in maintaining accuracy. I have also made every effort to separate fact from surmise and conjecture and to avoid presenting the last two as the first.

Partly because so many human figures participate in it, the history of the computer, like any other branch of history, may be viewed and recounted from many different, and often conflicting, viewpoints. Sometimes the final result is universal agreement on what really happened, but more often the outcome reminds one of Kurosawa's film *Rashomon:* five different witnesses to an event will relate five different impressions of it.

This "Rashomon effect" often leads to controversy in cases where two or more individuals have strongly dissimilar recollections of the same person or event. Where disagreements exist, I have tried to present information from all relevant viewpoints, in the interest of both fairness and accuracy.

Some of what is written here will probably set off heated dispute. Therefore I hope readers will keep in mind that this project was intended not to ignite controversy or anger but to bring the written history of computers closer to "the reality that was."

*Hampton, Virginia*
*January 15, 1985*

*Invention breeds invention*
*—Ralph Waldo Emerson,*

*"Works and Days"*

# 1
# FROM ABACI TO NUMBER SIEVES

In 1938 the Works Progress Administration (WPA), one of the federal agencies set up to provide employment during the Great Depression, launched its Mathematical Tables Project. As its name indicates, the project involved boiling down large amounts of statistical data into tabular form. Most of the work was the purest drudgery—scribbling calculations on sheets of paper—and to do it the WPA hired several dozen New Yorkers from the unemployment rolls.

These men and women worked in a New York City stable that had been abandoned by its previous tenant and taken over by the government. Equipped only with pencil and paper the human calculators sat in four groups, facing the walls of the room, carrying out arithmetic. The first group handled addition, the second group subtraction, and the third group multiplication; the fourth group carried out division and checked the work of the other three. The WPA workers used black pencil to write

down positive numbers and red to indicate negative numbers.
Posted on the wall in front of each group was a set of simple
instructions. Those for the addition group read:

> Black plus black makes black.
> Red plus red makes red.
> Black plus red or red plus black,
>     hand the sheets to group 2.

Such was computing before the age of the modern computer.
The computer as we know it was unknown when Herbert
Hoover occupied the White House. At that time a "computer"
was not a machine at all, but rather a human—in most cases a
woman—who sat at a desk doing arithmetic on a hand-cranked
adding machine or desk computer, as it was sometimes called.

To carry out a long addition, the operator had to punch in
numbers, turn the crank, read the total off a paper-roll printout
or set of dials, and write down the total for accuracy's sake. This
was known as leaving an audit trail, and it was essential for re-
tracing her steps if the calculation later went awry and had to be
redone. Then she would reenter that total, punch in the next
number to be added, and repeat the whole process. The operator's arm got tired after a few hours of cranking and scribbling.
It was like trying to start a balky Model T and write a letter simultaneously.

Around 1930, electric motors were added to some of these
adding machines, but computing remained a tedious and error-
prone process. Mistakes increased dramatically over time. After
a few hours, it was all too easy to misread a 6 as a 0, or hit the 9
key instead of the adjacent 8, and throw off the calculation.
When that happened, one had to follow the audit trail backward, find the error, and start again from that point.

This eye-straining and arm-breaking labor was measured in
units called girl-hours. The primitive mechanical calculating
devices of the late twenties have since developed into electronic
marvels that, in a fraction of a second, can carry out feats of calculation that would have required a whole girl-hour in 1925.

Between about 1925 and 1950, a set of computing devices
smoothly spanned the chasm between the purely mechanical

computers of the 1800s and early 1900s and the digital electronic computers of today. Each of these transitional machines, some made in Europe but most of them built in America, was unique; each contributed something to the computers we now find in our offices, homes, and pockets; and together these devices form the nucleus of one of the most fascinating stories in the history of science and invention. Since that story has its roots in events of the past few centuries, a little background is in order.

The word *computer* is not of recent coinage. It is actually several hundred years old. The earliest known reference to computers in the English language appears in the writings of Sir Thomas Browne, who in 1646 described "computers" (which then referred to persons who reckoned the passage of time) drawing up calendars.

Though calculating devices, as opposed to flesh-and-blood computers, are at least as old as the Chinese abacus and probably older, the direct ancestors of the modern computer did not start appearing until the European Renaissance. These were all mechanical analog calculators, *analog* meaning they substituted a device, or process, such as the turning of a wheel or the sliding of a ruled stick, for operations on numbers.

Among the first to try his hand at inventing a computer was the early-seventeenth-century German mathematician and clergyman Wilhelm Schickard. A close friend of the astronomer Johannes Kepler, who formulated the laws of planetary motion, Schickard designed and built, late in 1623, a mechanism that could add, subtract, multiply, and divide. The Schickard machine was similar in operation to the slide rule but also incorporated a set of metal wheels that carried out arithmetical operations.

Schickard planned to send Kepler a copy of his invention, but fire destroyed its component parts before they could be assembled, and Schickard died soon afterward in an epidemic spread by troop movements during the Thirty Years' War. What happened to his original model of the machine, no one knows. Possibly it was put in storage and is still gathering dust in an attic somewhere in central Europe. Schickard's rough sketch of the calculator survived, however, and was used to reconstruct the device in the 1970s.

The French mathematician and philosopher Blaise Pascal, in whose honor a modern computer language is named, contrived a calculator much like Schickard's and had it built between 1642 and 1644. Pascal's creation was called the *arithmatique* or *Pascaline*. It was roughly the size of a shoebox, housed a set of numbered dials, and could handle numbers up to 999,999.999. The Pascaline worked well but was so expensive that Pascal's project ended in commercial failure.

About thirty years after Pascal, Newton's great rival, the German mathematician and diplomat Gottfried Wilhelm von Leibniz, designed a mechanical calculator comparable to those of Pascal and Schickard. Leibniz's machine was completed around the year 1673 and was dubbed the *Leibniz wheel,* because it was dominated by a large wheellike mechanism reminiscent of a nineteenth-century meat grinder. The Leibniz wheel could handle modest arithmetic problems but was too limited in its capabilities to be of much use to scientists, so in a sense it was obsolete even before it was built.

Though the Leibniz wheel had a negligible influence on the development of computers, another of Leibniz's contributions did much more to direct the computer's evolution. Among Leibniz's papers at the time of his death were some notes he had written on the subject of binary, or base-2, arithmetic. This is a counting system that uses only ones and zeroes in place of our familiar base-10 counting numbers. In base 2, 0 remains 0 and 1 is still 1, but 2 is 10, 3 is 11, 4 is 100, and so forth.

Leibniz reasoned that since everything in the universe either exists or is nonexistent, the whole of existence could be reduced, through binary arithmetic, into a universal calculus where being would be symbolized by one and nonexistence by zero. Leibniz never succeeded in working out this all-encompassing branch of math, but almost two centuries later someone else did, with tremendous implications for the growth of computer science and technology.

That someone was the nineteenth-century English mathematician George Boole. He devised a revolutionary algebra based on the numbers one and zero, which Boole interpreted respectively as "universes" and "nothingness." His system was published in 1854 and is now called Boolean algebra in his honor.

As Leibniz did before him, Boole postulated that anything and everything could be described in equations using binary arithmetic, since any given thing either is (constituting a little universe designated by one) or is not, (its nonexistence being represented by a zero). This seemingly simple-minded way of looking at the world was really a great and subtle advance in mathematical thought, and later in this chapter we see how Boole's one-and-zero reckoning system came to the aid of computer designers in the twentieth century, by converting information into terms that a machine could understand.

One of Boole's contemporaries, Charles Babbage, is widely credited with designing the first modern computer. Notorious for his irascible personality, and said to have served as the model for the eccentric tinkerer Daniel Doyce in Charles Dickens's novel *Little Dorrit*, Babbage envisioned a steam-powered calculator as big as a present-day football field. He called this monstrosity his Analytical Engine. It included many features found in modern home computers, including the Victorian equivalent of a printer: a typesetting machine.

The British government took an interest in Babbage's machine and appointed a committee to study his proposal for it. The committee was impressed with Babbage's prospectus and, in 1823, advised the government to give Babbage money to build a more modest version of his giant computer, known as the Difference Engine. The Chancellor of the Exchequer hoped that Babbage's invention "would place a new and most valuable computing power at the disposal of analysts and physicists."

But Babbage's great computer was never constructed. Even with financial backing from the Crown, Babbage was unable to complete more than a few components of his machine, and the government, seeing no results after nineteen years of work, cut off Babbage's funding in 1842. Babbage continued working on his own, but the project drove him so deeply into debt—living "on bread and cheese," as his mother once put it—that he died in virtual poverty in 1871.

Though Babbage's machine was never built, its influence turned out to be almost as great as if he had completed it, because it set the pattern for many of the computers that followed. The logical design of the Babbage computer was especially important to later computer designers. Babbage's machine employed a feature known today as conditional logic or branching logic. *Branching logic* can be summed up roughly by saying that if something happens (or does not happen), then something else will happen (or not happen).

One may illustrate branching logic with the analogy of a motorist on a highway journey. The motorist comes to an intersection where one road branches off from another. The first road leads to Smithville, the other to Jonesburg. If the motorist takes the first road, then he will wind up in Smithville. But if he takes the second road, then Jonesburg will be his destination. This kind of logic gives the computer a certain freedom of choice and is represented in home computer programs today by the familiar "IF . . . THEN" statements.

Babbage contributed so much to the design of computers that it would take too long to list all his accomplishments here. Perhaps his most famous contributions to computer architecture are the two divisions of his machine: the "store," which in later computers would be known as memory, and the "mill," a processing unit in which data from the store were operated on. For this achievement alone, Babbage is often cited as the "father of the computer," and some histories of computers are written as if all modern computers were descended directly from his Analytical Engine, in the manner of a canine pedigree. But that is a misconception. As we shall see later, Babbage's influence on twentieth-century computers, though great, was not as widespread as some of his more worshipful biographers have claimed.

A few years after Babbage's death, an American inventor named Herman Hollerith saved the U.S. Census Bureau from drowning in a sea of demographic data in the 1880s: he built a tabulating machine that added up census figures automatically. The Hollerith tabulator was about the size of a small office desk and took its *input,* figures fed in for analysis, from cards punched with holes that stood for population data such as age, gender, and number of children. The cards were floated on a bath of electrically conductive mercury, and an array of spring-loaded pins was lowered onto the card to read the data. Wherever there was a hole in a card, a pin made contact with the mercury, completed an electrical circuit, and added one more datum to the total.

Hollerith's tabulator was a tremendous success. His machine allowed the census bureau to finish tabulating the 1880 census data in the then unbelievable span of two years. (The 1870 census was still being tallied up when 1880 rolled around.) Even better, the machine virtually eliminated human error from the tabulating process.

Soon everyone was clamoring for a Hollerith machine. Hollerith founded a company to build and market his invention and began automating the offices of America's biggest corporations. His company eventually became a giant corporation itself. A series of mergers transformed it into International Business Machines (IBM), whose familiar IBM cards of recent years are essentially the same as those Hollerith used to feed data into his tabulating machine a century ago.

Another computer pioneer of the late 1800s was the famous Victorian physicist William Thompson, Lord Kelvin. He looked like a very determined Santa Claus and was known for his meat-cleaver wit. Once Kelvin posted a notice on his classroom door, "The Professor will not meet his classes today." When he returned, he found that a student had crossed out the *c* in classes. Kelvin retaliated by crossing out the *l*.

Kelvin wanted to substitute "brass for brain" in the computational process, and he designed and built a number of successful computing devices, including a tidal harmonic analyzer that could forecast the rise and fall of tides at British seaports for any date in the future. The Kelvin tide predictor worked by breaking down tidal patterns into their different *harmonics*, or component cycles, and then using the harmonics to model the tides.

Encouraged by the success of that machine, Kelvin made plans for a differential analyzer that could find solutions for differential equations, a fiendishly difficult branch of math which deals with variations in given quantities—such as volume or voltage or velocity—over time.

Differential equations commonly come in sets of twenty, thirty, or even more, with dozens of unknowns to be determined. One solves the first equation, then takes that solution and applies it to the next equation, and the next, until a final solution is achieved. Often the equations are so complex that they cannot be solved in the ordinary sense of the word, but can only have their solutions approximated. Even a ballpark solution might take a human mathematician using pencil and paper several months of continual labor.

So a machine like the one Kelvin planned was needed desperately. Kelvin came very close to making his differential analyzer work, but he failed because the machine was weak in one small but very important part: the integrator.

The integrator was supposed to help reach the solution by finding the area underneath a given curve (the process known in calculus as integration). The integrator contained two wheels tilted at right angles to each other. One wheel rotated horizontally, the other vertically. The vertical wheel slipped inward across the horizontal wheel's face as the latter rotated, and turned a horizontal output shaft attached to the vertical wheel.

The Kelvin differential analyzer contained a series of integrators. Each one would contribute a little to the solution of a set of equations. The first integrator would get the job started, then pass its results to the next integrator by way of the rotating output shaft. The second integrator would then pass its output on to the third, and this process would continue until the problem was solved.

On paper, it all worked fine. In practice the integrators failed, however, because the output shafts lacked the "muscle"—what engineers call torque—required for their task. The vertical wheel would have to be pressed down very hard on the horizontal wheel to give the output shaft enough torque to run the next integrator; and that much pressure would prevent the first integrator from working at all.

If this problem is hard to visualize, imagine taking the gearbox off your car's rear axle and replacing the gears in it with smooth glass discs. In that case, the driveshaft would have a hard time transferring its torque to the axle, because the glass discs would tend to slip. The rear wheels would not move, and the car would go nowhere.

Much the same thing was happening inside Kelvin's computer. He could not use gears to solve the problem, because the discs had to move freely, not mesh together. Nor could he press one disc down harder on the other, because that would restrict their movement and throw off the solutions to equations.

By 1880, Kelvin had given up. Victorian hardware simply was not ready for the job he had in mind. But Kelvin's scheme was not forgotten, and shortly after World War I a canny New England inventor named Vannevar Bush saw a way to strengthen the weak spot in Kelvin's design and build a computer like the one Kelvin had in mind.

Bush was an engineer at the Massachusetts Institute of Technology (MIT) in Cambridge. He wore spectacles perched on a long and bony nose and resembled a beardless Uncle Sam. Bush had one of the most versatile and practical minds of the twentieth century. He understood politics and finance as well as he knew engineering, and he had a genius for administration. In World War II, as organizer of the National Defense Research Committee (NDRC), Bush took charge of America's research and development effort and did much in that capacity to ensure the Allied victory. After the war Bush became one of the elder statesmen of American science and was frequently sought out by the press for comment on this or that invention or discovery. Unlike some of his less enlightened colleagues, Bush was aware that science and technology were part of society, not separate from it, and he warned time and again that scientists and inventors must consider the possible impact of their work on society. If scientists today have more of a social conscience than they used to, Bush's influence must be one of the reasons why.

In the 1920s, however, Bush had not yet become the conscience of the engineering fraternity. He was pondering Kelvin's dream of a differential analyzer and wondering how a Kelvin-type machine might be built.

Bush knew how badly such a device was needed. The mathematical problems involved in science and engineering had grown faster than the ability of calculating machines to handle them. Many crucial problems in engineering—far more than in Kelvin's day—involved big sets of differential equations that only a very rapid, automatic computer, like a desktop calculator but hundreds of times faster, could solve. Without such an aid to calculation, engineers and scientists found themselves in much the same position as a swimmer trying to dog-paddle across the Pacific. A vast ocean of equations and variables stretched out before them and could never be crossed without some kind of mechanical assistance. Kelvin had come close to building such a machine. Was technology finally up to completing that job?

It was. Bush saw where Kelvin had failed. The output of the integrators was too feeble and needed beefing up. The hardware of Kelvin's day had been inadequate for that task, but Bush now had a tool denied to Kelvin: a small, reliable electric motor, or servomotor, which could give the integrators' output shafts the extra kick they needed to communicate with one another. So Bush attached an electric servomotor to the Kelvin integrators, and at last, in 1930, Bush built the machine that Kelvin had envisioned.

The servomotor worked in much the same way as power steering works on a car. It took the output from one integrator and amplified the torque so that that integrator could work the next one in series, and the pattern would keep going until the equations were solved. What Bush actually did was more complicated than this brief summary indicates, but his innovation worked, and the result was a smoothly functioning differential analyzer, sometimes called an integraph because of its integrative powers.

Bush's integraph bore very little resemblance to the computers of today. It had no keyboard, no flashing lights. It sprawled out over several hundred square feet of floor and looked like a cross between a billiard table and a printing press. The Bush integraph contained hundreds of parallel steel rods supported by a tablelike metal frame and turned by a set of gears and axles driven by an electric motor. The rotations of the rods simulated operations on numbers.

One could not set up a problem on the integraph with a few keystrokes, as on a modern computer. Users of the Bush machine had to wield screwdrivers and hammers to prepare the machine for a run. It was programmed, an observer quipped, "with a wrench in one hand and a gear in the other." The Bush differential analyzer looks almost comical today, but for its time it was a marvel, not to mention a godsend to anyone who, like most of the MIT engineers, had to deal with large numbers of long and involved calculations.

Among Bush's colleagues on the MIT faculty was Norbert Wiener, a mathematician who would play a small but important role in the making of the modern computer. A stout and absent-minded man with thick glasses and a white goatee, Wiener waddled like a duck and would sometimes forget, while running an errand, what business had brought him out in the first place. "Where was I going?" he would ask passersby, hoping they could enlighten him.

Born in 1894, Wiener was the scion of an intellectually distinguished New England family. His father raised him with the goal of making him a genius and succeeded. Wiener had learned the alphabet at the age of eighteen months. Four years later he was reading the works of Charles Darwin. Wiener enrolled at Tufts University at age eleven and had his Ph.D. from Harvard—a double degree in mathematics and philosophy—in hand when he was only eighteen years old. The boy's academic brilliance was a monument to his father's guidance, but Wiener gave his parent only part of the credit. "I became a scholar," he wrote, "partly because it was my father's will but equally because it was my internal destiny."

Wiener went on to study mathematics at Göttingen, the German mecca of mathematical research, under such teachers as the great David Hilbert. Not everyone enjoyed Wiener's company. Hilbert disliked him, and Bertrand Russell took offense at what he saw as Wiener's incredible arrogance. Russell once complained that Wiener "thinks himself God Almighty."

Wiener's hubris was in fact the defense mechanism of a shy and insecure man. He knew how odd and awkward he looked and how his intellect set him apart from others (Wiener once described himself as "an outsider at the feast [of life]"), and, as was said of Samuel Johnson, he sometimes made himself a boor to avoid being made a butt.

Before joining the MIT faculty, Wiener spent part of the First World War as a mathematician at the U.S. Army's ballistics research laboratory at the muddy Aberdeen Proving Grounds in Maryland. Ironically for a man who hated militarism and spent much of his career denouncing the growth of the military-industrial complex, Wiener at Aberdeen helped the Army compile firing tables for artillery.

The firing tables consisted of simple tables of numbers (elevation, range, and other data) that soldiers could use when aiming their guns before firing. Tables drawn up prior to the First World War were mostly useless by the time hostilities commenced, because new guns could fire much farther. So the firing tables had to be revised. The revisions were monumentally difficult and time-consuming, because 10,000 to 100,000 calculations were needed to accurately work out the trajectory of a single shell. A woman would sit at a table with a desktop computer, push buttons, scribble down results, punch the results back into the machine, and continue that way for days on end. She might need two or three weeks to work out the trajectory of a single shot. This was repeated on every shot, and hundreds of thousands of shots were required to amass enough data for the firing tables.

To make matters worse, designers kept improving the guns to increase their range. Just as one set of firing tables was completed, a new gun would come along and make those tables obsolete. The mathematicians must have felt like the mythical figure of Sisyphus, who was doomed forever to push a huge rock up a hillside, only to have it slip from his grasp and roll back down before he could reach the hilltop.

To help with this labor, Wiener's boss at Aberdeen—Oswald Veblen, a gifted mathematician who would later play an important role as a catalyst in the development of electronic computers—put Wiener and about a dozen other mathematicians to work on trajectory analysis.

Aberdeen seems to have been an unpleasant experience for Wiener, whose strange appearance and mannerisms made him the natural target for his co-workers' pranks. Knowing how he prized his handsome mustache, they once tricked him, by citing nonexistent Army regulations, into shaving it off. When Wiener learned of the deception, he was furious.

After leaving Aberdeen, Wiener taught briefly at the University of Maine, where raucous students practically hooted him out of the classroom. He worked even more briefly for the Boston *Herald*, which fired him after only a couple of reporting assignments.

In 1919 he landed at MIT, where he made a friend in Vannevar Bush. The lean Yankee engineer liked the round little mathematician with the bulging eyes and strange beard, and he called on Wiener for help in understanding the mathematical principles behind the design of computing machinery. Their collaboration pleased them both. "I did not know," wrote Bush later, "that a mathematician and an engineer could have such good times together."

While working with Bush, Wiener was thinking about the workings of computers and other data-processing systems such as the brain. He saw similarities between them. He also saw past the similarities and eventually had an idea that would change the world. He called that idea cybernetics (from the Greek word *kybernetes*, "steersman") and defined it in general terms as "the science of control and communication in the animal and the machine." The cybernetic principles described by Norbert Wiener helped to free computers from the confines of mechanical technology and usher in the electronic age in computing.

Wiener realized that any information processor—an adding machine, a brain, an abacus, or whatever—not only handles information but also, in a sense, *is made of* information. Anyone who sees a computer merely as a mess of gears or wires or discs, according to Wiener, fails to grasp the computer's true nature. The mechanism, or hardware, is ultimately unimportant. What counts is how the machine processes information.

What Wiener believed, then, boils down to this: the computer is, in the final analysis, a system of and for information transfers. As long as the data get where they are supposed to go within that system, the mechanism, the actual body of the machine, may be almost anything. There is no absolute need to build computers out of wire and glass and silicon. Toothpicks would work. One MIT professor built a simple working computer out of stones and toilet paper rolls to demonstrate this point, and John Searle of the Berkeley philosophy department once proposed building a computer out of empty beer cans.

So there are very few restrictions on how to build a computer. It need not be full of moving mechanical parts. Any arrangement that can move the information properly is fine.

That, in a nutshell, was Wiener's great insight, and in the years after Bush built his integraph, computers would demonstrate the truth of Wiener's vision. They would evolve from mechanical devices into electronic ones and would go through many other metamorphoses along the way. Yet they would remain computers, and the more they changed, the more they remained true to Weiner's ideas.

In the thirties, Wiener was thinking of ways to edge the computer out of the mechanical era and into the electronic age. "I suggested," he said in a speech given in 1955 at a meeting of the MIT Faculty Club, "(a) that the machines be digital (that is, they work with a succession of quantities with a small number of values), and (b) that they be electronic, that you use the tremendous advantage that you have from the speed of electronic apparatus."

Wiener was talking here about machines quite different from the analog machines that had dominated computing technology in the early twentieth century. Instead of substituting the turning of gears or the rolling of discs for operations on numbers, digital computers would work directly on the numbers themselves. They would use digits, the familiar counting numbers zero through nine, and juggle those quantities around. Humans do the same thing when counting on their fingers—the origin, in fact, of the words *digit* and *digital*.

"Then it occurred to me," Wiener went on, "that electronic machines by their very nature don't work well on the scale of ten. The ordinary desk machine has gears with ten teeth in it to give you the various digits. But there is no natural way of getting electronic impulses with ten alternatives."

Wiener proposed using a different counting system, based on binary arithmetic, the same system used in Boolean algebra. The electronic computer, Wiener decided, "should be not only digital but digital on the scale of two."

He advised setting up the computer to read a dot (or some other, equivalent symbol) as a one and its absence as a zero. Computers naturally "prefer" this kind of arithmetic because it is best suited to their operation, just as humans prefer base-10 arithmetic because they have ten fingers. Time and again between 1925 and 1950, computer designers would try to make computers work in base 10 and would discover (as Wiener did) that computers are much "happier" with the binary system of counting. In those years the computer makers would also discover that Wiener was right to favor electronic machines.

While Wiener pondered the nature of computers, Bush was working on other data-handling devices. One was called the Rapid Selector. It was designed to retrieve and photocopy data stored on reels of microfilm, and it incorporated features that would play an important role in the building of other computers—notably a data-input system which consisted of tapes and tape readers.

The tapes were made of backing tape from ordinary photographic film and were punched with holes that stood for characters the computer was supposed to recognize. Sprocket wheels like those on ordinary movie projectors moved the tape along through the machine. In effect, the tapes told the machine where to look for given items on microfilm. The punched tape entered a tape reader and passed between a light bulb and a photoelectric cell. Patterns of light passing through the punched holes told the computer, in code, what to look for.

The Rapid Selector was akin to another device called a number sieve. A sieve is used to sift through material in search of something, and that is exactly how a number sieve worked. It sifted through large masses of numbers looking for *primes*, numbers divisible only by themselves and the number one.

Prime numbers start out 1, 2, 3, 5, 7, . . . and continue indefinitely. They have fascinated mathematicians since the days of ancient Greece and have many practical uses, such as the making and breaking of codes. Over the centuries, prime-seekers have used mechanical means to isolate primes. About three hundred years ago, a German and an Austrian mathematician developed the stencil method. It involved putting perforated stencils over a sheet of ruled paper and marking spots on the paper through the holes in the stencils. The mathematicians used the stencil method to produce a list of primes exceeding the number 400,000. They would have gone higher, but the Austrian government confiscated their paper supply to make rifle cartridges for a war against the Turks.

In 1794, a French mathematician named Legendre devised a strip method that substituted strips of paper for the cumbersome stencils. Both the strip and stencil methods were awkward and time-consuming, however, and mathematicians knew they had to automate the prime-seeking process if the study of prime numbers was ever to advance.

Part of the problem was the sheer size of the numbers. The bigger a number, the more difficult it is to tell whether or not it is a prime. One can see that 210 may be broken down into 2 x 3 x 5 x 7, but what about a gigantic number like 9,999,000,099,990,-001?

That number happens not to be a prime. It is divisible by 1,-676,321 and 59,648,480,781. It was broken down in about two hours by a computer devised in 1926 by the American computer pioneer Derrick Henry Lehmer, son of the well-known mathematician Derrick Norman Lehmer.

Lehmer's number-sieve computer looked nothing like a computer as we know it today. It resembled a highway barrier sign draped with bicycle chains. The chains substituted for the strips in the strip method and were cranked around by a motor-driven shaft. There were nineteen chains altogether, and they could analyze 3,000 numbers every second in search of primes.

The bicycle-chain computer was built in LeConte Hall at the University of California in Berkeley. Unfortunately, that number sieve was destroyed. A later model that Lehmer built was more sophisticated. It used punched film and made electrical connections through the film, in much the same manner that Hollerith's tabulator read punched cards, to signify when a prime had turned up.

Next Lehmer added a photoelectric cell to his apparatus. Whenever holes in the moving tapes lined up, a beam of light would shine through and activate the photoelectric cell, which would send out an electrical signal to mark the isolation of another prime number. That sieve was built in 1932 and could carry out 5,000 operations per second, a performance that made it, in Lehmer's words, "the first high-speed computer, I guess." He had built a photoelectric tape reader. A few years later in Britain, a similar device incorporated in a giant electronic computer would help the Allies win the war against Hitler.

Lehmer's number sieves were special-purpose computers. Unlike the general-purpose computers in use today, they were designed to carry out one particular task (finding primes) and no other. The number sieves were also parallel computers. They were so called because they could carry out several different operations—"chains of thought," to use an anthropomorphic analogy—at the same time. In the case of Lehmer's sieves, the chains were literal, and each one represented a separate prime-seeking operation. Parallel computers are roughly comparable to the human brain, which can handle many different operations at once.

The opposite of a parallel computer is a serial computer. *Serial* is the adjective form of *series*, and that is how a serial computer operates. It carries out one, and one only, predetermined string of instructions, one after another, straight through from beginning to end. It can "think" about only one thing at a time. If parallel computers work like a brain, then serial computers function more like a bloodhound following a scent. They proceed single-mindedly down the trail until the end is reached.

Most computers in use today, from giant supercomputers down to pocket-sized calculators, are serial machines. Possibly this is not for the better but for the worse, because parallel computers have many advantages over serial computers. Unlike their serial cousins, parallel computers are not confined to a narrow, one-step-at-a-time method of operation but can make better use of time by working on several things simultaneously.

For years after Lehmer devised his parallel-processing number sieves, computer technology seesawed back and forth between parallel and serial processing. Had computers and their designers followed the lead of Lehmer and his number sieves, the computers we use today would probably be quite different from what they are. Eventually, however, computers went the serial route, in a move that Lehmer thought ruined the machines.

Between 1925 and 1950, computers evolved in several important ways:

• They went electronic and digital, as Wiener advised.

• They became automatic, to speed up calculations and eliminate human error from the computing process.

• They progressed from doing special, highly limited jobs to serving a general purpose, being fit for many different calculating tasks.

• They achieved *program control*, meaning a human operator could give the machine a set of instructions and turn the computer loose to carry them out on its own.

• Computer programming evolved, too, from a tiresome mechanical process involving screwdrivers and wrenches into almost a literary art.

• Finally, computer programs became self-modifying and, one might say, part and parcel of the computers themselves.

This quarter century was a tumultuous time in which computers were shaped by worldwide depression, global war, and numerous lesser conflicts waged in every arena from college faculty meetings to courtrooms. And the computers, in turn, transformed completely this world that made them.

# 2
# GEORGE STIBITZ AND THE BELL COMPUTERS

As the WPA workers did their figures in the New York stable, George Stibitz, a phone company employee in nearby New Jersey, was making their methods forever obsolete.

A pipe-smoking man with a whimsical sense of humor and an independent turn of mind, Stibitz worked as a mathematician at the Bell Telephone Laboratories in Holmdel. He had grown up in Ohio and attended a high school where the curriculum had been weighted heavily in favor of math and the sciences. In college he specialized in physics and mathematics, and in 1927 he took his master's degree from Union College.

He spent the following year working for General Electric (GE), measuring the propagation of radio waves. Stibitz performed this work at a farmhouse far out in the country. Stibitz and his co-worker devised a remote-control system to open the damper on the fire in the farmhouse stove, so the place would be warm when they arrived on cold mornings.

After his year with GE was over, Stibitz got his doctorate and went to work for Bell Labs. He soon found himself using phone components to fabricate a calculator that could do the work of a hundred or more human computers in a small fraction of the time. Though Stibitz was unaware of it just then, he was picking up where Charles Babbage had left off a century before. He was working out a new technology that would make Babbage's dream a reality.

Stibitz's computer ideas started taking shape during the last few weeks of 1937, when he was asked to investigate the design of phone relays. The relays were metal devices, somewhat like clothespins, that clicked open and shut to control electrical circuits.

Electromagnetism operated the relays. An electric current would pass through ferrous metal in a relay and briefly create an electromagnet that would snap the relay shut. When the current was cut off, the magnetism would vanish, and the relay would open. A closed relay let through a call, while an open relay meant no call was possible.

Stibitz was interested in the logic functions demonstrated by the relays and saw a parallel between their on-off operation and the binary counting system, which he had studied years earlier in a math course. It occurred to Stibitz that the relays might be used to represent mathematical operations such as addition and subtraction; and if a relay-equipped machine could add and subtract, then it could also multiply and divide, since multiplication and division could be transformed respectively into strings of additions and subtractions. Stibitz thought it sounded like fun and decided to try.

The idea of using a machine to solve binary math problems was very much in the air about this time. Claude Shannon of MIT published a paper in 1938 suggesting that a computer could be built using on-off switches to handle Boolean logic and calculations. A few months before Shannon's paper appeared, Stibitz began thinking about the same kind of setup, using switches like those found in telephone equipment.

Each switch had only two "states"—on and off. Stibitz saw how the states of a contact could thus be made to represent the value of a binary digit, either zero or one. Arbitrarily he made zero the state of an open contact; one became that of a closed contact. Thus the relays were made to represent binary arithmetical operations.

As he sat in his kitchen, one November evening in 1937, thinking of telephone relays clicking open and shut, something clicked in Stibitz's mind as well. He conceived the design for a binary adder, based on relays, that could do anything a desk calculator could.

Stibitz went into his workshop, took some relays salvaged from Bell Labs' junk pile, and brought the equipment back into his kitchen, where he spread the components out on the table and devised a few circuits. Input consisted of a couple of strips of metal cut from coffee cans. Output was a pair of flashlight bulbs that lit up or stayed dark to indicate the results of binary calculations. The components were mounted on a piece of plywood about a foot square and looked more like a grade school science project than the beginning of a revolution in computing. Stibitz's wife christened his gadget the "K-Model," after the kitchen table where it was assembled.

Stibitz hooked up batteries to the relays and found that the relays could indeed be wired together to add binary digits. In his own words, it was "just fun seeing what could be done with very simple things."

He took the K-model to the Bell Labs and showed his coworkers what he had built. At that time Stibitz had no idea that his work would help to usher in the computer age. "So, unfortunately, there were no fireworks, no champagne," he recalls.

Instead, there were chuckles. When he suggested a whole calculator could be built of relays, his colleagues were amused. It seemed absurd to think of a gadget that calculated in the old, esoteric binary notation. But Stibitz did not think the idea was necessarily funny and for the next few weeks he pondered it.

Soon afterward, Stibitz says, his relay-based computer "turned serious." What helped to turn it serious was the Bell system's own need for long, complicated, and accurate calculations involving complex numbers. Once considered mere curiosities "dreamed up by long-haired professors" (as Stibitz puts it), *complex numbers* are a special category of numbers that incorporate the imaginary number *i* (which is, the square root of negative one, or $\sqrt{-1}$. It is called an imaginary number because it exists only in the human mind: that little *i* stands for a value—the square root of one less than nothing—that cannot exist in the real, physical world we live in.

When an imaginary number is multiplied by a real number, such as 2 or 10 or 1,956, it becomes a complex number and has many practical applications in phone engineering. Complex numbers are used to represent current, voltage, and other parameters.

At Bell Labs and just about everywhere else, groups of women called computists were hired to carry out this work on mechanical desktop calculators. Their workload was tremendous and kept increasing until, early in 1938, a Bell employee proposed that two desk calculators be linked mechanically to simplify complex calculations. Ganging up the smaller machines would result in a supercalculator that, in theory, could save human operators time and labor. But the supercalculator would be complicated to build and cumbersome to operate, and at that point Bell Labs turned to Stibitz and his K-Model.

In the summer of 1938, Stibitz's supervisor in the mathematics division asked if Stibitz's tiny relay calculator could do arithmetic with complex numbers. "Could it!" Stibitz remembers. He already had thought out most of the components for what he called a complex calculator, and soon he had drawn up circuits for such a device using standard relays and other widely used equipment. "Not a pretty machine," Stibitz describes it, "but one I thought would work."

His drafting was unconventional, but a circuit designer deciphered Stibitz's diagrams and pronounced them workable. The circuit designer made a few changes in the plans, and soon work was under way.

"All the angels were with us," according to Stibitz, and the project—what would later be called the Bell Telephone Laboratories Model 1 Complex Calculator—commenced in September 1938. Mechanics began assembling the machine the following spring.

Before construction could begin, there were big design barriers to be overcome. One was the matter of input. Obviously strips of tin can were unsuitable for use with a machine like this one.

The Bell engineers considered several arrangements and finally settled on an ordinary ten-key setup. The ten-key board required more memory and was more expensive than other schemes, but it was also simple to use and therefore worth the extra cost. The board had extra keys for entering mathematical operations and the positive and negative values of $i$.

Then there was what Stibitz called the "problem of interface." He was talking not about interfacing machines with machines but machines with humans. How could someone thinking and punching keys in decimal notation, as humans do, "talk" understandably with a calculator that used only binary notation?

It seemed impractical to train users to convert decimal into binary in their heads, because the conversion process would be too tricky and prone to error. Stibitz says that the notion of teaching binary notation to operators was appalling, so that plan was rejected. Instead he came up with a mixed binary-decimal system, as he called it, that allowed the calculator to convert decimal numbers into binary form. Numbers would be entered in decimal form on the ten-key, and the machine would translate them automatically into one-and-zero code. As the interface problem demonstrated, binary arithmetic was not as familiar a concept then as it is now. Hardly anyone outside a small circle of mathematicians had even heard of it.

Nor had anyone but a handful of historians and mathematicians heard of Babbage and his early computer. Stibitz confesses, "I did not know I was picking up where Charles Babbage in England had to quit over a hundred years before." Stibitz also recalls that no one in the Bell group mentioned Babbage until the Model 1 had been built and was running.

The Model 1 required some special tricks of arithmetic that at times forced the machine to operate backward from the way a human would calculate. Consider a simple division problem involving complex numbers: $2i/4 = 0.5i$. A human would first write down the top number, the dividend, and then put in the bottom figure, or divisor, and work the problem. But that approach was unsuitable for the Stibitz calculator.

In complex calculations it was simpler to enter the divisor first, so that the computer could start working on the real and imaginary numbers as soon as the division slash was typed in. That meant the slash had to be turned around to allow the divisor to be slipped in before the dividend. For that purpose the computer had to have a special reverse-division symbol added.

Like the Lehmer number sieves, the Model 1 was a parallel computer. It had two units that operated simultaneously. One carried out operations on real numbers, while the other handled imaginary numbers. When visitors to the lab were shown the latter unit and told it dealt with imaginary numbers, they would say something like, "It *looks* real!"

The timing of relays caused innumerable headaches while the Model 1 was being assembled. Accurate timing was all-important, because each relay had to connect at just the right moment to allow another relay to carry out the next step in a calculation. Even a little delay—no more than the blink of an eye—would spoil the whole procedure.

One way around the timing problem was to slow down the relays, but that in turn slowed down the computer. Timing created what Stibitz calls "profane moments" for the Bell Labs staff. Eventually they got everything right, however, and the Model 1 was able to carry out an addition in the then phenomenal time of one-tenth of a second.

The Model 1 was completed in November 1939, approximately two years after Stibitz started thinking about the use of phone switches for calculating. Stibitz found it "a spine-tingling experience" to see the machine of his dreams finally assembled and working. Now and then a little bug would turn up, but its effects were usually minor, and sometimes amusing. Once a bug caused the Model 1's teletype to print out "BOO" repeatedly. Stibitz jokingly wrote it off as "witchcraft."

The Model 1 was perhaps the first time-sharing computer system in the world. As word of the computer's capabilities spread outside the mathematics department, other sections of Bell Labs wanted access to the Model 1, too. So a couple of extra teletypes were added in other locations, and the time-sharing computer was born.

At first the computer could only multiply and divide. Those were the most time-consuming operations, so the Model 1 had been made specifically to deal with them. As soon as the computing groups at Bell found how convenient the computer was, however, they wanted to make it add and subtract as well. The Model 1 was modified for those functions, and in a couple of days the Bell Labs calculator was ready for just about anything.

The calculator had 440 relays. They worked fine. In fact, the system performed so well that its makers were invited to show it off at a meeting of a section of the American Mathematical Society at Dartmouth College in Hanover, New Hampshire, in September 1940. The computer at that time was installed at the Bell Labs building on West Street in New York City, but a telegraph link with Dartmouth was possible, and wiremen arranged the hookup on the Dartmouth campus the day before the mathematicians gathered.

At the meeting, the Model 1 performed admirably. A problem was typed out and transmitted to the Model 1 in New York. Less than a minute later, the teletype began printing out the answer.

The Dartmouth demonstration turned out to be a historic event, for it was the first time a computer was controlled by long distance. The meeting was also noteworthy because of the people who attended it. Norbert Wiener was in the audience that night, peering at Stibitz with bulbous, heavy-lidded eyes. Also present was John Mauchly, a then obscure scientist who would become one of the most famous figures in the history of computing.

A lanky man with a prominent nose and spectacles, Mauchly was trained as a meteorologist and taught physics at Ursinus College in Pennsylvania. He was interested in using automatic computers to solve problems in atmospheric physics and weather prediction and about this time was putting together small computing devices comparable to Stibitz's K-Model. A few years later Mauchly would participate in the making of a much more powerful wartime computer; but at the time of Stibitz's speech, Mauchly could afford only the simplest of computing equipment on his meager salary as a professor. (Mauchly's work is the subject of later chapters.)

After Stibitz had given his talk, members of the audience were allowed to play with the teletype and see what results they could get from the computer. Mauchly noticed Wiener punching away at the teletype and becoming very angry and frustrated. When Mauchly walked up to Wiener and asked if something was wrong, Wiener grumbled, "No problem with the machine."

That, to Wiener, was the trouble: there *was* no problem with the Model 1. Wiener had been performing a test: he wanted to trick the machine into dividing by zero, an inadmissable operation in arithmetic. Naturally, Stibitz had anticipated that possibility and made sure that the Model 1 would not commit such a schoolboy error. Mauchly and Wiener chatted briefly and agreed that electronic computers were "the way to go."

At that time, "electronics" meant vacuum tubes. Though seldom seen today, having been supplanted by transistors and integrated circuits, vacuum tubes were once the workhorses of electronic technology. Sometimes called electron tubes, they were invented by Lee De Forest, an American, and patented by him in 1907. (In fact, he did not invent the vacuum tube from scratch but merely modified an already existing component created by an Englishman named John Ambrose Fleming.)

The vacuum tube could take many different forms, but essentially it was a device for controlling the flow of electrons through a circuit. It consisted of a closed tube of glass or metal containing either a vacuum or a gas under very low pressure and a set of two or more metal *elements* (wires and grids) that emitted and/or soaked up electrons. The electrons would leap across an open space between the elements and while in flight could be channelled in ways that would alter the flow of current through circuitry outside the tube. This process was somewhat like turning a valve to control the flow of water through a pipe, and for that very reason the British preferred to call vacuum tubes by the more descriptive name of "valves."

Vacuum tubes could do marvelous things. They could pick up radio signals, or any other kind of electromagnetic signals, and amplify them. That made the tubes perfect for use in radios, phonographs, and many kinds of military equipment, such as antisubmarine listening devices. Vacuum tubes could also duplicate electronically the on-off, open-shut action of relays—but much faster, because the vacuum tubes did not need a whole twentieth of a second to open and close a physical switch. Electrons can move at the speed of light (about 186,000 miles per second), so a pulse of electrons or the absence of them could signify one or zero much more rapidly than the motion of a relay could. That made vacuum tubes ideal for the calculating machines Mauchly and Wiener had in mind.

But vacuum tubes had drawbacks. One was their fragility. Their brittle glass shells were easily shattered. More troublesome was their unreliability. The tubes were so complicated to make—each one was an intricate work of art—that no two vacuum tubes behaved in quite the same way. They could be so idiosyncratic that one tube might work fine in a circuit, while another, seemingly identical tube would be no use at all. A given vacuum tube might roar, or whisper, or cough; you couldn't tell beforehand. Often engineers who designed circuitry had to first find out the quirks of each vacuum tube in the system and then design the system around them.

In the eyes of most engineers, then, vacuum tubes were too undependable to serve as components of computing machines. Nonetheless, Wiener and Mauchly thought electromechanical machines like the Bell Labs calculator eventually would be superseded by all-electronic machines. In that assumption they were correct. But in 1940, that triumphant day at Dartmouth belonged to Stibitz, his Bell co-workers, and the electromechanical Model 1.

Model 1 was the first computer in a series of five, but it was the only one to be designed and built solely by Bell Labs. When the company saw the bill for the Model 1, a then frightening sum of $20,000, Bell Labs decided against building any more computers. Stibitz reported that the total horrified the upper management. (Nowadays some companies will spend ten times that much for a single software package.)

The line did not end with Model 1, however, because the gov-

ernment took a keen interest in Stibitz's work. Shortly after the
Model 1 was completed, he was approached by Duncan Stewart,
a representative of the National Defense Research Committee,
which Vannevar Bush had helped to organize.

Stewart explained how NDRC was meant to marshal
America's scientific genius for national defense. There was no
prospect of financial gain, for NDRC policy stated that its employees would neither make nor lose money by their work with
the committee. Would Stibitz, Stewart asked, be willing to work
with them as a technical aide under those circumstances?

At first glance Stibitz did not seem the kind of scientist who
would agree, or be invited, to join what he calls the establishment. He was often critical of authority, and, in his own words,
"certainly a poll of the establishment in the years 1930–1945
would have placed me among the dissidents."

Establishment material or not, Stibitz liked "Dunc," whom he
describes as "a forceful person," ordinarily quiet but "capable of
breathing fire" if frustrated by bungling or official stupidity. In
Stewart, Stibitz had found a kindred spirit, and he accepted
Stewart's invitation to join the NDRC.

Stibitz appreciated the people at NDRC, and he admired the
way its members cooperated to put science at the service of the
U.S. war effort. "They didn't wave flags; they didn't make
speeches about patriotism; they lived it," writes Stibitz.

But Stibitz had less admiration for some of the military men
he encountered. He has particularly harsh words for one general
who called away a group of soldiers who were assigned to perform a badly needed test on antiaircraft equipment. The general
insisted the soldiers be drilled in how to salute properly. Stibitz
also has sour memories of officers who could not be bothered to
attend an important conference because "it conflicted with their
customary afternoon tea."

Stibitz shared with Stewart an impatience with martinets and
bunglers in authority and made no secret of it. Consequently,
Stibitz admits, "I was accounted one likely to be at liberty rather
early during the firing process."

A different kind of firing process gave Stibitz one of his first
projects for NDRC. He served as a technical aide in the division

dealing with antiaircraft gun directors, or AA directors, analog devices that helped aim guns at enemy aircraft.

AA directors were needed because planes were small, fast-moving targets and therefore very difficult to hit. The trick was to aim the gun not directly at the plane—which would be long gone by the time the bullet reached the spot where the target had been—but at the point where the aircraft would be when the bullets arrived. The director had to estimate that point on the basis of the airplane's previous course and tell the gunner where to aim.

The problem with AA directors was that they worked well only at close range. They had to be improved for greater accuracy at long ranges. It was a challenging problem that required new technology, and perhaps the most challenging part of the problem was testing the AA directors once they had been designed and built.

Tests on actual aircraft were of course out of the question. Stibitz writes, "Pilots are understandably averse to being shot at, even with the purest research motives, and some other method of testing was needed."

So Stewart came up with an analog device that he called the dynamic tester. It used foot-wide cams, specially shaped plates of metal, to simulate the path of an imaginary plane swooping in for an attack. The cams were machined to a tolerance of 1/2000 of an inch—less than the diameter of a human hair. The dynamic tester worked well but was time-consuming and costly to manufacture, and the skilled workers needed to build it were in great demand and short supply because of the war.

Stibitz thought there might be other ways to do the job, and he designed a "cheap competitor," as he calls it, to the Stewart machine. Stibitz's device was called the punch-tape dynamic tester and, instead of metal cams, used ordinary teletype tape with the necessary information recorded on it in the form of punched holes that were read at a speed of ten characters per second. That was slow by 1940 standards, but Stibitz devised a scheme that allowed the tester to read the punched tape at ten readings per second while following the hypothetical target correctly to within a few thousandths of a second. This was roughly equivalent, in carnival terms, to a marksman shooting the fuzz off a falling peach at fifty paces.

The tester incorporated three different innovations. Stibitz describes them: "It turned from mechanical to electrical data storage, from decimal to binary representations, and from continuous to digital data handling." There, in one machine, were most of the criteria that Norbert Wiener had laid down for the modern computer.

Stibitz's tester had two great advantages over the cam-operated machines. Punching paper tape was easier than cutting mechanical cams, and programming the tester by tape was quicker and easier than designing new cams for different runs. Soon several of Stibitz's testers were working away for NDRC.

The tester had to figure the plane's position at thousands of individual points along its imaginary path, and it had to do the job fast, accurately, and reliably. That was a tall order indeed. Stibitz had solved the speed and accuracy problems but needed reliable hardware to carry out the calculations. Here his experience with the phone company came in handy. He used U-type telephone relays as elements in a binary computer.

The relays looked like little horseshoes about the size of a baby's hand. Stibitz found these relays "awesomely reliable" and thought they would work well as computer components. If "awesomely" sounds like hyperbole, Stibitz points out, then one must realize that if a set of U-type relays had started in the year 1 A.D. to turn a contact on and off once per second, they still would be clicking away reliably. Their first contact failure, or misfire, would not be due until more than a thousand years from now, around the year 3000.

So Stibitz and his co-workers put the relays into a computer called the Relay Interpolator, or Model 2. *Interpolate* means to fill in gaps between measurements with estimated data points, and that is what the computer did while working out the flight paths of hypothetical aircraft.

Model 2 used punched tape and contained six *registers*, or number-holding units, to carry out what mathematicians call iterative operations on data. In *iterative operations*, a procedure is broken down into brief, simple tasks that are performed again and again until the final answer is reached. For example, the equation $4 \times 1 = 4$ can be transformed into an iterative string of additions: $1 + 1 + 1 + 1 = 4$.

The Model 2 was a general-purpose computer, for it was not restricted to data interpolation but could also handle many other jobs, such as harmonic analysis like that carried out by Kelvin's early computer. Most of Model 2's time, however, was spent interpolating data instead of solving what Stibitz calls "fancy problems."

The Model 2 was installed at Bell Labs' West Street offices in late 1943, in a room decorated, in Stibitz's words, "avant-garde style." The decorations consisted of spare paper tapes hanging on wall pegs near the computer. Stibitz describes how the computer worked in that room, all day, every day, for years, "with human attention for only a few hours a week, when someone put problems into it." Watching the machine go through its paces unattended by humans was "exciting and a bit weird" for Stibitz.

Stibitz and company had created, in the Model 2, one of the first programmable computers, if not the very first one. The Model 2 also incorporated features that would become standard equipment on home microcomputers in later years—notably error detection, which the NDRC workers called self-checking. (Stibitz had proposed this feature in a memorandum written in 1940.) If something went wrong, the computer would shut itself down until the problem was corrected.

The self-checking circuits helped the Model 2's operators entertain visitors. Guests at the lab were invited to stick a toothpick in any of the madly clicking relays during a computation. The computer would stop when that blocked relay was needed. When the toothpick was removed, the Model 2 went on with the job unperturbed.

Even before Model 2 went into service, Stibitz and his colleagues were preparing its successor, Model 3, a bigger and more versatile machine—"a real show piece," Stibitz describes it—with several times more registers than the Model 2 and a special "hunting" feature that allowed the Model 3 to search for any bit of information requested. (This feature is of course familiar to modern microcomputer users who ask their computers to locate specific programs on tape or disc.)

The Model 3 could carry out a search while simultaneously engaged in solving a problem. It also had a genuine multiplication table built into its circuitry: a rare feature that meant the machine could carry out multiplications directly, without having them broken down into iterative strings of additions.

Like Model 2, Model 3 took its input from paper tapes and sat in a room decorated in similarly avant-garde style. Tapes lay all about the floor. Occasionally visitors would carelessly step on a tape and provoke indignant howls from the programmers. Stibitz remarks that "lively conversation" ensued.

The Model 3 seemed to have an almost human personality. It was nicknamed "the baby" because its trouble alarm sometimes went off in the middle of the night and awakened a sleeping attendant. Model 3 was followed by Model 4, which was essentially the same machine with a few extra capabilities added, such as being able to calculate certain trigonometric functions.

The next computer, Model 5, was a giant that occupied some 2,000 square feet of floor space and could handle calculations so huge that its designers actually had to set arbitrary bounds for infinity! Stibitz remembers fixing positive infinity at $10^{64}$ and negative infinity at $10^{-64}$. By comparison, the universe is thought to be only about $2 \times 10^{18}$ seconds old.

Two Model 5s were built, one for the National Advisory Committee for Aeronautics (NACA) at Langley Field in Virginia, and the other for the Army ballisticians at Aberdeen. The Model 5s were highly reliable. In one week the Aberdeen Model 5 averaged more than twenty-three hours per day of *up-time*, meaning steady, trouble-free operation. Together the Aberdeen Model 5 and its counterpart at Langley did the work of more than 400 human computists with desktop calculators.

The Model 5 still is a clear memory to the men and women who worked with it at Langley. When the Model 5 arrived there in 1945, the airfield was a quiet little place compared to the mammoth aerospace installation at Langley today. Seen from the Hampton shore across the river, Langley afforded a pleasant vista of well-watered lawns and officers' homes built in Tudor style. A block or two beyond officer country, NACA territory began.

NACA (later to become NASA, the space agency) was, in 1945, a small and highly professional group of mathematicians and engineers whose brilliant work in flight research had helped America win the war and would assist the United States in maintaining its world lead in aviation for a quarter century afterward. The spirit of camaraderie—and lack of personal rivalries—at NACA made the Langley group a model of progress and productivity. "Everyone knew each other well and worked together as a team to get the job done," says Thomas Andrews, who helped maintain the Model 5.

NACA was also a colorful and individualistic society. One high-ranking NACA engineer lived in a tin-roofed shack and subsisted largely on candy bars and on fish that he caught from the muddy Back River. He refused to drive or ride the bus to work; instead, he rowed his tiny boat from his home on the Hampton shore to the NACA buildings across the river and back every workday, regardless of the weather. He was delighted when the river rose during hurricane season and flooded the parking lot, because then he could row right up to the front door and moor his boat to the handrail on the steps. "And he wasn't the oddest," says one mathematician who worked at Langley during the forties.

The NACA employees worked in a landscape out of a science fiction film. Giant silver cylinders—the casings of wind tunnels—snaked around the grounds and into and out of buildings. Spherical tanks like steel basketballs five stories high created the intense pressure gradients that sent air rushing through wind tunnels at high velocity. The tunnels were up to nineteen feet wide. In them model aircraft were tested to determine how full-scale planes would hold up under the fierce blast of wind during flight.

The engineers who designed and tested those models had to deal every day with long and mind-numbing strings of equations that described such processes as airflow over a wing or the flexing of a fuselage in flight. For years those equations were handed over for solution to a computing pool of women armed with desktop calculating machines.

One former member of the Langley computing pool, Kathleen Wicker, recalls: "The engineers at the wind tunnels brought their computing to the pool to be done. It was in the old nine-teen-foot tunnel building. When I came there to work in June 1945, I hardly knew what a computer was. Until then we had been using Monroes." (The Monroe Calculating Machine Company manufactured a line of desktop calculators that made "Monroe" practically a synonym for such machines for many years.)

A couple of days after starting work at Langley, Wicker learned that "this big huge computer was coming in, and I was slated to work on it." The "big huge computer" was of course the Model 5, known to the Langley group simply as the Bell Machine.

The Model 5 was installed on the ground floor in a large partitioned room. The partition was needed to isolate the Model 5's relay elements—which "looked like a telephone switching office," Wicker says—from grit and dust that might foul up the relays. The Model 5 also had its own air-conditioning system for protection against the tropical heat of the Virginia summers, which could have caused the metal to expand and thus throw off calculations. "We considered ourselves lucky to have an air-conditioned office," says Wicker, "but it wasn't for us; it was for the computer."

On the near side of the partition, separate from the relays, stood a row of several large cabinets, about the size of soft drink machines. Atop the cabinets were beehive lights, similar in shape to beehives or fat Christmas tree bulbs, that glowed green when everything was running smoothly and red when problems arose. "We worked on the night shift," says Wicker, "and after we left, while waiting at the bus stop across the street, we could see the green lights glowing through the windows."

The green lights glowed most of the time, for the Model 5 was highly reliable, as Stibitz had figured it would be with relay technology. "In all the time we used it, it never made a mistake," says Wicker. "You could run the same problem again and again and always get the same answer. When there was a mistake, it was a human error."

Andrews concurs: "We used this thing for eight or ten years and never detected it making an error—not in all the millions of calculations it made. Everyone was proud that it could run almost unattended around the clock. We were spoiled by its reliability. The electronic computers that came later were faster but not as reliable."

The beehive lights were about the only colorful parts of the Model 5. Everything else in the room, chairs and consoles and all, was gray, except for the white paper tapes that were used to feed the computer. The tapes were similar to those used in the Relay Interpolator, or Model 2, and were about the width of a man's thumb. They were pulled through the computer by sprockets like those on motion picture projectors. Down the middle of each tape ran a row of sprocket holes, on either side of which were punched holes representing data or instructions.

As in the New York office, tapes tended to proliferate, and the Langley group used special filing cabinets to keep the tapes in order. "We had cabinets with numbered wooden pegs," says Andrews. "Routine instruction tapes were stored in the back of the cabinet, while the data tapes were hung on the doors. They were categorized by problem numbers and delivered to the machines on a rolling cart."

Two tapes were needed for each run: a looped *program tape* that told the computer what to do and how to do it, and a *data tape* that contained the information to be analyzed. For generating tabular data, there was also a *table tape* that could be run either backward or forward through the machine, as necessary. The tapes were prepared on a punching device that looked much like an ordinary typewriter.

The program and table tapes "could be used over and over," says Wicker, and in fact they had to be, since the Model 5 had no setup for storing programs inside itself. Computers with that facility, known as stored-program computers, were not yet a fixture of modern technology. Often several copies of a tape were prepared at the same time, because spares were needed in case the originals broke or wore out from mechanical use. Besides getting yanked around by the sprockets, the tapes were poked by little fingerlike pins that jutted through the holes in the tapes and made electrical connections to register data, in much the same fashion as Hollerith's tabulating machine did more than half a century earlier. Sometimes the pins wore holes in the tape where no hole had been intended to be. Then the tape became useless and had to be discarded.

The Model 5's users heard a continual whirring from the sprocket wheels and a soft clatter from the relays in the next room. When the clatter ceased, it usually meant that dirt had found its way into a relay and shut the machine down.

"Despite the air-conditioning, some dust would get in," says Andrews. "Also, there was no prohibition on smoking, and so smoke could get in the relays, too. You couldn't rub the relays with a cloth to clean them, because the cloth would leave lint, and that was as bad as dirt. We had special relay-cleaning strips made of plastic that we pressed between the relay contacts to clean them. We were told the best thing for cleaning relays was a dollar bill. You put it between the contacts, and it would leave no lint." He chuckles. "We didn't really use that."

Despite its size, the Model 5 could not hold much data by the standards of modern computers. Each of its registers, which were arrays of relays mounted on frames about the size of a shirt box, could only contain a single number. "To add A + B = C," says Wicker, "you had to tell the machine to add the contents of the A register to those of the B register and put the result in the C register. So you couldn't handle many numbers, and there was a limited number of mathematical operations that you could do." Yet she thinks the Model 5's limitations made it "a good experience that made for better programmers," because the Model 5 taught programmers how to do a lot with a little, so they could accomplish much more with the increasingly powerful machines that succeeded the Model 5.

A typical run of the Model 5 went as follows. An engineer would bring in a problem to be solved. The problem would not go directly into the machine. First a programmer had to break down the equations into the simplest possible operations: addition, subtraction, multiplication, and division. The "predigested" equations would then be entered in punched code on the tapes and be sent whirring through the computer. The output would appear on a printer similar to an electric typewriter.

The computer "was slow," Wicker recalled one day in the kitchen of her home in Hampton. She was holding one of the few surviving pieces of the Model 5, a round spindle about the size of a hockey puck. It was used to run the tapes through the computer. "But," she added, "it could keep going for hours and hours without stopping to rest, and that was more than a person could do."

Sometimes the machine would halt because a flawed program had gone in, and the program would have to be debugged. Then as now, debugging was an ordeal. The mistake would sometimes be apparent just from looking at the program, but when it wasn't, the Langley team had special debugging techniques to fall back on. They could duplicate the machine's calculations on their desktop machines to see where things went wrong. Another trick was to put more print statements into the program, so that the computer printed out its results automatically at every step along the way and thus brought the error to light.

If nothing else worked, a Model 5 program could be debugged by "stepping it through" the computer. This was a matter of putting the machine in manual mode—that is, turning it into a giant desktop calculator, albeit without a hand crank—and carrying it through the program step by step, watching all the while for the bug.

There was some initial resistance to the Model 5 among the Langley engineers, for engineers have always been arch-conservatives with a skeptical attitude toward innovation. This was especially true among aeronautical engineers, who knew that a newfangled idea might cost some pilots their lives before it was thoroughly tested in flight. But the Model 5's tireless and accurate operation dispelled the engineers' doubts and convinced them to use the computer instead of desktop machines. It was hard to believe that less than a decade had passed since George Stibitz presented his crude K-Model to his colleagues at Bell Labs.

Both Model 5s were decommissioned in the fifties. The Aberdeen Model 5 was donated to the University of Arizona. NACA's Model 5 was given to Texas Tech, but it never reached its destination—at least, not intact. The truck hauling it to Texas tipped over, and the computer was damaged beyond repair. It wound up providing spare parts for the Arizona machine.

Stibitz went around the country lecturing about his computers. He took pains to point out that the computer was "not basically numerical but logical, so that nonnumerical subjects such as musical composition were within its purview." A few years later, computers would be helping composers create electronic music.

While Stibitz worked on his relay computers, other experts in computing science were designing and building their own computing machinery. Among them was a Harvard mathematician who seemed to stand for almost everything the free-thinking, antiestablishment Stibitz opposed. His name was Howard Hathaway Aiken, and he created Harvard's famous Automatic Sequence Controlled Calculator (ASCC), or Harvard Mark I.

# 3

# AIKEN AND ZUSE: THE HARVARD MARK I AND THE Z-SERIES

A towering figure literally as well as figuratively, Howard Aiken has become almost legendary. Half genius and half bully, Aiken had an explosive temper and is sometimes described as a man who looked like an approaching thunderstorm. His colleague Garrett Birkhoff of the Harvard math department describes him as "exceedingly disagreeable." Aiken was known to do violence to desks when something displeased him.

At times the only way to deal with Aiken's bellicosity was to return shout for shout and blow for blow. Birkhoff recalls a pertinent anecdote about Aiken and Dean McGeorge Bundy, who went on to become an advisor to President Lyndon Johnson. Bundy told Birkhoff that he had no trouble dealing with Aiken, because (in Birkhoff's words) "as soon as Aiken started pounding on the table, Bundy pounded right back, and Aiken got the point." Birkhoff also recounts what happened when a faculty committee tried to assert its authority over Aiken and harness his computing machinery for the service of the Harvard faculty. Aiken, says Birkhoff, took only one meeting to "disrupt the faculty committee totally" so that it "never had any control whatever on anything that he did."

Yet in the right company, Aiken could relax and reveal a more genial facet of his personality. Maurice Wilkes, who after World War II would write his own glowing chapter in computer history, describes Aiken as "bluff and uncompromising, but a delightful companion."

Aiken began thinking about calculating machines while a graduate student in physics at Harvard in the late thirties. The road to Harvard was long and arduous for Aiken. He grew up in Indianapolis and had to go to work after the eighth grade. But his stamina was tremendous, and he held down a job with the local gas company at night while attending the Arsenal Technical High School during the day. An enlightened superintendent of schools arranged for him to take a set of special exams that gave him credit for much of his schoolwork so that he could graduate early. Aiken then went to work for the gas company in Madison, Wisconsin, while working toward an undergraduate degree from the University of Wisconsin. He received his B.S. in 1923. The day after graduation, he was promoted to chief engineer of the company.

The next twelve years were busy for Aiken. He went into business for himself and became a professor at the University of Miami. Then, in 1935, he decided it was time to get his Ph.D., and he came to Harvard by way of a graduate program at the University of Chicago.

Aiken's dissertation at Harvard required a plethora of long and tedious calculations, and he began looking into ways to ease the burden of figuring by use of an automatic machine. He proposed his computer in a 1937 memorandum. A model of scientific exposition, it began: "The desire to economize time and mental effort in arithmetical computations, and to eliminate human liability to error, is probably as old as the science of arithmetic itself. This desire has led to the design and construction of a variety of aids to calculation . . . "

Aiken continued with a brief homage to Babbage and other

early pioneers of the computing art; then he outlined the design and construction of a computer that could be built using hardware right off the shelf and which would be capable of "fully automatic" operation "once a process is established."

He listed some of the operations the machine would be expected to perform, including trigonometric and probability functions, and pointed out how little effort would be needed to modify existing punched-card calculating devices, like those manufactured by IBM, into "machines specially adapted to scientific purposes."

Initially Aiken found little support at Harvard for his proposed machine. At that time Harvard still had its head in the clouds and its nose in the air and was reluctant to sully its reputation for "pure" research by getting involved with tinkerers working on computer hardware. Aiken had no more luck, at first, with private industry. He asked the Monroe Calculating Machine Company, famous for their desktop calculators, for support. Monroe's chief engineer, G. C. Chase, liked Aiken's proposal and did his best to get it approved by the firm's management, but the company turned Aiken down because the top executives thought Aiken's machine would be impractical if built.

Fortunately Chase had a contact at the Harvard Business School who put Aiken in touch with IBM, and when that happened, Aiken's fortunes started to rise. IBM was taken with Aiken's idea and agreed to help back the construction of the Mark I.

IBM expected no direct financial gain from this project, for IBM was not in the computer business then. Its principal products were office machines, such as tabulating machines. Only a few years earlier, IBM had been manufacturing Hollerith-type equipment with claw feet. IBM's management was interested in encouraging research in new and promising studies, however. In addition, the Mark I project would give IBM the prestige of being associated with America's most prestigious university.

The project brought Aiken into close contact with IBM's leader, Thomas Watson, Sr. A kindly-looking man with heavy features and a sad smile, and the author of the famous motto

"Think," Watson is one of the most renowned figures in the history of computing, and also one of the most misunderstood.

It is widely believed, for example, that Watson raised IBM from a relatively small tabulating machine maker into the mighty multinational corporation it is today. In fact, he did not; his son, Thomas Watson, Jr., who took over the helm in 1946, presided over IBM's rise to glory. IBM under Watson Sr.'s leadership was still so small (only about $40 million in annual sales) that around 1938 the editor of one British newspaper killed a story about IBM on the ground that IBM was an "unsuccessful company which . . . is never going to amount to much."

Neither was Watson the great inventor he is sometimes described to be. He himself built not a single machine. Though a brilliant manager and salesman, Watson was not a technologist in the same class with Edison or Charles Steinmetz. Nor did Watson spearhead the development of large electronic computers, as is sometimes claimed. He and his company in fact were slow to realize the merits of the new computing technology. It was almost 1950 before IBM inaugurated its first big computer, and that machine (which is discussed in a later chapter) was only slightly advanced over Aiken's Mark I.

The Mark I was a completely mechanical computer roughly fifty feet long and eight feet tall. Whereas Stibitz's machines had electromechanical relays that opened and shut by induced magnetism, Aiken's computer was more like Bush's differential analyzer in that the Mark I's relays were activated by motors.

Aiken's machine contained three-quarters of a million parts—many of them moving—and roughly five hundred miles of wiring, enough to stretch from Harvard Yard to Richmond, Virginia. The Mark I had approximately the dimensions of a small locomotive and looked somewhat like a long stack in a library, until one realized that the books on the shelves were actually rows of relays. When in operation the Mark I made a twittering, clicking noise like that of ten thousand grandmothers all knitting at once. The staff called the computer "Bessie" for its work in computing Bessel functions, which are solutions to certain kinds of differential equations.

Bessie was built around a set of seventy-two IBM rotating registers, which whirled around like robot dervishes to carry out operations on numbers. Each register could store a single twenty-three-digit number and "remember" whether the number was positive or negative. The registers communicated with one another by electrical signals.

A 1946 article in the journal *Electrical Engineering*, co-written by Aiken and Hopper, describes the Mark I's operation thus: "The development of numerical analysis . . . and methods for solving ordinary and partial differential equations have reduced, in effect, the processes of mathematical analysis to selected sequences of the five fundamental operations of arithmetic: addition, subtraction, multiplication, division, and reference to tables of previously computed results. The Automatic Sequence Controlled Calculator was designed to carry out any selected sequence of these operations under completely automatic control."

The Mark I was fed instructions and data punched out on four long paper tapes: one control tape for instructions and three others for data input. The tapes looked like rolls of toilet tissue and were simply continuous strips of IBM punch-card paper. There were also two IBM card readers and a card punch for feeding data into the Mark I, and the machine used two electric typewriters as printers for its output.

Aiken's creation had no keyboard like that on Stibitz's Model 1 or on modern home computers. Instead the Mark I was set up for a run by adjusting some 1,400 rotary switches, knoblike devices similar to the tuners on old-fashioned radio sets. When working properly, the Mark I—reading its instructions one at a time from the control tape—could add 2 + 2 in a third of a second, and 2 × 2 in a second or so. A complicated division problem might take fifteen seconds or longer, while a trigonometric function (sine or cosine) might require a whole minute. This performance made Aiken's machine a bonanza to scientists and engineers, but the Mark I was not restricted to calculations in engineering and the sciences. After the war Bessie helped categorize Greek manuscripts, among other jobs.

Aiken's staff seldom saw the "delightful" side of him. Sometimes he drove them like slaves, twenty-four hours a day. Yet their respect for him was so great that nothing deterred them from carrying out his orders. Once Aiken's group was working to complete a project as a hurricane approached. They kept working even after the storm struck. By the time they finished, fierce winds and torrential rains were lashing the vicinity. To get out of the building and back to the their quarters, the team had to form a human chain and inch their way from tree to tree.

Aiken had a gift for seeing the quick and easy way to do things—a gift that some of his colleagues lacked. Once he was talking to an engineer who wanted to build binary division into a computer so that the machine could compute the quotient of $a/b$. "You don't need to do that," said Aiken, and pointed out that $a/b$ is algebraically equivalent to multiplying $b^{-1}$ x $a$, something then existing computers could do with ease. The engineer was at first unable to comprehend this simple trick of mathematics. He went over to a blackboard, inserted values for $a$ and $b$ into the formulas, and got identical answers. "You're right," he told Aiken. "We'll do it."

Aiken knew how to get the maximum performance from his subordinates. He found out a person's limits, and then pushed him or her beyond them. Once he walked up to Lieutenant (later Captain) Grace Hopper, a former teacher of math at Vassar who became one of the world's leading authorities on the military uses of computers, and told her she was going to write a book. Hopper protested that she didn't know how. "You're in the Navy now," Aiken reminded her.

Hopper wrote the book. It was one of the most famous documents in the literature of computers: the manual for the Mark I Automatic Sequence Controlled Calculator (ASCC) which Aiken built for Harvard in collaboration with the Navy and IBM.

Like any other major R-and-D project, the Mark I was plagued from time to time by visiting VIPs who came to gawk. Once Hopper's quick thinking saved the staff from embarassment when a contingent of admirals dropped by Aiken's lab to see the wonder machine at work. The brass had appeared at the worst possible moment. A component in the Mark I had failed and was causing the computer to shut down every several seconds.

Hopper's remedy was simple. She leaned against the machine and kept her finger discreetly on the start button the whole time to keep the computer running. The Mark I made one mistake after another, but the admirals didn't notice. They departed thinking they had witnessed an error-free run.

The Mark I was formally presented to Harvard at a dedication ceremony in Cambridge in 1945. Aiken and Watson were present, along with Thomas Watson, Jr. Up to that time, the Watsons' firm had invested half a million dollars in the Mark I. That was a huge sum for those days, and especially so in view of IBM's rather small sales. Without IBM's input of cash and technical expertise, there might never have been a Mark I. At the very least Watson deserved a loud public expression of thanks for his company's generous contribution. Aiken was not about to share the limelight with anyone, however, and at the ceremony he barely mentioned IBM's contribution to the project, making it sound instead as if all the laurels belonged to himself and Harvard.

The elder Watson was incensed, to put it mildly. "You can't put IBM on as a postscript!" he shouted at Aiken. Before walking out on the ceremony, Watson told Harvard President James Conant, who was also present, that IBM would back no more research at Harvard. Aiken growled: "The president of IBM can't tell the president of Harvard what to do!" Thomas Watson, Jr., recalled later, "If Aiken and my father had had revolvers, they would both have been dead."

The feud between Aiken and IBM simmered for decades after that incident. Katherine Davis Fishman (see Recommended Readings) tells how IBM's then chairman of the board, T. V. Learson, saw a picture of Aiken in an exhibit during the 1960s and burst out: "That sonofabitch!"

Other IBM executives put Aiken down in more genteel language. In a series of lectures delivered at Columbia University's graduate business school in the early sixties, Thomas Watson, Jr., mentioned Aiken only once and then did his best to make Aiken sound like both a bit player and a piece of ancient history. "The first large-scale computer, the Mark I, built by IBM in collaboration with Dr. Howard Aiken . . . was capable of three calculations per second," Watson said. "The first commercially available large-scale IBM computer . . . did 16,000 per second." So much, Watson implied, for the Mark I.

The Mark I and its three successors, numbered II through IV, had their share of bugs. Not only did Aiken's team contend with bugs, but it also apparently coined the word "debugging." A quite literal bug was responsible. Hopper recounts how, in the summer of 1945, Mark II was housed in a World War I temporary building without air-conditioning. One hot summer day, when all the windows were open, Mark II stopped. Hopper and her co-workers found the source of the trouble. Inside one relay was a moth that had been beaten to death when the relay closed. The dead moth was removed with tweezers and placed in the Mark II logbook, which recorded all activity on the machine.

Shortly afterward, Aiken strode into the room and demanded, "Are you making any numbers?"—his expression for running the computer. He was told they were "debugging" the Mark II. (The expression "bug" was already in common usage a hundred years ago to describe failures in mechanical systems. It appears in the writings of Thomas Edison.)

The Mark II logbook is preserved in the Naval Museum at the Naval Surface Weapons Center in Dahlgren, Virginia. The entry at 1545 hours (3:45 p.m.), September 9, 1945, reads: "Relay #70, Panel F, (moth) in relay. First actual case of bug being found." Thus the Mark II gave computers an entomology as well as an etymology.

Aiken conceived the Mark II, like the Mark I, as a mechanical-relay computer. Besides being moth-killers, the Mark II's relays were exceptionally large and expensive, costing the then exorbitant sum of fifteen dollars each. The Mark II was faster than the Mark I, though slow by electronic standards. An addition on the Mark II took about one-eighth of a second, and twelve seconds could be required for a square-root extraction or logarithmic calculation. Only after the Mark II did Aiken start building electronic machines.

Why did Aiken hold out so long before switching to electronic equipment? He had good reason for sticking with the tried-and-true mechanical relays. Despite his flamboyance, Aiken was a highly conservative and cautious engineer, and he hesitated to trust electronic parts when they were still uncertain quantities. No one could be sure they would work reliably.

Though electronic technology worked faster, Aiken decided to sacrifice speed for reliability and make his early computers mechanical. After the war, he explained that he knew electronic hardware "was the way to go." He added that as soon as he saw electronic components working reliably on other projects, "I went electronic too."

Aiken's move into electronics resulted in the Mark III. Finished in the autumn of 1949, it stored data and instructions on magnetic drums. It had a capacity of 4,350 sixteen-bit words and roughly 4,000 instructions, which is close to what one would expect from a modest home computer today. Access was restricted to drums seven and eight. Data from other drums was transferred onto them, a few words at a time, as needed. Here again, Aiken was concerned more with reliability than with speed, and he jokingly called the Mark III "the slowest all-electronic machine in the world"—it needed almost thirteen thousandths of a second to do a multiplication.

In fact, the Mark III was not completely electronic. In its final version the machine contained some 5,000 vacuum tubes but had approximately 2,000 mechanical relays as well. Neither was the Mark III reliable at first; it crashed frequently and appeared to prove Aiken's wisdom in choosing mechanical relays for the Mark I.

Eventually, however, the Mark III lived up to its famous predecessor's standard of reliability. The Mark III's makers soon realized that heating and cooling were to blame. Electronic components were failing because of thermal expansion and contraction caused by powering up and down. When the computer was turned on and then off, the hot and cool cycles wore out the hardware fast. The solution: leave the computer on constantly. Thereafter the Mark III worked fine. The Mark IV was similar in many ways to the Mark III but calculated more rapidly.

The star of the series was the Mark I, even though, since it used only off-the-shelf hardware, it contributed very little in the way of new technology. It was in many respects a modernized version of Charles Babbage's Analytical Engine, driven by electricity instead of steam. The Mark I was a beautiful blind alley of computer technology, but a blind alley nonetheless, for the old-fashioned mechanical relays of the Mark I were about to be superseded by electronic circuitry.

Aiken's principal contribution was to demonstrate, through his Mark I, that such a big computer could be built and could lead to much larger and better computers. *The Journal of the Franklin Institute* summed up the Mark I's importance in 1952 by pointing out that "it was the first large-scale digital calculator ever built and also . . . stimulated the imagination of the world and thus gave impetus to the desire for more and better computing machines."

While Aiken roared at his staff in Cambridge and listened to the clicking of relays, that same desire—for better computing machines—was driving a young engineering student in Germany, Konrad Zuse, to invent an amazing series of computers that equaled and in many ways surpassed the capabilities of American-built computers of the same generation.

Zuse developed an enthusiasm for engineering at an early age. One story has it that he was inspired to become an engineer when he saw Fritz Lang's classic science fiction film *Die Frau im Mond (The Woman in the Moon)* in 1929. That romantic story may or may not be accurate. What is certain is that Zuse grew up to become one of the most honored figures in the history of computing, even though the Second World War limited his influence on computing in Britain and America.

Zuse was born in 1910 in Berlin-Wilmersdorf but grew up in East Prussia, where his family moved shortly after his birth. East Prussia was conservative, as was the school in Braunsberg where he received his early education; the curriculum was based on the classics and revolved around the use of Latin. Before long Zuse left that backward-looking environment for a more progressive school, and about this time, in his mid-teens, Zuse developed his fascination with engineering. In 1927, at age seventeen, he enrolled in the Technical University (Technische Hochschule) in Berlin. Eight years later he graduated with a degree in civil engineering.

Zuse found engineering school a disillusioning experience. There the romance of engineering was soured for him by the "long and awful" calculations he had to perform. Even the simplest feats of engineering involved huge sets of differential equations that might contain twenty-five variables or more. A single set of these equations might take the better part of a year to solve on a desktop calculator, if indeed they could be solved at all; some sets were so fearsome as to be virtually beyond solution.

After graduation Zuse took a job with the Henschel Flugzeugwerke (aircraft factory) in Berlin, where he worked as a stress analyst, trying to figure out just how much punishment a plane in flight could take before falling apart. Here the differential equations were horrible, and Zuse had the same idea as Aiken: build a machine to do the calculations automatically.

Zuse began sketching machines for this task. He knew that the big problem lay not in the calculations themselves—the additions and subtractions and so forth—but in the steps in between, the recording and transfer of intermediate results. (These results were the numbers that human "computers" had to scribble down on note pads while leaving an audit trail.) And the bigger the set of equations, the more difficult the transfer.

Zuse knew he had to find a better way of getting those intermediate results from one part of a problem to another. At first he thought of printing up special sheets of paper with boxes on them. Each box would hold an intermediate result, and the figures in the various boxes could be passed along to a mechanical calculator by means of a punched-card system. But that setup was too clumsy.

Next Zuse considered something very much like the Stibitz Model 1: a calculator with a mechanical keyboard. Before long he came up with an arrangement similar to, but advanced over, Babbage's Analytical Engine. This was a doubly impressive achievement because Zuse—unlike Aiken, who was well aware of what Babbage had done—had no knowledge of Babbage's work. He was, in effect, rediscovering it on his own, as Stibitz and his colleagues were doing at the Bell Labs about the same time. In a speech delivered twenty years after the war, Zuse admitted, "I did not know anything about computers, nor had I heard about the early work of Charles Babbage."

Babbage had intended a "mill" and "store" to hold data and perform operations on them. Zuse's plan called for a storage unit (Speicherwerk), an arithmetic unit (Rechenwerk), a selection mechanism (Wahlwerk) to link the two, and a control unit (Planwerk). The control unit would be directed by punched tape, as in Stibitz's designs, and would deliver instructions to the selection mechanism and the arithmetic unit. With the design of his machine clear in mind, Zuse decided to devote full time to making it come true, and he set up his workshop in the living room of his parents' apartment near Tempelhof Airport.

Zuse was competent as a draftsman and skilled at mechanics, but he was handicapped as a computer designer by his relative ignorance of electrical engineering. Moreover, he knew very little about how mechanical calculators were built. His lack of knowledge turned out to be a blessing in disguise, however, because he went into the project unburdened by conventional ideas that might have stifled his imagination. "Thus—unprejudiced—I could go new ways," he said after the war.

One convention that Zuse discarded was that of counting in base 10, using toothed gears or whatever to represent the ten digits. Like Stibitz and Wiener, Zuse was familiar with binary arithmetic and found it simpler and more attractive than decimal counting. Zuse reasoned as Norbert Wiener did: why represent ten numbers when two will do just as well?

So Zuse decided to make his first machine a binary device. He was encouraged in this choice by the writings of Leibniz, who several centuries earlier had imagined the whole universe reduced to binary values. Zuse titled one report on his work "Hommage à Leibniz."

Binary arithmetic had the advantage of simplicity, but it also presented to Zuse the same obstacle that Stibitz had faced at Bell Labs, namely, translating base 2 into base 10 and vice versa. Base 2 was, as Zuse put it, "unfriendly." Luckily the base would only have to be converted twice—once when data went into the computer and again when the results came out. For the rest of the time the binary numbers would be "among their fellows," as Zuse said.

Zuse designed and built, with the help of friends, a computer with a mechanical memory unit that used movable pins in slots to indicate, by their position, zeroes and ones. This binary approach made possible a surprisingly compact memory that occupied only about a cubic meter. In 1938 Zuse connected this memory with a crude mechanical calculating unit to produce his first computer, the Z1.

Zuse's second computer carried the hardware one step forward and incorporated electromechanical relays like those in the Stibitz computers. Zuse's friends helped him lay in a supply of secondhand telephone relays, and soon the Z2 took shape.

Problems with the relays made the Z2 less reliable than the Z1, but it worked well enough to interest the German Experimental Aircraft Institute, or Deutsche Versuchanstalt für Luftfahrt (DVL), the German equivalent of America's NACA. The DVL was trying desperately to overcome *flutter*, a shivering of aircraft wings, and saw in the computer a possible means of speeding up the extensive calculations required to tackle the problem.

Not everyone in German aviation thought the computer was needed. One Luftwaffe major reportedly protested, "There is no need for a computer! The German aircraft is the finest in the world!" But DVL provided money for the design and building of a relay computer, and Zuse, still laboring in his parents' living room, set to work on the Z3. Completed in 1941, the Z3 had two thousand relays and could multiply, divide, or extract a square root in only three seconds.

Like the Bell Labs computers and the Mark I, the Z3 had program control. Unlike them, it was a compact machine that occupied only the volume of a closet. The Z3 had a sophisticated push-button control panel that allowed the user to carry out operations just by lifting a finger. With a single keystroke one could convert decimal numbers into binary and with another keystroke switch them back again.

The Z3 could handle imaginary numbers, and it lit up a bulb to indicate when $i$ appeared in a calculation. Zuse devised an elegant programming notation for his machine, including the now familiar symbols $= >$ (greater than or equal to) and $< =$ (less than or equal to). Input for the Z3 took the form of punched motion picture film. One of Zuse's input tapes showed a couple at the beach—when Zuse was finished with it, they looked as if Al Capone had just passed by.

While Zuse was carrying computer technology forward, he was doing the same for programs. Up to this point, computer programs had been manually controlled. One just punched them in, as on an ordinary calculator or on the Bell Labs Model 1. Zuse's Z3 was more advanced. It achieved automatic control of a sequence of calculations and was, as far as is known, the first computer to do so; no longer did a computer need someone standing right there to punch in numbers continually. Now the computer could carry out a string of calculations automatically, thanks to Zuse's tape mechanism. Stibitz's later machines also had this capability, but they came along slightly after the Z3. So the honor of this invention must go to Konrad Zuse.

Though Zuse thus became a software pioneer, the concept of *software,* as distinguished from the *hardware* of a computer, was still unknown as the Z3 came together. In the early forties "nobody knew the difference between hardware and software," said Zuse in a postwar speech to an American audience. "We concentrated ourselves on purely technological matters, both logical design and programming."

Nothing of the Z3 survives. It was totally destroyed when an Allied bomb fell on the Zuses' apartment building in 1944. Indirectly, however, Zuse had his revenge for that bombing when another of his computers—the special-purpose relay computer S1, a non-programmable version of the Z3—was used to design terrifying weaponry.

The S1 looked like a coffin set on end, with an array of relays where the deceased's face would ordinarily have appeared. A cable connected the "coffin" with the control panel, a compact affair like a small writing desk with push buttons.

This sober-looking system was used in the making of the German glider bombs, unmanned aircraft that were filled with high explosive and carried aloft by a bomber. The bombs were then dropped and directed by radio control to their targets, usually British ships. The Britons feared the glider bomb above almost any other aerial weapon. The glider bomb could not be disabled by shooting the pilot, for it was pilotless, and when it hit a vessel, the concussion was so terrific that the explosive in the ship's magazines was liable to go off and thus destroy the ship with its own firepower. Glider bombs were used to good effect against Allied shipping in the Mediterranean in the last two years of the war.

Because glider bombs were built as cheaply and crudely as possible, so their aerodynamics were unpredictable, the S1 was needed. The S1 helped to figure out how much a glider bomb's actual flight path would deviate from the path expected. Once that was known, the Germans could adjust control surfaces on its wings and tail to ensure a steady flight—and a sure kill.

When the Zuse family lost its home, the Third Reich had only a few months left. As British and American armies were moving in from the west and the Russians from the east, Zuse completed work on the Z4, an advanced mechanical computer comparable to the Bell Labs Model 3. Several times Zuse had to move the Z4 around Berlin to escape the damage caused by Allied bombs.

Early in 1945 Zuse put the Z4 on a truck and transported it from Berlin to the university town of Göttingen, about two hours' drive to the west. In Göttingen, where Norbert Wiener had studied only a few years previously, Zuse handed his machine over to the care of the Experimental Aerodynamics Institute, or Aerodynamische Versuchanstalt (AVA). As Germany crumbled before the Allied advance, however, Zuse relocated the computer yet again, this time to a little Alpine village called Hinterstein, where he hid the machine in a barn.

That move was unnecessary, for Göttingen was left undamaged. Had Zuse stayed there, the world would soon have known what marvelous things Zuse and his co-workers had achieved during the war. As it happened, however, because of his retreat to Hinterstein, his work was virtually ignored outside Germany until years after Germany surrendered.

French troops occupied Hinterstein several days after Zuse and the Z4 arrived. Soon thereafter word of the computer reached the British and Americans. They sat up and took notice, for in the latter part of the war the Z-series had acquired the prefix V—the Allies thought Zuse's computer might have something to do with the V-weapons, the German rockets that bombarded Britain in the final months of the war. In fact there was no connection between Zuse's computers and the missiles. The V in the rockets' names stood for *Vergeltung,* or "vengeance," whereas the V on Zuse's machines simply meant *Versuchsmodell,* "research model."

Two British secret service officers came to the barn for a look at the Z4 but were unimpressed. They had no way of understanding that Zuse's computers were every bit as impressive as the Nazi missiles, for Zuse had designed and built his machines practically from scratch. He had no knowledge of other, previous computer designs to guide him and no information at all about contemporaneous computer projects in the United States and Britain. More knowledgeable observers who saw the Z4 in operation later were astounded at what Zuse had accomplished. After seeing a demonstration of the Z4 in Zurich in 1951, one of them wrote, "I could not believe it."

The isolation of Hinterstein was not the only reason that the rest of the world took so long to hear about Zuse's wartime achievements. The Z4 did not look very impressive at first glance, and the fact that it resembled a typesetting machine more than the giant American machines may have led the Allies to assume the Z4 was unimportant. Also, Zuse was a loyal German and resented the Allies; after all, they had defeated his nation and destroyed his home. Consequently he did not cooperate with Allied investigators who came to Hinterstein asking for information about his machines.

After the war Zuse learned what the Americans, particularly Howard Aiken and his Harvard team, had accomplished during the war years. They had built computers bigger than Zuse thought anyone could. Yet Zuse had carried computer design farther than they had—so much farther that his Z-machines are not too much different, except in size and the nature of their circuitry, from the microcomputers we use today.

Had there been no war, Zuse and his associates in Berlin probably would have made the jump quickly from electromechanical relays to electronics; they could have given the world its first programmable, high-speed, all-electronic computing machinery. In fact, they were making plans for such a machine about the time the Z3 was conceived but had to abandon those projects because wartime shortages made it impossible to get the needed parts.

The British and Americans did have the needed parts, however, and between the mid-thirties and the war's end, Anglo-American computer pioneers produced a set of machines that led directly to the digital electronic computers of today.

# 4
# BOMBE AND HEATH ROBINSON

If one had to name the individual who did the most to speed the development of the electronic computer, a case could be made for choosing Adolf Hitler. He initiated a war that called for quantum advances in science and technology, which called in turn for greatly improved data-handling equipment, which spurred the development of the electronic computer.

As the Nazis advanced west across the Continent, a now legendary team of scientists and engineers, known officially as the Government Code and Cypher School and informally as the "Golf Club and Chess Society," gathered at the manor of Bletchley Park, just north of London, to devise machines that could solve the secret ciphers used in Nazi military communications. Once the German signals could be decoded and read, Britain could stand a fighting chance of keeping the Nazis at bay.

With the shadow of the German behemoth looming over

them, the Bletchley Park team knew that codebreaking was vital to Britain's survival. As one Bletchley Park alumnus, the mathematician I. J. Good, said after the war, "If you hated Hitler enough, you would fight on against fearful odds." Good's co-worker Allen W. M. Coombs described the Bletchley mind-set more poetically when he called the codebreakers "a happy few, a band of brothers." Coombs added that he and his co-workers at Bletchley Park were "inspired simply by the firm belief that this could be done, that it was the right thing to do, and that by guess or by God we were the people to do it."

"It" was the breaking of the Enigma code. Enigma was a cryptographic machine used to communicate in code between military headquarters and units in the field, both on land and at sea. The immediate ancestor of Enigma was invented by an American named Edward Hebern in 1915. Hebern took the then new electric typewriters and rewired them so that they could transform typed messages into ciphered ones via a simple substitution code. For example, the Hebern machine could transform the word *America* into *Zutopaz.*

The Hebern machine could be used to decode messages as well as encode them, provided the sender and the recipient had machines with identical wiring. The wiring was fixed to deliver only one cipher unless one went to the trouble of switching the wires around. However, Hebern saw a way around this shortcoming and used rotors to rearrange the connections when a key was pressed.

At last he had a rotor-equipped electric code machine (as he called it) built and working. The machine looked much like a typewriter but had some unusual features. Its keyboard had no numbers, but only the twenty-six letters of the alphabet, arranged as on a conventional typewriter. Directly above the keyboard was an array of twenty-six small glass windows, each with a letter of the alphabet printed on it. The windows were illuminated from behind by small electric bulbs.

Where the roller would be on a modern typewriter, the Hebern machine had five rotors; each rotor had the letters of the alphabet enscribed on it and twenty-six contacts on either face of the rotor—one for each letter. The rotors were wired together in pairs, and the wiring carried out the enciphering process. Each single rotor could provide twenty-six different ciphers.

Together the rotors could generate $26^5$ unique ciphers, or almost twelve million of them. This vast multiplicity of ciphers meant that codebreakers would have to work tremendously hard and long to break a machine-made code. By the time they could succeed, the information in the coded message would have been useless.

The Hebern machine was easy to use. One simply chose a *headcode*, meaning a certain starting order for the rotors, such as RFPQB, and tapped out a message in *plaintext*, ordinary language. Then the intended recipient of the message could enter the same headcode into an identical Hebern machine, type in the encoded text of the message, and read out a decoded plaintext as it appeared, one letter at a time, in the little lighted windows. Hebern was granted a patent on his invention, and sold a few code machines to the U.S. Navy in 1928.

In 1919 a Dutchman named Hugo Koch patented a similar device that he called the "secret writing machine." Though Koch designed the equipment, it was actually built by a German engineer named Scherbius, who bought the patent rights in the early 1920s and renamed the machine Enigma.

The Scherbius Enigma differed in a few respects from Hebern's device. For example, Enigma had only three rotors instead of five, but it routed a cipher twice through the same set of rotor wheels, giving it the equivalent of six rotors. The wheels differed in size but averaged about the diameter of a small pancake. Each wheel had studs or cams mounted at intervals around its rim on both sides. These studs could be set by hand in two positions, protruding either on one side of the rotor or the other. Thus they represented elements of a binary code, which was determined by the setting pattern of the cams on the wheels. To make codes as obdurate as possible, two of the wheels spun erratically and introduced a random element into the cipher.

Scherbius's machine was such a success that it attracted the attention of the German armed forces, which knew of many uses for such a codemaking system. In the 1920s the Germans were still suffering from their defeat in 1918, a disaster they owed in part to the highly effective British codebreaking effort of the First World War. The British codebreakers operated out of Room 40 in the Old Admiralty building and, at the height of their success, broke the German diplomatic codes that allowed the decryption of the famous Zimmerman telegram that did so much to draw the United States into the war and ensure the Allied victory.

The Germans saw Enigma as a good protection for their military codes, and before long Scherbius's device made its way to the offices of the *Chiffrierabteilung* ("Chi" for short), the Cipher Department of the German Army, or *Reichswehr*. For military uses Enigma was perfect. It generated seemingly unbreakable codes, was easy to use, and could be carried and set up on the battlefield as conveniently as an ordinary typewriter. When the German Army saw Enigma's potential, the machine was withdrawn from the commercial market and put into production for the military.

The civilian Enigma was improved for military use by the addition of a plugboard—a smaller version of the kind used in telephone switchboards—to add a final layer of encryption to the code rung up by the rotors. Eventually the number of rotors was increased from three to five for added complexity and security. Then Enigma was capable of 1,000,000,000,000,000,000,000, or one sextillion, initial settings. By comparison, there were then only about three billion persons on earth. That was encryption with a vengeance.

The British and the Germans were not the only people interested in codes. The Poles also had superbly skilled code experts on their side, and their equivalent of Chi and Room 40 was the *Biuro Szyfrow 4*, or BS4. The BS4 team had an unexpected stroke of good luck one Friday in 1928 when a mysterious crate addressed to the German embassy in Warsaw found its way into the railway customs office there.

The Germans seemed very eager to get their hands on whatever was in that crate, for they demanded that it be cleared through customs at once. Suspicious, the customs officials told the Germans to come back on Monday, since the office was getting ready to close.

Immediately the customs men got in touch with BS4. When an intelligence team arrived, the crate was opened and found to contain a brand-new advanced model of Enigma. Over the weekend the Poles had a chance to study the device thoroughly. Then they repacked it carefully and handed it over to the anxious Germans on Monday morning.

Even that brief look at Enigma told the Poles that new codebreaking techniques would be required to keep up with the Germans. BS4 had been helped partly by stolen German documents passed along by the French and partly by electromechanical codebreaking machines known as *bombas*, after a brand of ice cream.

Little is known about the bombas today. None of them appears to have survived the war, and the only physical evidence available is a crude sketch drawn more than three decades after the Allied victory. The drawing shows a boxlike contraption, apparently the size of an apple crate, with a motor inside. The motor is linked by a drive shaft to a set of wheels atop the box. Evidently those wheels duplicated the action of the Enigma rotors. One bomba was used for each rotor in the Enigma, so six altogether were required.

The bombas' output was passed along to experts who used it to work out code solutions manually on a light table, an internally illuminated, glass-covered table on which one moved around perforated sheets of cardboard similar to those used to isolate prime numbers in the old stencil method. When juxtaposed in certain ways, the holes in the stencils would line up and light would shine through to indicate a rotor setting.

This system worked well for several years. The Poles were able to read much of the Reichswehr's radio chatter. Sometimes the messages were humdrum, but at other times they were chilling. On June 30, 1934—the infamous Night of the Long Knives, when Hitler wiped out SA leader Ernst Röhm before Röhm could pose a threat to his authority—the Poles deciphered a message from the Air Ministry in Berlin: "TO ALL AIRFIELDS. BRING IN ERNST RÖHM. DEAD OR ALIVE."

For four more years, while the Germans continued to use the three-rotor configuration on their machines, the Poles were able to eavesdrop on German Enigma communications. Then the Germans added two more rotors to their Enigma in 1938, and Poland's listening line to Germany was effectively cut.

At a secret meeting between Polish and British officials in 1939 in Paris, the Poles passed their machines and codebreaking know-how over to Britain. One member of the British delegation was a mysterious figure known only as "Professor Sandwich." His actual identity is still a British state secret, and he appears to have been wearing a disguise, so it is impossible to say with certainty who Professor Sandwich was. He may have been one of the makers of an early electronic computer at Bletchley Park.

Several books have been written about the Bletchley Park team and its role in the war, but relatively little has been written about the machines developed there. Though some of the material on those computers is still classified, much has been released by the British government in the last decade, so we now have something approaching a comprehensive picture of how the British codebreaking computers came together.

The Bletchley team was a colorful group of mathematicians, engineers, chess experts, and amateur actors and musicians, with a vast accumulation of experience in everything from wiring to exotic algebras. The diversity—and occasional eccentricity—of the Bletchley team impressed Winston Churchill. On one visit to the manor the prime minister turned to an aide who had helped with recruiting for Bletchley, and said, sotto voce, "I told you to leave no stone unturned. I did not expect you to take me so literally!"

Some of Britain's most gifted academics worked at Bletchley. There was the brilliant and impatient mathematician Max Newman, who had a gift for seeing straight to the heart of a mathematical problem or any other situation. Newman had a keen wit and frequently aimed it at his peers. When he learned, after the war, that a colleague was traveling the length and breadth of

Britain giving talks on computer development in the United States, Newman growled, "He's getting twenty pounds each time for delivering the same speech!"

Newman was an outstanding lecturer. Once while delivering a talk on the "ham-sandwich theorem," a point of mathematics dealing with the division of masses into equal parts by a hypothetical plane, Newman explained the theorem so lucidly that the audience burst into applause before he had finished—an almost unheard-of tribute in the sober society of mathematicians. (Newman's expertise with the ham-sandwich theorem naturally makes one wonder if Newman was the shadowy Professor Sandwich who met with the Poles in 1939. The answer will probably remain a mystery unless and until the British government declassifies the remainder of its files on Enigma.)

Newman and his subordinates were known as the "Newmanry." They worked in close association with the "Testery," a group of mathematicians under the direction of one Major Tester. Prominent among their Bletchley co-workers were C. E. Wynn-Williams, of the Telecommunications Research Establishment (TRE), who in 1929 had invented the first electronic particle counter for use in physics research, and Allen W. M. Coombs, a Ph.D. from Glasgow University, who worked in the Dollis Hill Research Station of the British Post Office and believed God made the cosmos "with Rugby Union football in mind."

Also present at Bletchley Park were D. W. Babbage, a distant relative of Charles Babbage who went on to become the president of Magdalen College; Ian Fleming, who is best known today as the creator of James Bond; another Dollis Hill expert named Sidney Broadhurst, whom Coombs described as a wizard who could design complicated circuits "at the drop of a hat" and get it right on the first try; and Lewis Powell, who later became a justice of the U.S. Supreme Court.

Perhaps the strangest and most brilliant of the Bletchley group was the mathematician Alan Turing. Some historians consider him to be the greatest single figure in the history of computer science. Other students of computer history are waiting until all the facts on his career, some of them still classified, are available before making a full appraisal.

Turing was born in 1912. His father was an employee of the Indian Colonial Service. At Cambridge, Turing studied under Max Newman, whose lecture one day gave him a tantalizing idea. Newman was talking about the solution of mathematical problems: what the Germans called the *Entscheidigungsproblem,* "calculating problem," which dealt with the issue of what calculation could and could not do.

Newman discussed the view, held by the German mathematician David Hilbert, that any mathematical problem can be solved by a fixed and definite, "purely mechanical" process, as Newman described it. The word *mechanical* intrigued Turing, for to him it signified a process that some kind of automatic computing machine could handle. But what kind, specifically?

Turing sketched an outline for such a device. He dubbed it a *universal automaton* and proved it could solve any problem that depended on mathematical computation, as long as the machine was properly fed with information.

This hypothetical device, now known as the Turing machine, consisted of an apparatus that scanned an endless tape that was divided up into squares. Each square would be either blank or marked with symbols. Turing suggested the symbols be written in binary code. The machine would read the squares individually, in series, and could move the tape either ahead or backward one square at a time.

This arrangement was essentially the same as the one Vannevar Bush had used in his Rapid Selector (and Lehmer in his number sieves). The similarity of these different machines reflects the universality of the computer that Turing imagined. Historian Brian Randell points out the universal-automaton concept made Turing one of the first to grasp the "universal nature" of the concept of digital computers and that Turing probably understood the universality of that idea even more clearly than Babbage had a century before.

Turing presented his idea of a universal automaton in a paper published in 1937. The following year he made a voyage to the

United States. He lugged a heavy sextant aboard ship to keep track of his position at sea. Soon after his return Turing was employed at Bletchley Park and began converting his abstract ideas into working machinery.

At Bletchley, Turing was an object of wonder, not only because of his obvious brilliance but also by what Randell calls his "outlandish" personality and his bizarre mannerisms. I. J. Good tells how, in between sentences, Turing would make an odd stuttering noise—"Ah-ah-ah-ah-ah"—which made it difficult to get a word in edgewise "or even to have a line of thought of one's own!" Good recalls that another quirk of Turing's was to chain his coffee mug to a radiator pipe to keep the mug from being stolen.

Not all Turing's precautions against theft were successful. Once he took his family's cash reserves and buried them in the woods for safekeeping, then was unable to relocate the money. Turing never would have made a successful pirate. He was an equally untalented administrator and preferred leaving the running of his section to someone else. Possibly he hated having obligations to other people—Brian Randell once noted that Turing had an "obsession with self-sufficiency"—or perhaps he simply felt more comfortable in the role of inventor.

Many of Turing's inventions at Bletchley are still official secrets, including his contribution to the codebreaking computers called the Bombes, a code name derived from the Polish *bomba*. Because *Bombe* connoted atomic-weapons research, a subject the Germans were pursuing avidly, Good thought it a poorly chosen code name, for the manor probably "would have been blitzed to pieces" if the name had leaked out.

The Bombe was an electromechanical relay machine that housed a set of wheels comparable to those in Enigma. From the outside the Bombe must have looked impressive, but exactly what it looked like is uncertain. F. W. Winterbotham, who with his 1974 book *The Ultra Secret* was among the first to reveal the successes of Bletchley Park to the public, compared the Bombe to an "Eastern Goddess" with a "bronze-coloured face" and referred to the machine as Bletchley's "oracle." Bombe stood about eight feet tall and eight feet wide at its base and had the profile of "a keyhole," according to Anthony Cave Brown in his book *Bodyguard of Lies.*

Cave Brown's description of the Bombe is at variance with the image drawn up by the BBC for a television series in the 1970s. Working from the recollections of Bletchley team members who had seen and worked with the Bombe, the BBC produced an artist's conception of the machine. This sketch of the Bombe depicted a big boxlike cabinet about six feet high, ten feet long, and two or three feet deep, mounted on wheels and hooked up to an electric typewriter. The BBC artwork showed, on the Bombe's side, a set of plugboards, similar to those on the Enigma itself. However the Bombe appeared, its electromechanical relays are said to have made a noise similar to that of the Harvard Mark I. Cave Brown likened the sound to that of knitting needles.

The Bombe was to a large extent Turing's creation. Precisely what Turing contributed to the Bombe's design is uncertain and will remain so until material now secret is declassified, but Good reports that Turing suggested an improvement that increased the machine's computing power greatly. It seems reasonable to think Turing helped devise an algorithm to aid in sifting through all the many possible combinations of settings.

An *algorithm* is a mathematical concept that might be described as the best possible way of doing something. The familiar traveling-salesman problem, in which one has to work out the most profitable route through a number of towns, is an example of a search for an algorithm. In this case, the best algorithm is the one that nets the salesman the biggest profit for his time and labor.

The goal of the Bombe algorithm, if that was really Turing's contribution, was to work out the solution to the German cipher as quickly and accurately as possible. Turing's idea was so effective that Good once said Britain "might have lost the war" without it. Turing also invented a special device, described as an "ingenious set of rods," that unraveled the coding procedure of the Enigma plugboard.

Turing is not always given credit for his original contributions to the Bombe. It has been widely reported that the British merely took the already existing Polish bomba and modified it. A 1981 exhibit of wartime computing machinery, at the Smithsonian Institution in Washington, D.C., informed viewers that the Bombe was "first developed in Poland . . . [and] perfected by the English."

One reviewer of the exhibit took exception to that claim and cited a 1980 article in the journal *Cryptologica* which listed Alan Turing "among the architects of the bombe's design" and asserted that "the British bombes were not technological descendants" of Polish devices. Good's memories are consistent with this appraisal. He describes the Polish bomba as "primitive."

How many Bombes existed is still a secret, but they seem to have been numerous and were dispersed at sites around the country. Besides the machines at Bletchley, there are known to have been a large number of Bombes at the manor of Gayhurst Court, where they operated twenty-four hours a day. The manor was perfect for such secret activities, for it was isolated and accessible only by a long narrow drive. The only outward sign of its military importance was a barbed wire barricade and sentry at the entrance.

Like its Polish predecessor, the British Bombe did not itself decode messages. It only worked out the initial positions of the Enigma rotors. If that information led to a successful decryption, the codebreakers reported a "good stop." At that point cries of "Reds up!" or "Greens up!" would ring out. The messages were color coded, red ones being of maximum importance.

The intelligence provided by the Bombes was known by the code name Ultra. News in the deciphered signals often was grim, especially during the Blitzkrieg. One of the architects of the Blitz, General Guderian, traveled along with his fast-moving troops in a special command car equipped with Enigmas, and his messages were decoded and read in Britain almost as soon as they were sent. The signals told a gruesome tale of defending French troops smashed by the attacks of screaming, gull-winged Stuka dive bombers and overrun by the Nazi infantry that moved in behind the planes.

Gloomy though its burden might have been, Ultra brought joy to the Allied commanders. General George Patton was espe-

cially thankful for Ultra and traveled with his own Ultra intelligence truck. (Curiously, Field Marshal Montgomery disdained
Ultra and preferred not to use it.)

The Bombes probably saved thousands of lives at Dunkirk
alone. German messages unscrambled by the Bletchley computers made it clear to the British War Cabinet that the situation in France was hopeless and there was no point in continuing
to fight. So the British Expeditionary Force troops were ordered
to evacuate from the French beaches. The early warning provided by Ultra and the Bombes allowed time for a rescue force
to gather and set sail for France. Some 340,000 men were
plucked off the shore. Without the intelligence from the Bletchley machines, those men might have perished.

All the information in the decoded messages was written
down and stored in a huge cross-indexed card file. Eventually
the file reached a mammoth size. No information was ignored or
discarded. Brian Johnson, in his account *The Secret War*, says the
file contained "hundreds of thousands of names, units, postings,
supply requisitions, details of promotions, courts martial and
leaves of absence. A transfer of a single Air Force lieutenant
could reveal an impending attack." The Bombes had caused an
information explosion.

The Bombe was only one of several computing machines
designed and built at Bletchley Park. Two later generations
of Bletchley computers were made necessary when the Germans started using a new cipher machine, known to the British as "Fish," that was more sophisticated than the Scherbius
Enigma.

Essentially, Fish was a teleprinter that utilized both the Hebern wheel mechanism and another American invention called
the Murray telegraph code. The Murray code had been in widespread use before the war and included thirty-two different elements that could encode letters, numbers, punctuation, and
teleprinter functions. Each of the code elements was broken
down into five elements of about one-fiftieth of a second each
and could exist in only one of two states, on or off, referred to
respectively as *mark* and *space*.

So the Murray code was binary. It represented letters as

strings of ones and zeroes. *A*, for example, was 11000. These binary letter-equivalents could be added together to generate a message. Their binary character led to Fish's downfall, for those strings of ones and zeroes were something a computer could solve as well as generate.

The Germans seem to have used Fish rarely in the early days of the war. Enigma was suitable for most uses. When the Germans did turn to Fish extensively, beginning in 1942, they usually sent its messages by wire rather than by radio. That made Fish signals hard to intercept.

Fortunately for the Allies, one of the cables bearing Fish messages ran through neutral Sweden for a short distance, and the Swedes were able to tap in and listen to the Fish cipher. A Swedish teleprinter mechanic devised a machine, apparently a backward-working version of the Fish itself, that would convert Fish messages into plain language, but advances in Fish encryptions soon made his invention obsolete.

The Fish mystery made its way to Bletchley Park, where a mathematician with the Testery, W. T. Tutte, solved some of the Fish ciphers by time-consuming manual methods—pencil and paper.

Newman thought he saw a better way. He knew Fish could be deciphered by some manual process like the strip method or stencil method, but Newman didn't like hand processing because it was too slow and difficult. Instead he thought the job could be done with the aid of an automatic device like Lehmer's number sieves, using perforated paper tapes punched out in code.

Two tapes would do it. One would be a key tape that copied some characteristic of the coding machine and was glued together at the ends to form a loop. The other tape, designated the message tape, would also take a loop form and would contain a message to be cracked.

The procedure was to whirl the tapes around until they had achieved every possible position relative to each other; then if the tapes were kept in synchrony—that is, in step—somewhere along the way the tapes would line up so as to isolate the key to the cipher, just as the number sieves picked out primes. The computer could then read the key and hand it over to the code-breakers for use in reading coded messages.

This is how the binary, digital nature of the Fish messages made them suitable for analysis by a binary, digital computing machine. Although the principles and mechanisms involved in Newman's decoder and Lehmer's number sieves are similar—isolating prime numbers in one case and a cipher in the other—it seems unlikely that Newman had the number sieves specifically in mind.

Newman's theory seemed sound. Now he wanted to test it on a machine. Purely mechanical devices were out of the question, for they were incapable of the terrific speeds required to go through all the possibilities in a reasonable time. So the test device had to be electronic.

At this point Bletchley was lucky to have on its staff a quiet genius named Thomas Flowers, who had been thinking about electronic data-processing equipment for years. Described by his Bletchley colleagues as a modest, bespectacled man with the air of a kindly but resolute schoolmaster, Flowers had worked before the war at Dollis Hill.

Unlike its U.S. equivalent, Britain's post office handled both mail delivery and telephone service. That service was not always good. Often calls went awry. A caller might get a wrong number even when the correct number was dialed, or the call might not connect at all. What was wrong? Flowers thought the electromechanical switches in the phone system—the same kind of switches that Stibitz used in his K-Model and Zuse in his home-built computers—might be at fault.

Vacuum tubes, Flowers believed, could replace electromechanical relays and be made to work more reliably than the clattering little switches. In Europe as in America, this was a minority view in the late 1930s and early 1940s, for phone switches were tried and tested—unlike the vacuum tube, which had yet to prove itself. Moreover, vacuum tubes were much more fragile than the rugged metal relays. One engineer known to the Bletchley Park team summed up prevalent feelings when he said (using the British world for vacuum tube, "valves"), "Valves? Don't like them. Nasty things. They break."

Yet Flowers remained convinced that vacuum tubes could perform both reliably and rapidly in a computer. Though before the war he had never heard "computer" used except to describe someone who did calculations on a desktop machine, he now was sure that he could build an electronic equivalent of any data-processing machine then in existence. That prospect, he recalled after the war, filled him with elation. He was unaware while at Bletchley of similar ideas being pursued elsewhere by Stibitz and Zuse and Aiken. Conversely, the rest of the world would know little of Flowers's work on electronic computers at Bletchley until long after the war, because of official secrecy.

Flowers, Wynn-Williams, and several other electronics experts went to work on the project, and soon Heath Robinson, an electronic machine with five or six dozen vacuum tubes in it, was born. Heath Robinson was named for a British cartoonist who, like America's Rube Goldberg, was famous for his drawings of fanciful machines doing improbable things.

Unlike Bombe, which was strictly an electromechanical device, Heath Robinson incorporated several dozen vacuum tubes as well as a tape-recording feature similar to Lehmer's number sieves. Heath Robinson occupied a hut, or temporary one-story wood frame building, on the grounds of the manor. The exact appearance of Heath Robinson is not public knowledge, but it is said to have been a much more compact machine than the mammoth Mark I at Harvard.

Heath Robinson contained a pair of synchronized photoelectric paper tape readers that could read two thousand characters per second. (A human reading at that speed could finish this entire book in just over five minutes.) The readers resembled little movie projectors built backwards. Instead of shining a light out from within the machine, as a projector does, Heath Robinson aimed a beam of light into the machine from outside. At the receiving end of the beam of light was a set of photoelectric cells. In between the cells and the bulb stood a special glass plate that was completely opaque except for some odd-looking transparent holes shaped like reversed parentheses: )(. These double crescent masks, as they were called, came into play whenever holes in the tapes lined up and let through a flash of light. The holes "molded" the incoming light beam into a roughly square configuration that was easy for the photocells to register. One might say the masks were Heath Robinson's spectacles.

The loops of tape were made of standard teleprinter tape and were about three-quarters of an inch wide and many thousands of characters long: far too long to hang freely, so they had to be strung on an eight-foot-tall metal carriage with movable pulleys, called a *bedstead*. The bedstead was about as tall and wide as a modern garage door and sent the tape on a giddy ride "up and down and in and out," as the Gilbert and Sullivan song says.

Heath Robinson's output appeared on what Good called a "primitive printer" that clattered away at fifteen characters per second. The output consisted largely of numbers, but not exclusively. Letters made up some of Heath Robinson's "speech" too. Heath Robinson did not itself produce a decoded message; that was supplied later by the Wrens (Women's Royal Naval Service, or WRNS), who also handled the preparation of the tapes. The Wrens were officially assigned to H.M.S. *Pembroke* to conceal their work at Bletchley, and worked in three shifts of eight hours each, around the clock, feeding Heath Robinson tapes and data. The men at Bletchley tried occasionally to help with making up the tapes but always caused trouble, and soon they learned to leave the task entirely to the Wrens.

Heath Robinson housed a component that shows how strong Boole's influence on computers turned out to be. Inside the machine was a *modulo-2 adder* that carried out binary calculations utilizing the one-and-zero Boolean algebra system. This adder helped unscramble the binary codes produced by the whirling German rotors.

Coombs describes the circuitry of the adder as "very ingenious" in theory but "in practice . . . a nightmare." It had to be adjusted with surpassing care and even then did not always work. Sometimes it operated as desired for a while and then shut down inexplicably. Once a despairing Coombs went to Flowers for advice after two weeks of fruitless struggle.

"Change the frequency," Flowers told him. Coombs did as told. "It worked," wrote Coombs in a memoir of the project after the war. "I still don't know why. Nor, he tells me, does he."

Heath Robinson was built with more emphasis on speed than on reliability, and for a while the machine seemed to demonstrate Murphy's Law. Everything that could go wrong did, at the worst possible moment. The paper tapes kept breaking. When a tape snapped, the whole job had to be started over from the beginning. Heath Robinson also had a tendency to seize up, overheat, and catch fire. Operators could tell things were amiss when they scented the computer burning. At times Heath Robinson seemed nearly human, Good writes, for one of its troubles "could be diagnosed by smell!"

Less dramatic but equally troubling was the stretching of tapes. Every trip through the sprocket wheels would pull the tape slightly out of shape, and before long one tape might be half an inch longer than the other. Then the tapes could no longer be run in synchrony. New tapes would have to be made—a long, tedious, messy business that ended with snowy mounds of little white punchings scattered around the hut floor.

For a while Heath Robinson's temperamental nature made the fate of Newman's team seem dubious. It appeared that the computer might never work properly, and the Bletchley group would be condemned to labor for the rest of the war in rooms littered with the wadded-up paperwork of previous failures.

Yet Heath Robinson's creators overcame its troubles and soon had it running smoothly. Then the computer relieved the codebreakers of some of their tedious manual labor, such as the stencil technique. This involved sliding one stencil across another to identify repeating ciphers. It was boring duty. Once Good fell asleep while moving a stencil around. When he awoke, he accidentally slid the top stencil one space to the right, and in so doing he uncovered a twenty-two-letter repeat of the same cipher. That was the longest such repeat ever found at Bletchley.

Heath Robinson's total output was small. Though the machine was rushed into service in the phenomenally short period of eleven months, the machine's "teething troubles," as Flowers called them, restricted its operating time. So did other factors including tape length. Short tapes had to be run more slowly than long ones to allow sufficient time for the printing operation, while very long tapes placed great strain on the tape near the sprocket wheels and had to be run at reduced speed to keep the tape from tearing.

Only rarely did Heath Robinson reach its turnpike speed of two thousand characters per second. But in spite of the fact that Heath Robinson processed relatively little data, it was an invaluable aid to the Bletchley Park team, for Heath Robinson and its several companion machines (which had names like "Peter Robinson" and "Robinson and Cleaver" in honor of well-known London stores) proved that high-speed electronic devices could be built successfully for cryptanalytic work.

Bletchley Park's success was due partly to the fact that the codebreakers could get almost anything they needed at any time. Sometimes their requests sounded excessive. Brian Randell (see Recommended Readings) relates how once Bletchley Park asked the Ministry of Supply for yet another shipment of several thousand vacuum tubes. The official at supply replied, "What the bloody hell are you doing with these things, shooting them at the Jerries?" Some parts were hard to find at times, notably resistors because Germany had been the principal prewar supplier of them. But it was no great problem to have equipment flown in from the United States under the lend-lease agreement.

The cryptanalysts at Bletchley Park were short of nothing but time. Consequently, life could be hectic in the extreme. Flowers mentions that many of the staff worked steadily "for weeks and months on end," save for a few hours per week allotted to talk with spouses and get haircuts. Sometimes the staff used unusual time-saving measures: Flowers once drew up a rough draft of a projected new machine, then simply tore the draft into pieces, handed them out to his co-workers, and told them to get busy.

Even at the height of a war there is time for romance, however, and at Bletchley love had its effects. One circuit bore the same initials as Coombs, AWMC. When Coombs became engaged to be married, Sidney Broadhurst commemorated the happy event by designating another, closely associated circuit with the initials of Coomb's fiancee, VJB.

To relieve the often intense pressure, Bletchley left time for recreation. The group had an active dramatic club, and sometimes odd things happened as its members slipped into and out of their stage roles. One of the codebreakers had a marked nervous twitch, but it would disappear completely as soon as he stepped on stage. Other entertainments included dances at nearby Woburn Abbey, a beautiful deer-stocked estate where the Wrens were billeted. The men were bused there from Bletchley for the dances. They speculated about living conditions at the Abbey, particularly a report that the Wrens bathed in pairs for economy. On the way back, the Bletchley men would indulge in bawdy songs.

Ribaldry at Bletchley was not confined to singing. Sometimes it showed up in messages as well. The Germans prefixed messages with four-letter identification codes. The male mind being what it is, German operators made some of those codes obscene. Their vulgarity increased until the high command sent down a directive—also received and decoded at Bletchley—to watch their language. That incident gave the Wrens at Bletchley great satisfaction.

Almost as entertaining were the visits Bletchley received from the leaders of the Allied war effort. Once Field Marshal Alexander stopped at Bletchley to give the team a pep talk and got a good laugh when he mimicked the characteristic half-wave, half-salute of Montgomery, the field marshal who had looked down his nose at Ultra. U.S. Army Air Force General Jimmy Doolittle also paid Bletchley a call and, in a typically American analogy, told the Britons their work enabled the Allies to "see the other fellow's cards."

Churchill himself stopped by to meet and talk with the men and women who, with their computers, provided him with so much of his priceless intelligence. He referred to Bletchley as "the goose that lays the golden eggs but does not quack," and had his own cryptic way of demanding Bletchley's decryptions: "Where are my eggs?"

Once Churchill stood atop a stump on the lawn outside the manor house and addressed several dozen of the codebreakers. The prime minister glowered at the youthful faces before him and said, "You all look very innocent." Good remembers Turing being very nervous about meeting Churchill that day. (Good relishes Churchill anecdotes. He tells of one occasion when someone wrote underneath a photo of Churchill, instead of *Balls,* the words *Round Objects.* When Churchill saw it, he said, "Who is Round, and to what does he object?")

Good arrived at Bletchley fresh out of Cambridge. "I arrived at Bletchley Park on May 27, 1941, which was the day that the *Bismarck* was sunk," he recalls, "though that was not cause and effect." He was billeted for a while in Fenny Stratford, a small nearby town that was dominated by a tanning factory described by Good as "both the smelliest and the ugliest building in England." Viewed from one angle, the factory looked as if a bomb had scored a direct hit on it, but it was actually undamaged.

Among Fenny Stratford's residents was a retired banker who told Good one day about the Enigma his office had used before the war to encipher confidential bank transactions. "Fascinating," said Good. "Of course," he recalled years afterward, "I told him nothing about the work I was doing at the office!"

Today Good serves as professor of statistics at Virginia Polytechnic Institute in Blacksburg, a tiny community nestled in the Blue Ridge near the Carolina border. Good came to Virginia Tech almost two decades ago. He had a choice between Virginia and a position at a Scottish university, and chose Tech partly because he liked slides of its campus buildings.

A slightly built man with still-dark hair and mustache, Good seems to take an interest in practically everything from space travel to nutrition to what he sees as the deterioration of the English language. He wages a one-man campaign for precision in speaking and writing (he has issued a circular on the proper use of "denote" versus "designate") and has served as advisor to science-fiction filmmakers. Once he inquired about taking out life insurance for space flight. The insurance company turned him down.

Good occupies a small office at Virginia Tech. A portrait of Bertrand Russell glares at visitors. A huge desk fills the middle of the room, and file cabinets and bookshelves cover all but a few square inches of the walls. To fit anything else into the office, you would have to suspend it from the ceiling—and indeed Good has hung up one of his most prized possessions: the Good dream figure.

The dream figure looks like a hunk of Swiss cheese designed by an engineering student. Roughly spherical and about the size of a beach ball, it is built of hundreds of domino-sized plastic rectangles salvaged from a child's game. From one angle the dream figure looks amorphous. Then a breeze through the office window catches the dream figure and rotates it slowly, until the object all at once reveals a neatly symmetrical array of tunnels running through its body. "It's fantastically complicated," Good says. "A crystallographic figure made up of alternating triangles and octagons. The final version came to me as I dreamt. It proved conclusively for me how powerful the unconscious mind really is."

Heath Robinson, for its part, proved conclusively how powerful and fast electronic computing machinery could be. Great as its achievement was, however, Heath Robinson was inadequate for the demands made on it. The Bletchley team needed a bigger, faster, more powerful computer, which soon appeared in the form of the famous Colossus.

# 5
# COLOSSUS AND THE PILOT ACE

While Heath Robinson took shape, the Blitz was on. Huge Heinkel and Dornier bombers pounded London with tons of high explosive. British pilots in Spitfires and Hurricanes mauled the German bombers and their Messerschmitt fighter escorts, and the wrecked Nazi aircraft plummeted to earth amid the craters their own bombs had made. From high ground near Bletchley, one could see the city burning at night. There was also a threat, toward the end of the war, from German V-weapons. Bletchley Park came through the war unscathed, but German bombs did some damage at Dollis Hill. Yet the Bletchley team had little time to spare for worry about descending bombs and missiles. The codebreakers and their machines were preoccupied with cracking the ciphers of the tyrant across the Channel.

Nothing illustrates the difference between British and German society in the 1940s better than the organization of their research establishments. The Bletchley organization was reasonably democratic. Good remembers that suggestions for research or for improving day-to-day operation were written up on a blackboard in the research room and discussed at informal tea parties, which he describes as "free-for-all" gatherings where "many decisions were made." It is interesting to contrast this arrangement with the situation in many German research and development centers during the war. As Arthur C. Clarke, who helped develop Britain's early radar, once pointed out, everyone benefited from the free give-and-take of ideas in meetings like those at Bletchley. Relatively low-ranking members of the group could talk openly with their superiors and, if the occasion called for it, correct their errors for them. The Germans, on the other hand, had a much more rigid hierarchy in which a correction or suggestion might take weeks to reach the attention of the lofty Herr Doktor Professor in charge of the work. Bletchley illustrated how flexibility and informality could bring rich rewards.

Bletchley also demonstrated how the inventive process had evolved since Babbage's day. Up to the end of the nineteenth century, many inventions that changed the world were solo efforts. They were put together by one individual, or perhaps two, working in many cases during spare moments in a private shop or even a basement. Thus arose the legend of the Yankee inventor, an inspired handyman tinkering for the betterment of the world. Vannevar Bush, for one, liked to think of himself as an inventor in this tradition, and in his early years at MIT it was still possible for one person working alone to give technology a big shove ahead. By the time Bush was building his differential analyzer, however, the Yankee inventor was dying out. Invention was becoming more and more a team effort like that at Bletchley, because the increasing complexity and sophistication of machines made them too much for one person's mind to contain. New machines required input from five, ten, even a hundred minds or more. The result is that almost all the major inventions of our century, from the atomic bomb to the microchip, have been team achievements, of which the computers conceived at Bletchley are classic examples.

If teamwork was a way of life at Bletchley, then so, paradoxically, was secrecy. To foil enemy spies, work was split up so that only a few groups knew what other groups were doing. Except for the close ties between the Newmanry and the Testery, it was rare for anyone in any division to discuss his or her work outside the division. One did not talk shop at meals. Hardly anyone at Dollis Hill, where part of Heath Robinson was assembled, knew what was going on at Bletchley Park or even that the code-breaking school existed.

For the same reason, nothing was put on paper unless absolutely necessary. When diagrams were written down, it was often impossible to tell what the devices shown were supposed to do, or even what they were. Brian Randell describes how individual plans from which machines were built were made so small that it was impossible for the workmen who assembled them to determine what the circuits were supposed to do. Coombs relates how one worker familiar with radio took a close look at the circuits he had been wiring and realized he had merely been making a bunch of direct-current amplifiers, "which of course he had."

Soon after Heath Robinson went into service, Flowers realized that the breakage of its punched-hole tapes was causing tremendous problems. Flowers wanted to get rid of the tapes or at least reduce their number, and he thought he saw a way to do it.

The key tape, he decided, was unnecessary. It could be replaced by a device called a *bit-stream generator,* which would generate the equivalent of a key tape in the form of electronic pulses, inside the machine. The bit-stream generator would save precious time by eliminating the need to prepare and install a key tape. It would also make the remaining tape more reliable, for the message tape could be pulled around by smooth-faced pulleys, instead of sprocket wheels, so that the tape would stand less chance of snapping.

Flowers described what he had in mind, but his proposal met with "considerable skepticism." That was understandable. Electronic components still had a dubious reputation. But Flowers pointed to his post office experience with tubes and maintained that electronics would do the job reliably.

He was right. The tubes held up well, because they were not

jarred by moving around (no computer of this size could go anywhere) and because the tubes were left on constantly, thus avoiding the stresses of warming up and cooling down—which caused such trouble for Howard Aiken's first electronic computer.

In short, the bit-stream generator was a success. It involved a counter, much like the one Wynn-Williams devised years earlier for physics research, and a set of special tubes called *thyratrons*. A thyratron holds an ionized, or electrically charged, gas under very low pressure and is similar to a vacuum tube but responds a little less quickly. The thyratrons were part of an increase in electronic hardware to handle high-speed operations. The electronics also had to be supplemented by electromechanical telephone-style switches for more leisurely duties.

The result of these and other advances was the giant electronic machine Colossus. Its name was appropriate, for Colossus was the largest machine Bletchley Park had ever tried to build.

The first Colossus occupied a brick building near the manor house. On entering a large room one saw Colossus looming up against one wall. Tapes were prepared in an adjacent room and handed in to Colossus's operators through a portal, or hatch, in the wall. The hatch was at an inconvenient level, and Good recalls one could easily bang one's head on its upper edge. There was some practical joking between the two rooms; once Good's magnificently long scarf was rolled up and passed through the hatch in place of a message.

In contrast to the improvised Heath Robinson, Colossus "looked more like a finished production," says Good. It was as long and wide as a small highway billboard and roughly one meter deep. On the left-hand side, beneath a wall clock and next to the windows, stood Colossus's bedstead, festooned with tape and pulleys. To the right stood the teleprinter, about the size of a big manual typewriter, on top of a metal stand that resembled an infant's high chair. One would sit on a tall stool to read the printout, which rolled out of the printer on strips of paper about the width of one's hand.

A fat cable connected the printer to the main body of Colossus, which had a face covered with vacuum tubes and toggle switches similar to everyday light switches. The toggles were used to set up programs. They were supplemented by plugboards like those used by phone operators. The plugboards consisted of arrays of jacks, each array roughly the size of a serving tray, into which cables were plugged to put one part of Colossus in communication with another. Setting up Colossus for a run was like arranging a hundred-party call to all corners of Britain at once. The plugboards on Colossus's face were supplemented by others in the rear, so the machine had crisscrossed wires running over it almost anywhere one looked.

The first Colossus was basically a bigger and faster version of Heath Robinson—but it was not quite the supercharged vehicle its designers had hoped it would be. Colossus's makers once tried to run it at five times Heath Robinson's speed, or about 10,000 characters per second; that test was unsuccessful. At 9,700 characters per second, the tape fell apart. Flowers described how the pieces, traveling at nearly sixty miles per hour, came to rest in "all sorts of curious places."

Colossus's maximum safe speed turned out to be only about 5,000 characters per second. That was a letdown, because speed was vital to the codebreaking effort. Machines had to work as fast as possible to give Britain the greatest possible chance of cracking the Nazi ciphers.

Was there anything that might be substituted for mere speed? Fortunately there was: parallel processing.

A parallel-processing computer makes good use of time by carrying out several different operations at once instead of plodding along in serial fashion, one step after another. So Colossus became a parallel-processing machine.

Bletchley Park gave Colossus five different processors which worked in parallel fashion. Each processor handled a tape at about 5,000 characters per second, for a total of some 25,000 characters per second. With the addition of components called *shift registers*, which enabled Colossus to read all five tapes simultaneously, the computer was in business. The first Colossus went into operation in December 1943.

Colossus was remarkable for many reasons. For one, it had an internal clock that kept all parts of the machine working together. This was absolutely necessary when Colossus had five different "trains of thought" going at once, which all had to be kept apace of one another.

Also interesting was how Colossus used thyratrons to simulate the whirling of the cipher rotors in the German machines. The thyratrons were linked up in "rings" that substituted electronic operations for the mechanical motion of the wheels. (These setups were rings only in the sense that they were hooked up in a circuit; the tubes were laid out in straight rows.) Only one valve in a given ring would be conducting at any particular moment. After that valve finished, then its neighbor would take over, and its neighbor, and so on, thus copying in electronic fashion the rotation of the mechanical rotors. This circuit was somewhat like an illuminated clock face on which lighted bulbs mark the successive hours.

Signals from the thyratrons were passed along to other circuits that carried out complex Boolean calculations in ones and zeroes. Colossus could calculate Boolean functions containing up to approximately a hundred symbols, and it used binary vacuum-tube electrical circuitry on a grander scale than ever before.

The first Colossus to be built contained 1,500 vacuum tubes. Later models would have almost twice that many. The tubes gave off so much heat that it was once suggested the operators go shirtless. Howard Compaigne, a U.S. Navy communications expert, was assigned to Bletchley and remembers the tubes' heat output: "Ah, the warmth at two a.m. on a damp, cold English winter!"

Other, later computers had serious problems with circuitry "frying" in the machines, but Colossus was spared that problem for two reasons. First, the tubes themselves were so big—some almost the size of beer cans—that they could not be spaced closely enough for hot spots to form between them. Second, the tape seldom ran fast enough for the electronic components to "work up a sweat" and get overheated.

A description of a complete run of Colossus follows. When a tape was ready, and the switches and plugs had all been arranged properly, the message-tape motor would be turned on and the tape prepared by the Wrens would start rolling into the machine. Faint whirring and humming sounds would emanate from the computer as the tape drive warmed up.

Processing would not commence at once. It took a few seconds for the tape to reach its running speed. When the tape was moving fast enough, Colossus's operator would press a manual start switch, and processing would begin as soon as the start-hole passed through the tape reader and told Colossus where the message began. Another, similar hole at the end of the tape would inform Colossus that the message was over. The Wrens left a gap of about 150 spaces between the start- and stop-holes on a tape, to allow Colossus enough time to complete all operations from the previous passage before the tape came around again.

The tape would go through the machine repeatedly until the cipher was broken. As the tape ran through the photoelectric tape reader, the passage of the evenly spaced sprocket holes would generate a string of signals called *clock pulses* (symbolized as *CL1*) that provided the "beat" for the processing operation.

Simultaneously, the five-hole message tape would generate five streams of pulses designated $c1$ through $c5$. The digits in these bit streams would pass along into the shift registers in accordance with the tempo supplied by the clock pulses. The shift registers held six bits each and would make six consecutive bits of the message available to the five parallel processors for analysis. Here the thyratrons helped by keeping the parallel processors working in exact time with one another. The shift registers were connected by switches to function units that handled much of the actual processing of the data.

Ultimately the data would all be passed along to a base-10 counter that was hooked up by a set of twenty-eight wires to a read unit and then to the printer. When a decryption was done, the printer would begin to clatter. From beginning to end, the processing was under the guidance of a master-control device that used CL1 and a second, slightly delayed set of pulses called CL2 to keep everything working in synchrony.

When the computer reached a solution, the printer would start typing out the answer. How fast it typed depended in part on how quickly the computer deciphered the message. Colossus did not always process tapes in huge chunks. Sometimes the computer looked at message tapes one character at a time, and while doing so Colossus once appeared to be calling for its friend Good. The printer typed out: "I . . . J . . . G . . . O . . . O," stopping only one letter short of completing Good's name.

Colossus's output was not plaintext but something in between plaintext and code that had to be interpreted by specialists. An analyst would look over the output as it emerged from the printer and would tell the Wren in charge how to alter the program if necessary. Colossus's operation required a close cooperation between the machine and its operators, and more than three decades passed before humans and machines again attained this degree of closeness, or "synergy," as Good calls it.

The first Colossus worked so well that the government demanded more of them. The volume of German teleprinter traffic was increasing, so more machines were needed to decipher the texts. At the same time, the Germans were coming up with better operating procedures, and more computer power was required to outfox them.

So, in late February of 1944, Flowers was flabbergasted to learn that a dozen more Colossi were to be built and running by the first of June. Flowers replied that the task was impossible, but the Bletchley Park group went to work on more Colossi and by late May had a second Colossus operating—though only intermittently.

That Colossus was temperamental and seemed to have a perverse mind of its own. Its makers struggled with it right up to midnight on May 31, the day before the deadline. Then they gave up and went home for much-needed sleep. When they returned the next morning, a miracle appeared to have taken place: the Colossus was up and running.

In fact, good luck had happened along the previous evening in the person of a Dollis Hill night-shift engineer. He had found the trouble to be parasitic oscillation—a condition comparable to epilepsy in a human—within some of the tubes. He corrected the problem by adding a few resistors. The machine went into service on schedule.

Epilepsy was not the only health problem that the Colossus seemed to mimic. Occasionally it suffered "eyestrain" as well. The photocells in the tape readers became desensitized after a few days of steady use and had to be put in a dark cupboard for a rest before they could be used again.

On the whole, however, the electronic elements of Colossus held up admirably—better, in fact, than the relays and other electromechanical components. Colossus proved the superiority of electronics over machinery for computing. Whereas Heath Robinson occasionally erred because a relay misfired, Colossus's electronic codebreaking operations were virtually error-free. Mistakes crept in only through human failure—when someone at Bletchley took down a message inaccurately, or an operator on the German side made a blunder in transmission.

Evidently the Germans never concluded that their messages were being routinely intercepted and read. If they had, they appear to have blamed treason rather than the existence of sophisticated codebreaking systems across the Channel. Though the existence of Britain's codebreaking computers was known to more than a thousand individuals, from Churchill to the Wrens who prepared the paper tapes, no word of Colossus and Heath Robinson ever seeped out to the Germans. The computers and their work remained an ironclad secret until the British government declassified information about Colossus in 1975.

That the Germans never learned of Colossus and Heath Robinson is a testimonial to the patriotism and devotion of the men and women involved with the monster machines at Bletchley. But patriotism alone did not preserve secrecy; fear played a part as well. Winterbotham describes how, when new sergeants joined the Ultra organization, he made them swear they would never divulge Ultra's secrets. Then an officer would pull out a revolver, point it at the frightened sergeant, and say: "If you ever do, I personally shall shoot you."

The burden of security sometimes caused persons privy to the Bletchley secrets great anxiety, even long after Germany's defeat. Historian Ronald Lewin has described how, twenty-five years after the war ended, a former member of Field Marshal Alexander's intelligence staff suffered a brain hemorrhage and had to be rushed to the hospital. Though she came close to death and was saved only by a long and delicate operation, her main concern was not for her own condition but for the secrets she carried. She was frightened that she might lose control and babble, under anaesthesia, the secret of the Bletchley computers.

Thanks largely to Colossus and its cousins at Bletchley Park, Britain had the best codebreakers of the war. The U.S. brass from Eisenhower down got most of their decoded enemy messages from the British, and Churchill was able to read messages addressed to Hitler before Hitler had a chance to read them himself.

Yet the United States was not completely in Bletchley Park's shadow where the cracking of enemy codes was concerned. The Americans had brains and persistence on their side, if no wonder-working machines, and they achieved some miracles of cryptanalysis without Bombes to help. One of the largely unrecognized heroes of the war, for example, was the U.S. cryptanalyst William Friedman, who is often considered to be the greatest code and cipher expert of all time.

Friedman set about solving the Japanese Enigma code (Japan's armed forces used a variant of the German machine) with no tools to help him except pencil and paper. He worked virtually alone. At last he cracked the code. Then he himself cracked under the strain of his labors and had to spend several months in a psychiatric ward. Among his leading achievements was the Sigaba machine, comparable to Enigma, that protected American signals all through the war. Before the war, Friedman had taken an interest in Enigma and had tried to find reliable ways of breaking its ciphers but was unsuccessful because he lacked a high-speed mechanical codebreaking machine like Colossus.

At one point the United States came close to starting work on a machine for decryption similar to Heath Robinson. Shortly before Pearl Harbor, Friedman was approached by John Mauchly—the meteorologist who was present at George Stibitz's demonstration of his relay calculator at Dartmouth—about using an electric-powered computer of Mauchly's design to encipher and decipher coded messages. Had history taken a slightly different turn, America might have used Mauchly's gadget as the basis for a computer like Heath Robinson or Colossus. Mauchly had no luck interesting the government in his device, however, and so Britain was able to take the lead in the use of computers for cryptanalysis. But Mauchly would play an important role in the history of computing, as we will see.

If the ghost of Charles Babbage had hovered over Bletchley during the war, he would have been gratified to see his branching logic incorporated into the Colossus. Branching logic gave the computer the added dimension of "intelligence" that was needed to solve the devilish problem of Fish's eccentric rotors, which, as noted earlier, introduced an extra element of randomness and security into the cipher. So far as is known, the Colossus was the first computer to use branching logic successfully.

Many myths have grown up around Colossus since information on the computer has been made public. One of the grossest and most widely published untruths about Colossus has been that it led indirectly to the destruction of the cathedral city of Coventry in a German air raid on November 14, 1940.

According to the myth, Churchill was presented just prior to the raid with a deciphered enemy signal to the effect that Coventry was about to be attacked. Churchill allegedly decided to leave Coventry undefended rather than risk tipping off the enemy, by mounting a spirited air defense of the city, that the German code had been broken and Luftwaffe messages deciphered. In short, Churchill has been accused of sacrificing a city to preserve the secrecy of Colossus.

That is a fiction. The Germans attacked Coventry more than three years before Colossus went into operation. What really happened is a more interesting story, for it illustrates the limitations on what Bletchley and its computers could accomplish.

The British intercepted several German transmissions containing code names of cities to be hit in a series of nighttime air raids. One of the code names was *Korn*, "corn." The codebreakers could supply the code name of the target, but that was all. There was no way to tell which city the Germans actually had in mind.

At that time the most likely target for a German aerial assault seemed to be London, so Churchill assumed that the British capital would be the target. The actual target turned out to be Coventry, which had been left undefended—not because the British government was desperate to keep its computers secret (though it was), but because they had expected the blow to fall elsewhere. Also, sending up fighters at night would have been a futile gesture at best—British pilots were not trained for nighttime combat and could have hoped only for a few accidental hits on German bombers.

So Colossus and its precious decryptions were not the cause of Coventry's sacrifice, nor were the earlier Bletchley computers able to provide the actual meaning of the deciphered code names. There are some tasks no computer, however advanced, can do.

Another myth about Colossus has been that it was the first general-purpose electronic computer. Colossus was not made for general purpose. It was designed, as was the Bush differential analyzer, to handle a highly specific set of problems. The age of all-purpose electronic computers was inaugurated by a set of American-made machines, which is discussed in subsequent chapters.

Work on codebreaking machines ceased at Bletchley when Germany surrendered in 1945. As soon as the end of the European war was announced, Newman called the staff together to tell them that their job was done and they could go home. Newman added (according to Flowers) that to lose their fascinating jobs at Bletchley "was the price which we as individuals had to pay for peace."

Exactly what happened to the Colossi then, only the British government and some of the surviving Bletchley staff members know. Most likely the giant machines were taken apart and their components scattered. The Bombes were dismantled too. The Wrens showed up for work one day with screwdrivers and took the now silent machines apart, piece by piece, to be hauled away and disposed of.

The makers of Bletchley's machines went their separate ways after the war. Some went into government, others into academe, and still others into private industry. Coombs tried to carry the pell-mell pace of Bletchley over into other, more leisurely work in peacetime. He soon learned better. "War is one thing," he writes, "peace is quite another."

Turing's career had its ups and downs following the war. In 1945 he went to Britain's National Physical Laboratory (NPL) to work on an advanced computer known as the Pilot Automatic Computing Engine, or Pilot ACE. As the word *Engine* in the ACE's name indicates, Babbage had a strong influence on the making of the ACE. Turing was well aware of Babbage's pioneering work more than half a century earlier. He was also aware of the need to improve programming, and in a written proposal for the ACE, Turing expounded what would become one of the most important and controversial ideas in the history of computing: the stored-program concept.

The stored-program concept is so familiar today that it is hard to imagine a time when it did not exist. A stored program is one stored inside a computer, not in external memory arrangements like stacks of cards. The stored-program computer uses a program that includes data to be analyzed. Program and data are all mixed up together and can be fed in simultaneously through the same input organ.

In a modern home computer, the input organ is the keyboard. Machines like Colossus, however, did not have keyboards. Instead Colossus had big arrays of switches and phone jacks that were used to arrange the programming. The data were fed into Colossus separately by message tapes. Other computers such as Heath Robinson had separate input tapes for data and program. Mixing program with data promised to save a lot of time and effort, and it did. That is why the stored-program concept revolutionized computing.

The stored-program concept figured prominently in one of the most bitter disputes in the history of science: that of who originated the stored-program idea. Turing may or may not have been the first to think of stored programming, but he was among the first to explain it in print.

Turing was also among the first to imagine how subsidiary operations—what we call subroutines—could be included in a program. A *subroutine* is a highly useful trick of programming that may be thought of as a side trip or detour in a program. The computer reaches a certain point in the mainstream of a program, goes off and does something else on the side for a while, then comes back and resumes work at the point where it left off. This is accomplished in BASIC programming by the familiar "GOSUB . . . RETURN" loop. "GOSUB" sends the computer off on its tangential errand, and "RETURN" brings it back to the point where it departed. Turing explained the procedure this way:

When we wish to start on a subsidiary operation, we need only make a note of where we left off the major operation, and then apply the first instruction of the subsidiary. When the subsidiary is over, we look up the note and continue with the major operation. Each subsidiary operation can end with instructions for the recovery of the note.

Here "GOSUB" is the note, and "RETURN" looks it up when the loop's work is done. Turing, in language reminiscent of his unsuccessful treasure hunt in the woods, referred to this process as "burying and disinterring" data. He used "BURY" in place of "GOSUB," and "UNBURY" instead of "RETURN."

Turing wanted to eliminate the human element in computing as much as possible and that meant putting distance between the human operator and the machine's operation. What Good called synergy between human and machine had no place in Turing's design. Turing detested the "human element of fallibility," as he described it, which could result in misplaced plugs or wrongly flipped switches. He wanted to remove what he called the "human brake" on the operation of computers, so that error would be reduced and, in Turing's words, "the speed of the machine [would be] no longer limited by the speed of the human operator."

Turing had in mind a machine that could multiply two ten-figure numbers in half a second. "This," Turing wrote, "is probably about 20,000 times faster than the normal speed with calculating machines." At NPL Turing hoped to make his fast stored-program computer a reality.

The head of NPL, Sir Charles Darwin, grandson of the famous naturalist, noted Turing's arrival in a BBC address in 1946:

About twelve years ago a young Cambridge mathematician, Alan Turing by name, wrote a paper in which he worked out by strict logical principles how far a machine could ... imitate processes of thought. It was an idealized machine he was considering, and at the time it looked as if it could never possibly be made. But the great developments in wireless and electronic valves during the war have altered the picture. Consequently Turing, who is now on our staff, is showing us how to make his dream come true.

By 1946, as Darwin indicated, computer hardware had gone electronic. No longer were vacuum tubes seen as nasty things to be avoided. Turing's primary concern now was with programming.

Colossus and Heath Robinson had used clumsy arrangements of switches and plugs to set up programs. Turing was sure there were better ways to do it. He explained, "we are trying to make greater use of the facilities available in the machine to do all kinds of different things simply by programming rather than by the addition of extra apparatus." This was a goal of the Pilot ACE.

The Pilot ACE was a big machine by early postwar standards. It was to have a capacity of some 6,400 words of thirty-two binary digits each. (*Words* should not be confused with the modern expression *bytes*. A byte and a word are two different measures of data-holding capacity. Words are generally bigger than bytes—in this case, four times bigger than the eight-binary-digit, or eight-bit, byte commonly used in home computers today.) Turing drew up notes for four early versions of the ACE, but he was never fond of documentation and none of those notes has survived. The only ACE version of which we have substantial records is Turing's Model V.

The ACE project was troubled by friction between Turing and other members of the staff. Among other things, Turing appears to have resented the influence on the Pilot ACE of hardware enthusiasts who wanted more emphasis on that aspect of the work. He expressed contempt for what he saw as "the American tradition of solving one's difficulties by means of much equipment rather than by thought." Turing's NPL colleague J. H. Wilkinson claims that Turing had especially poor relations with an American expert in electronic computing, Harry Huskey, who spent a sabbatical year in 1947 at NPL helping with the ACE. Huskey, however, reports no great conflict with Turing. "In all my relations with him," Huskey writes, "I found him cooperative and helpful."

Turing's frustration may have had more to do with the fact that he wanted a big, powerful machine, and his NPL co-workers had in mind a smaller experimental prototype, or pilot. Finally Turing walked out, leaving his co-workers to finish the Pilot ACE. He returned briefly a year later, in 1948, but was again displeased with working conditions at NPL and chose not to rejoin the project.

Despite Turing's absence, the Pilot ACE eventually was completed and worked well. Among its early successes, in 1950, was a simple multiplication program known formally as Successive Digits. The staff shortened its name to "Suck Digs." NPL's director, Darwin's successor Sir Edward Bullard, was not impressed. He thought the program was "scarcely epoch making."

In fact, the program was significant. It demonstrated conclusively that the computer was working as it should; and only three decades later millions of home computer users would be using descendants of Suck Digs to test the capabilities of their desktop microcomputers.

A few years after Turing left NPL, the British nation turned on him and destroyed him for a crime that would be decriminalized in Britain only a few years later: homosexuality. Turing went cruising in London one evening and struck up a friendship with an unemployed nineteen-year-old. When their affair was discovered, Turing confessed everything to the police. "I really think he wanted to get caught," says a colleague who knew him during the war years. "It was either confess or live a life complicated immensely by lies and subterfuges."

Though Newman and others of his Bletchley colleagues testified as character witnesses in his behalf, Turing was convicted, as Oscar Wilde had been for a similar offense in the previous century. Wilde was sentenced to prison, but in the years since

Wilde's offense the art of criminal punishment had been refined, and the law had a truly fiendish fate in store for Turing.

He was given a choice between prison and hormone treatments. He chose the treatments. The effects were devastating. Turing's breasts began to grow. Finally he could stand the ordeal no longer and committed suicide, like a character in a fantasy, by biting into a poisoned apple. He made the cyanide himself in his home chemistry laboratory.

The British nation, which very likely owed its salvation to Turing's work on codebreaking computers during the war, showed him its gratitude by having him, in effect, tortured to death under medical supervision. Turing died in 1953. Four years later homosexuality was legalized in Britain.

In the peacetime autumn of 1945, Flowers visited the United States and stayed about six weeks. His itinerary took him to Aberdeen, Bell Labs, MIT, Harvard, and the Moore School. He visited Aiken and Hopper and saw the Mark I and had a look at the Model 5. Flowers was close-mouthed about his work at Bletchley Park, for the existence of Colossus, Heath Robinson, and the Bombe was still an official secret. Flowers expected to meet George Stibitz at Bell Labs but discovered he had taken a position at the University of Vermont, so the Briton boarded a train for Essex Junction and met Stibitz in Burlington for a weekend visit.

At the Moore School of Engineering at the University of Pennsylvania in Philadelphia, Flowers made the acquaintance of John Mauchly, who had spent the war years working on the computer that would be known as ENIAC. Maurice Wilkes, the British computer pioneer who found Howard Aiken's company so congenial, and of whom we will see more later, described ENIAC as the focus of "the big bang" that led to the explosive growth of computing technology in the postwar years.

Wilkes's description was accurate. In terms of its impact on later generations, both of humans and of machines, ENIAC was one of the two most important inventions to come out of World War II. The other was the atomic bomb.

Yet ENIAC did not appear with the suddenness of a mushroom cloud. Its genesis was the end product of two long and intertwined trains of events that began during the Great Depression in the environs of Philadelphia and the Iowa grain country.

# 6
# JOHN ATANASOFF AND THE ABC

While the Bletchley Park codebreakers were assembling the Bombe and Stibitz was converting phone relays into electrome-chanical calculators, a physicist and mathematician named John Vincent Atanasoff, at Iowa State College (now Iowa State University) spent the late thirties working on what would become one of America's first electronic computers, and one of the most famous computing machines in history.

A Southerner with interests ranging from the polarity of molecules to the history of alphabets, Atanasoff was born in 1903. He took an interest in calculating at age ten, when his father, an electrical engineer employed by a phosphate mine in Florida, acquired a Dietzgen slide rule. One could read a Dietzgen to an accuracy of one part in 2,500, or 0.04 percent—equivalent to about two feet per mile. Much of twentieth-century science and engineering was accomplished with the help of slide rules like this one, and a good slide rule opened up all kinds of discoveries to the young Atanasoff.

He had the device mostly to himself, for his father did not need it very often, and the slide rule became, in Atanasoff's words, "my meat." In a few days he was working simple mathematical problems with it. Before long he moved into the intricately scaled world of logarithms, where numbers, like quick-change artists, are transformed into fractions of powers of ten and then back again into their familiar form.

Atanasoff's venture into logarithms left him hungry for more. He found a college algebra text in his father's library and from the book learned about differential calculus, about derivatives and factorials and binary arithmetic.

In high school Atanasoff decided he would go into theoretical physics. It was an exciting study, because in the years since Atanasoff's birth the physical sciences had been transformed from top to bottom by Einstein's works on relativity and the photoelectric effect, both published in 1906. Into the fast-changing world of physics Atanasoff plunged as an undergraduate at Florida State, where during his first year he read a book showing a mathematical proof using binary arithmetic. Years earlier he had read about the binary counting system in a textbook belonging to his mother. In the entire class, he was the only one that had ever heard of base-2 numbers. Binary math would play an important part in the making of Atanasoff's revolutionary calculating machine.

Atanasoff was getting motivated to build that machine while doing his graduate research in physics at the University of Wisconsin in 1929 and 1930. Part of his work required him to calculate the polarizability of helium. His results were excellent, but the labor was tremendous—eight weeks of hard work using a Monroe desktop calculator—and he began to think about machinery that could do the job faster. He later said this research on polarizing helium was his "first experience in serious computing" and "polarized" him toward computers.

After taking his Ph.D. degree in 1930, Atanasoff joined Iowa State as an assistant professor of math. He rose quickly through the ranks of academe and was soon an associate professor of math and physics, supervising the research of several graduate students. Some of Atanasoff's students were interested in linear partial differential equations, which are especially daunting relatives of the equations that defeated Lord Kelvin in his quest for a computer.

Atanasoff saw that automatic computing machinery would be needed to solve equations like those. He described in a memorandum the many possible uses for such a device:

... In the treatment of many mathematical problems one requires the solution of systems of linear simultaneous algebraic equations. The occurrence of such systems is especially frequent in the applied fields of statistics, physics, and technology. The following list indicates the range of problems in which the solution of systems of linear algebraic equations constitutes an essential part of the mathematical difficulty:
1. Multiple correlation.
2. Curve fitting.
3. Method of least squares.
4. Vibration problems involving the vibrational Raman effect.
5. Electrical circuit analysis.
6. Analysis of elastic structures.
7. Approximate solution of many problems of elasticity.
8. Approximate solutions of problems of quantum mechanics.
9. Perturbation theories of mechanics, astronomy and the quantum theory.
This list could be expanded very considerably, for linear algebraic systems are found in all applications of mathematics which possess a linear aspect. . . .

In this way the solution of large systems of linear algebraic equations constitutes an important part of mathematical applications.

Mathematics, then, stood to gain much by the invention of a computing machine that could tackle those fearsome strings of equations. The question was, what kind of apparatus was best? What should the machine be like?

Atanasoff knew it would be either analog or digital. (He claims, incidentally, to have coined the word *analog.* Digital machines he called "computing machines proper.") Analog computers—which substitute a process like the sliding of a stick or the rotation of a gear for operations on numbers—had the advantage of long experience. So many analog computers had been built already that the principles behind them had been thoroughly tested.

The most famous example of an analog computer is, of course, the slide rule. Atanasoff thought of ways he might turn the familiar old Dietzgen into a bigger and more accurate calculating device. He considered replacing the slide with strips of 35-millimeter motion picture film rolled over sprockets. (About this same time Konrad Zuse in Germany was also putting movie film to use in computers, but he intended it as input to a computer, not as a mere analog of a slide rule.) The film-operated gadget could be made reasonably accurate. Any fairly long piece of film would have many thousands of individual frames in it, so that error could be reduced to perhaps one part in 100,000, or 0.001 percent. That was forty times better than the best accuracy one could get with a conventional slide rule; it was the equivalent of half an inch per mile. But Atanasoff soon rejected this plan because even that degree of accuracy was insufficient.

Were other analog machines any better? There was the Bush differential analyzer at MIT, but Atanasoff was not enthusiastic about it, for the integraph was too limited in its applications. It was built to solve one special category of problems and would have to be modified to handle any wider spectrum of uses. The U.S. armed forces were using a complex analog computer, the AA director, but it was successful only at near range, at least until Stibitz developed his punched-tape dynamic tester.

On the simpler side, there were harmonic analyzers, like Kelvin's, and a device that Atanasoff and one of his students created to solve a certain partial differential equation in two dimensions (that is, a plane). The machine molded a piece of paraffin wax into a shape that provided, when its height was measured, a solution to the equation.

Atanasoff devised another analog system to give him mathematical measurements of airflow out of pipes. The device substituted water for air and worked fine for its intended purpose. It gave Atanasoff the answers he was seeking, and a scaled-up version of this windy analog computer wound up heating and cooling his house.

Eventually, however, Atanasoff had to give up on analog computers, for their built-in inaccuracy, the inevitable result of substituting some physical process for operations on numbers, made them unsuitable for his purposes. That left him with digital machines. They were far more accurate than analog computers because digital machines avoided analog substitutions. A digital computer working out the decimal equivalent of two-thirds, for example, would get a decimal point followed by a theoretically endless string of sixes (0.666666666666 . . .), the last digit of which would be rounded off to seven to keep the calculation from running on indefinitely.

Digital machines included the old-fashioned Chinese abacus. An abacus was surprisingly fast in the hands of a skilled operator and could carry out calculations faster than many desktop adding and multiplying machines. There also were big digital tabulating machines comparable to, but advanced over, Herman Hollerith's model. The largest of these were made by IBM and Remington Rand and were fed information in the form of punched cards, each of which could hold several dozen base-10 numbers. As in Hollerith's device, the cards were read by sending electric current through the holes in the cards. Computing was done mechanically, not by electronics.

Like the analog devices, none of the digital machines was quite what Atanasoff had in mind for his computer, either. Digital devices then were very limited in their capabilities. The most powerful had an internal memory of only 266 bits, or less than one percent of what one finds in a low-priced home computer sold today.

Atanasoff thought the Bush machine might be modified suitably for solution of partial differential equations, but he had no chance of getting to use it, much less tinker with its structure. An IBM tabulator could have been revamped, but the overhaul would have taken a lot of work, and in any case Atanasoff had difficult relations with IBM. In his words, that "did not make the task seem easier." IBM seemed scared that Atanasoff might muck up one of its beautiful machines in his pursuit of differential equations. One IBM internal memo warned, "Keep Atanasoff out of the tabulator!"

Atanasoff spent 1935 through 1937 reviewing his choices and eventually found himself with what he called a "waning bag of concepts." He appeared to have only one hope left: maybe he could gang up thirty or so Monroe machines, arrange them all on a common drive shaft, and use this "aggregate machine" to solve sets of equations.

This was approximately what the Bell Labs people had been thinking of doing before George Stibitz came up with the relay-operated calculator. First the aggregate device would work out one unknown in the equations; then it would be set up again, by punching in data manually, to solve the second unknown on the basis of that first answer. The third, fourth, and subsequent solutions would follow one at a time until the whole set of equations was solved.

That approach sounded good in theory but was unworkable in practice, because too much effort would be required to enter all the data and keep up with the results at every step along the way. Worse yet, one little error at any point would ruin the whole calculation.

"Too cumbersome," Atanasoff decided. Thus ended his hope of using then existing hardware to build the computer of his dreams.

There things stood for a while. Unlike Wiener, Atanasoff was unsure which route computing technology ought to take. Atanasoff knew what kind of machine he needed. He knew it ought to be digital. It also had to be fast, accurate, and adaptable. Yet he had only the vaguest idea of how to build and operate such a machine.

Atanasoff was aware he would have to use something to represent numerical digits, but what? Would the computer use electrical or mechanical technology? Analog or digital operation? Base-2 or base-10 arithmetic, or some other base entirely?

That last question led Atanasoff to search for two numbers. One was symbolized $E$, the other $b$. The lowest possible $E$-value was what he ultimately wanted. It stood for the mechanical effort involved in computing—that is, how much work a machine must do to solve a given problem—and was dependent partly on $b$, the base number used for the computations.

JOHN ATANASOFF AND THE ABC    115

The mathematics of the relationship between $E$ and $b$ essentially comes down to this: if you use a big base, such as our everyday base 10, the operations will be harder to perform, but you will have to do fewer of them; on the other hand, if you use a relatively small base, like base 2 or base 3, you will have to do more individual operations, but they will be easier to carry out.

One can visualize this problem in terms of building a house. If you build the walls out of ten-ton slabs of stone, the individual slabs will be hard to lift into place, but you will not have to lift many of them. If you go to the other extreme and assemble the house out of individual grains of sand, gluing them into place one at a time, the individual grains will be easy to lift, but you will have to handle many more of them. In this case, the best plan—the optimum $E$-value—is to use reasonably small bricks, say, a couple of pounds each. Here the weight of the brick represents the base number $b$.

So Atanasoff had to find a $b$-value that would give him the optimum value for $E$, machine effort. Calculus was no help, because it provides no workable minimum value for $E$. But since computers naturally "prefer" small base numbers because such numbers are easier to juggle, Atanasoff saw eventually that the best $b$-value was either base 2 or base 3. He chose base 2, the same base Norbert Wiener had recommended. At last the binary arithmetic from Atanasoff's old math textbook was coming back to aid him in his quest for a computer.

Strange as it may seem today, when binary arithmetic is the basis for nearly all computers, Atanasoff's choice of base 2 was almost scandalous at the time. Back then, base-10 arithmetic was an idea you didn't find fault with: to mathematicians and scientists, opting for base 2 in a computer was like spitting on Old Glory or motherhood. Atanasoff consoled himself by rationalizing that his use of base 2 was strictly in the interest of science and would not spread far.

Choosing the base number was only one aspect of the computing process. Much remained to be settled before Atanasoff could start designing and building his machine. Chief among the unresolved issues, and closely tied to the chosen base number, was the matter of computer memory. (The word *memory* was

Atanasoff's choice. In the late 1930s Atanasoff had only a sketchy knowledge of Babbage's work and was unaware that Babbage, in his Analytical Engine, had dubbed the memory a *store*.)

Atanasoff planned for a big memory by depression-era standards, much bigger than the less than 300 bits available in the biggest commercial machines. There were several possible ways to build the memory device. He could use electromechanical parts like the relays in the Stibitz K-Model; iron-bearing magnetic material might work too, if one magnetized the material in different directions to represent the on and off states. The trouble with that scheme was that the elements would have to be so small that they could hold only a tiny charge.

Vacuum-tube circuits were practical, but they would be costly both to build and to operate, not to mention their being bulky. Far cheaper and smaller than tubes—and therefore more attractive—were paper electrical *condensers,* or *capacitors,* little components that looked like miniature cigarettes and could hold a reasonably strong charge.

Like any other device, condensers had their advantages and drawbacks. A memory built of condensers would save money but would have to be recharged from time to time, since the condensers lapsed (that is, leaked electricity) and could not keep their charge for long. So Atanasoff, if he went the condenser route, would have to figure out a way to refresh the computer's memory every so often.

Those were Atanasoff's options. Now how might he put them all together—base number, memory hardware, and so forth— to build a computer? He was going to have to make a lot of tradeoffs between ease and speed, cost and convenience, before his computer saw the light of day.

Atanasoff was in low spirits in 1937, because he was not eager to pioneer the new technology that his dream machine would require. He had many other things to do  and was unwilling to get involved with a complicated invention. Yet he had no other choice, if he wanted the machine he needed.

He was sustained in part by some advice he had received from a professor years before. "If you have to do something that is distasteful," the teacher told Atanasoff, "keep yourself at it; keep doing what you can do, and in the end you may enjoy it."

So Atanasoff kept plugging. He wrote down what he called a "hodgepodge" of concepts and tried to sort through them. Nothing seemed appropriate. His ideas, in his own word, refused to "jell." Several months passed. He recalled later that he became extremely distraught.

Here is part of Atanasoff's account of what he did next.

. . . I remember that the winter of 1937 was a desperate one for me, because I had this problem and I had outlined my objectives but nothing was happening, and as the winter deepened, my despair grew . . . I have told you about the kind of items that were rattling around in my mind, and we come to a day in the middle of winter when I went out to the office intending to spend the evening trying to resolve some of these questions, and I was in such a mental state that no resolution was possible. I was just unhappy to an extreme degree, and at that time I did something that I had done on such occasions—I don't do it anymore—I went out to my automobile, got in and started driving over the good highways of Iowa at a high rate of speed.

Bundled up in a heavy coat in his Ford V8, Atanasoff left Ames, Iowa, and drove hard, to take his mind off the dilemma of his computer. Whenever the computer began creeping back into his thoughts, he drove still harder. Several hours later, "I sort of became aware of my surroundings." Atanasoff found he was crossing the Mississippi River into Illinois near Rock Island. He had traveled almost two hundred miles that night, with the idea of his computer in hot pursuit. Now that idea was about to catch up with him, with historic results.

Atanasoff saw a light ahead. It was a tavern. "You couldn't get a drink in Iowa in those days," he points out, but in Illinois alcohol was available. Atanasoff stopped, got out of the car, and went inside.

After hanging up his coat, he sat down at a table and ordered a drink. Then he realized his mind was "clear and sharp." His ride had cleared the cobwebs away.

Atanasoff tells what happened then: "Now, I don't know why

my mind worked then, when it had not worked previously, but things seemed to be good and cool and quiet. There were not many people in the tavern, and the waitress didn't bother me particularly with repetitive offers of drinks." A couple of drinks later, Atanasoff had what he considered encouraging results. He worked for three hours on the design of his computer. Then he got back in his car and drove slowly home to Ames in the wintry night.

That night in the tavern, Atanasoff had decided what his computer should be like. As in Wiener's plan for computers, the Atanasoff machine would use electronics instead of mechanical technology and would operate on a base-2 system. It would use condensers for memory, recharging them as necessary.

Finally, Atanasoff decided his computer "would compute by direct logical action." That meant, in very simple terms, that the machine could handle the logic of arithmetic, not merely count off numbers one after another.

That last point—computing by direct logical action—was perhaps the weakest point in Atanasoff's scheme. He didn't know how to do it. He simply imagined "a black box that would do this" (*black box* being an engineer's expression for something one wants to build but doesn't know how to design).

Despite his vague vision of the black box, Atanasoff started drawing circuits for use with base-2 arithmetic. He knew something about Boolean algebra but did not use it to design the circuits. He designed, as he put it later, "by sheer awkward force" and then by "a kind of cognition."

Iteration helped. Atanasoff understood, as did Howard Aiken when writing his proposal for the Mark I, that even complex equations can be broken down into repetitive strings of comparatively simple operations that can be carried out easily by machine. To handle the iterative arithmetic, Atanasoff came up with a logic circuit that he called an add-subtract mechanism. It used vacuum tubes and could be used for multiplication and division as well as addition and subtraction.

Atanasoff also worked out a procedure for refreshing the condenser-built memory. He called it *jogging*. The computer would regularly jog its own memory, replacing data as fast as they were withdrawn from memory. This process is comparable to a person repeating a telephone number over and over ("555-1212— 555-1212") to keep from forgetting it. Jogging turned out to be one of the most useful and influential concepts in the history of computing and influenced the design of many computers built just after World War II.

By the spring of 1939, Atanasoff thought he could start building his machine. He had other duties as a faculty member, however, and could not devote full time to the making of his computer. So he decided to hire an assistant, preferably a skilled electrical engineer.

His choice of assistant was resolved one day while Atanasoff was walking across the campus. He happened to meet a professor of electrical engineering and asked him to recommend a student for the job. "I have your man," the professor answered, "Clifford Berry." Thus one of the most famous teams in engineering history was formed.

Clifford Berry was a gifted engineering student. He was enthusiastic about Atanasoff's project, and Berry and Atanasoff turned out to be a perfect match. "Absolutely tops," Atanasoff called him.

They set up shop in the basement of the physics building, a dry and cozy spot insulated from the rigors of the awful Iowa winters and steamy summers. Their work area was only forty feet from the machine shop: a perfect location, since they had to spend lots of time fabricating components.

In the autumn of 1939 Atanasoff and Berry went to work on the computer. Atanasoff ordered a shipment of angle irons for the frame. Other faculty members saw the hardware sitting at the rear entrance of the physics building and asked what they were for. Atanasoff heard someone answer, "Oh, Atanasoff thinks he is going to make a computer out of those angle irons."

Atanasoff did just that, but not immediately. First he and Berry built a prototype and by Christmas had it in operation. It was the beginning of what Atanasoff later christened the ABC, or Atanasoff-Berry Computer, to commemorate Berry's role in its creation.

Atanasoff and Berry were not trying for an elegant invention.

As Atanasoff puts it, "We realized ... that such a computer should be and must be a simple gadget." So they put together a rough-and-ready prototype built with a combination of condensers and vacuum tubes.

Many different kinds of vacuum tubes were available, so Atanasoff and Berry chose the "receiving" kind that consumed the least power. The tubes and condensers complemented each other nicely. The condensers provided enough voltage to actuate the vacuum tubes, and the tubes in return contributed enough voltage to recharge the condensers.

At this point Atanasoff and Berry came close to inventing one of the most famous items of hardware in history: the transistor, the little "three-wired hat" that revolutionized electronics in the fifties by replacing vacuum tubes with much smaller and longer-lasting equivalents.

Atanasoff mentions that he and Berry wanted something that would substitute for a vacuum tube yet be no bigger than "a grain of wheat." They knew that crystals of silicon carbide and certain other substances could act as solid-state counterparts of vacuum tubes, but their workload prevented them from investigating that possibility. Had Atanasoff and Berry had the opportunity to pursue this use of crystals, they might have invented the transistor a decade before William Shockley. Shockley produced the first working transistors at Bell Laboratories in 1949.

The prototype computer looked like a tiny amusement park, complete with Ferris wheel. In this case the wheel was something Atanasoff called an abacus. It consisted of a plastic disc mounted on a horizontal shaft turned by an electric motor. Gears set the wheel to rotating about once per second.

Either face of the disc held a circle of twenty-five condensers arranged in a radial pattern, like wheel spokes. The condensers were secured with separate connections along the outer rim; on the inner rim they were tied to a slip ring. This arrangement gave the abacus a capacity of twenty-five base-2 places, or the equivalent of a ten-digit number in base 10.

One set of condensers on the abacus was called the *keyboard abacus* because it served the same purpose as the keyboard on a desktop machine. (This computer had no handy keyboard, as the

Bell Labs Model 1 did, for entering data.) The other set of condensers corresponded to the wheels or counters inside a desktop
calculator and was therefore known as the *counter abacus*. Together these abaci were supposed to juggle back and forth the
coefficients of equations being solved. (A *coefficient* is the number preceding a letter variable in an equation; the coefficient of
6*x*, for example, is 6.)

The bright lights in this tabletop amusement park came from
vacuum tubes. Most of the tubes were found in the memory-re-
generating unit, which sent electric pulses through little brushes
mounted at the wheel's rim to jog the condensers as they passed
by, and in the all-important add-subtract mechanism, an arrangement of vacuum tubes mounted on a cadmium-plated steel
chassis about the size of a paperback book. The tubes were
linked together on the rear of the chassis by a rat's nest of wiring.
The add-subtract mechanism was the "manager," so to speak,
for it contained the binary number-juggling system.

There were no input or output devices, such as tapes, on the
prototype ABC. Before each run, numbers were entered on the
abaci by tapping their terminals with a negative electrode. Negative charges stood for ones; uncharged condensers represented
zeroes.

Atanasoff admits this prototype was crude. Yet it was a mile-
stone in the history of computing, because it was the dry run for
what some historians think was the first electronic digital computer ever built: the ABC. The prototype proved to Atanasoff
and Berry that a digital electronic machine utilizing binary
arithmetic and condenser memory was possible. It also showed
the feasibility of Atanasoff's jogging technique. A "new era in
computing," as Atanasoff puts it, was about to begin.

The next step was to build the ABC. Atanasoff and Berry
wanted the machine to be able to solve sets of thirty equations
for thirty unknowns. That was a lot of computing which would
require a lot of computer, and at first Atanasoff was unsure how
big the device should be. He guessed it would take up about as
much space as an office desk. That estimate turned out to be just
right.

Now, how many tubes would it need? For thirty equations in

thirty unknowns, thirty add-subtract units would be required. At seven tubes to an add-subtract unit, that made the total 210 tubes. A couple of hundred tubes represented a considerable investment in the late thirties, when a vacuum tube might have cost the equivalent of fifty dollars in modern currency.

Here the condensers proved useful, as their low cost offset the big bill for vacuum tubes. The condensers were arranged in thirty-two rings of fifty condensers each on abaci in the ABC's memory drums. The memory drums were two cylinders, about the size of large fruit-juice cans, mounted on a rotating shaft at the rear of the machine. The drums rotated once per second. Their rotation supplied the timing mechanism for the ABC.

Brushes made contact with contact studs on the drums and recharged the condensers even as the brushes drew electrical charges off them—the jogging process at work. The drums were sealed with wax to prevent moisture from getting inside and fouling up the condensers. Each drum could store thirty numbers of fifty bits apiece and could be loaded in a minute and a half.

Along the front of the ABC were mounted the add-subtract units. The vacuum tubes stuck out horizontally from their cadmium mountings. This arrangement, like base-2 arithmetic, was almost heretical (the tubes conventionally were supposed to be mounted standing upright), but it caused Atanasoff and Berry no trouble. Traditions were falling left and right as the ABC neared completion.

In building the ABC, Atanasoff and Berry had to deal with a problem they had not faced while working on the prototype. How were they going to switch back and forth between the decimal and binary systems while doing computations on the ABC? The computer could carry out calculations fine in base 2, but then it had to convert them into base 10 numbers more easily understandable to humans.

Zuse handled this conversion process through a set of mechanical linkages and relays set in motion by a switch on the control panel. Stibitz used his mixed binary-decimal system. The ABC's makers designed a special card reader and a conversion drum that translated input from base 10 into base 2 for the machine's convenience, and vice versa for the aid of the operators.

The ABC had two kinds of memory: fast (handled by condensers) and slow. The latter would handle base-2 numbers and serve, in Atanasoff's words, as a "scratch pad" for the computer's use while calculations were under way. Slow memory in the ABC served much the same purpose as the paper on which human computers left audit trails.

Though slow memory might seem easier to achieve than fast memory, in fact slow memory was harder to arrange, because there was no reliable technology for it. Today home computers use magnetic tape for slow memory, but in the 1940s magnetic tape had yet to be invented. Moreover, no one had yet devised a practical recording head to store magnetic signals on tape or wire. So Atanasoff and Berry had to think of something else.

They came up with a binary card-punch and card-reader system that would store the results of computations on the way to the eventual answer. Instead of punching the cards mechanically, Atanasoff and Berry had a better idea: they would punch the cards electrically, by burning holes in them with electric sparks. Cards would pass in between two tungsten electrodes and be zapped by electric arcs. The scorched areas around the holes had different conductive properties than the unaffected parts of the card, so cards could be read by applying electric current to them and reading the voltage.

The punching process was tricky because it had to be timed precisely. But Atanasoff and Berry put thyratrons—the same components that did yeoman duty in Colossus and Heath Robinson—to work on the punching, and soon everything was in order. To keep the movement of the cards from producing oblong holes, the arc was moved along with the card. The base-2 card punch and card reader sat side by side on top of the ABC, like Tweedledum and Tweedledee, and looked somewhat like the "in" and "out" paper bins on an office desk.

Ingenious as it was, the card system proved to be the Achilles heel of the ABC. The hole-punching setup was not completely reliable. It allowed errors to slip through about one in every 100,000 times. That meant the ABC could handle relatively brief sets of equations but was defeated by bigger bunches.

So the ABC fell short of Atanasoff's and Berry's expectations for it. But even its limited success represented a history-making triumph in the art of computing, and was reported in a news release that appeared as an article in the Des Moines *Register* early in 1941:

An electrical computing machine, said here to operate more like a human brain than any other machine known to exist, is being built by Dr. John V. Atanasoff, Iowa State Physics Professor. The machine will contain more than three hundred vacuum tubes and will be used to compute complicated algebraic equations. Dr. Atanasoff said it will occupy about as much space as a large office desk. The instrument will be entirely electrical and will be used in research experiments. Dr. Atanasoff said he had been working on the machine several years and will probably finish it in about a year.

Iowa State College did not patent the ABC, as it was entitled to do under the terms of its contract with Atanasoff. It is uncertain why the school failed to nail down the patent. Atanasoff claims he and Berry submitted more than enough information for a patent application, but the college thought more material was needed. This absence of a patent would later have a major impact on the history of computers.

The ABC was never completed. Working out a new technology took time, and time was in short supply for Atanasoff and Berry at the start of the forties. They had other duties at the college to take care of and could not spare much time for work on the ABC. Also, the United States was heading for war with Germany and Japan, and very soon the scientists and engineers at Iowa State would be swept up in the war effort to the exclusion of all other work. So the ABC never reached its intended goal of solving thirty equations for thirty unknowns.

The computer was put in storage in the physics building, and in 1946, after Atanasoff had left Iowa State, a graduate student came across the ABC and asked what it was. No one seemed to know. The space was needed, so the student took the ABC apart and threw the parts away. Only later did he find out he had destroyed a piece of history.

Though Atanasoff and Berry had taken a giant step toward the

advent of the modern electronic computer, not everyone realized the magnitude of what they had done. Other faculty members, Atanasoff found, were "not unduly enthusiastic" about the
computer. One of them told Atanasoff he doubted the machine
could "run a street car." Business also gave the computer the
cold shoulder. Companies that built calculating machines said
they were uninterested.

About the only party interested in the ABC, besides Atanasoff
and Berry, was John Mauchly, a Pennsylvania meteorologist.
Mauchly had an opportunity to see the ABC in action during a
visit to Ames in 1941. His meeting with Berry and Atanasoff was
quiet and cordial, yet it set off an explosive controversy which
even now has not been settled.

# 7
# ATANASOFF MEETS MAUCHLY

Reenter John Mauchly, the man who had seen Wiener lose his temper at the teletype machine at Dartmouth in 1940. Though Mauchly was destined to go down in history as one of the greatest of all computer pioneers, he never resembled an Olympian figure. He looked like what he was—a schoolteacher. He was neither a bigger-than-life personality like Aiken nor a supreme organizer like Bush or the elder Watson. A quiet, unassuming man with a liking for Bach, Mauchly is remembered with affection by associates who describe him as a devoted family man and an excellent listener. One of his acquaintances wrote of him in a note published after his death in 1980:

For most of his life, John Mauchly sought to guide, advise, and educate. He was a person with interesting and even exciting ideas, but he can best be described as highly intelligent, very warm, gentle, and honest. He was always eager to explain the vast potential of computers—especially microcomputers in recent years. . . . We have lost one of the key figures in computing history, and for those of us who had the privilege of knowing him, we have also lost a good friend.

Among the computer pioneers of our century, Mauchly's career is perhaps the most perplexing of all, fort it is shrouded in uncertainty and conflicting opinion, some of which he generated himself. Mauchly's memory ("gray-cell storage," he called it) was not always trustworthy, and his recollections could be so selective and self-serving that some who read them called them "fantasy in hindsight."

Mauchly was born in Cincinnati, Ohio, on August 30, 1907. His was a scientific family: his father, S. J. Mauchly, had a Ph.D. in physics from the University of Cincinnati and became head of the Terrestrial Electricity and Magnetism section at the Carnegie Institution in Washington, D.C. The Carnegie Institution is a nonprofit organization that was founded by steel magnate Andrew Carnegie in 1902 and supports research in astronomy, the physical and biological sciences, and archeology.

At an early age John Mauchly was tinkering with electric circuits. As a boy he put together a crystal radio set. It used a crystal of galena (lead sulfide, a heavy, silvery gray metal that occurs as cubic crystals about the size of dice) to intercept radio signals and turn them into electricity. One tuned the radio by moving thin wires known as cat's whiskers over the crystal's surface. When the whiskers hit the right point on the crystal, a station came in clearly.

The crystal radio was not very satisfactory. Later Mauchly won a vacuum-tube radio in a contest. The radio was called a WD-11 and had a single vacuum tube. Mauchly found it "a relief not to have to jiggle cat's whiskers on galena." Much later Mauchly would use vacuum tubes in computers that were as far advanced over previous mechanical and electromechanical machines as his vacuum-tube radio was over his first crystal set.

Mauchly already knew much about electric circuits when only eight years old. While visiting relatives, he showed them how to wire a pair of light switches so that a light could be turned on from either of two points in the house. Many years later Mauchly realized that this "lazy-man" switch, as he called it, had actually been a binary switching circuit similar to those incorporated later into digital computers.

Mauchly made extensive use of calculators while in high school. After school and on weekends he spent long hours seated in front of a desktop calculator, helping his father with geophysics calculations. The elder Mauchly then was working on machinery and techniques for measuring and mapping the strength of the electrical field in the atmosphere. That work was not merely a matter of noting where lightning bolts were crackling. Mauchly and son had to immerse themselves in long calculations involving temperature, humidity, electrical potential, and many other parameters. Sometimes the air seemed as tranquil as a bottle of milk. At other times it seemed to hiss and pop like the fur on a stroked cat in winter. All such changes showed up in the equations; all had to be calculated and reduced to numerical answers. Not everyone would have found it fascinating work, but John Mauchly did, and he developed twin interests—in meteorology and computing—that would last a lifetime.

Mauchly entered Johns Hopkins University in 1925, about the time Vannevar Bush at MIT was starting work on his differential analyzer. At first Mauchly planned to study electrical engineering, but before long his love of weather won out over his fondness for circuitry, and he transferred into the physics department to study meteorology.

The middle third of the twentieth century was a fascinating time to be a meteorologist. The stratosphere, the atmospheric layer immediately above the weather layer or troposphere, had been discovered only a few years before, and the mysterious phenomena of the upper air were just beginning to be studied. Physicists were finding that the atmosphere was linked together into one huge and staggeringly complex "weather machine" that encompassed the entire world from pole to pole. That machine, like any other, could be taken apart and understood, but only by collecting and analyzing mountains of statistics.

Mauchly had little time to help dissect the worldwide weather machine while he was in school. His Ph.D. studies and later his work as a research assistant required him to observe the spectra of molecules and calculate their energy levels. Only

during the summers did he get the wind in his face—he assisted
with measurements and computations at the wind tunnel at the
National Bureau of Standards in Washington, D.C.

As a grad student Mauchly had to struggle, as he put it later,
with "little calculating machines, mechanical types." The machines were slightly advanced over the common hand-cranked
desktop adding devices. Some of them had small electric motors
inside, so that instead of cranking the calculator like a slot machine, all Mauchly had to do was enter the numbers and press a
button, and the calculator whirred and clicked and eventually
spat out the answer. An addition might take ten seconds. That
was fast for the early 1930s but not fast enough for Mauchly. He
wanted a calculator that would give him answers as fast as he
could push the buttons.

At Johns Hopkins there was no shortage of equipment, and so
Mauchly had all the calculators he wanted. Things were different after he graduated in 1930. The stock market had crashed
and the depression was on. Jobs in academe were as scarce as
everywhere else, but in 1934 Mauchly had the good luck to get a
position in the physics department at Ursinus College near
Reading, Pennsylvania, not far from Philadelphia.

At Ursinus, Mauchly was known as an entertaining lecturer.
Sometimes his demonstrations were flamboyant—and risky.
Once he fell and broke his arm while riding a homebuilt skateboard in class to illustrate the relationship between velocity and
momentum.

Ursinus was a threadbare school compared to Johns Hopkins
and did not have an abundance of calculating machinery.
Mauchly had to go out and get his own. Here the depression
worked to his advantage, however, for many banks were folding
and putting their calculators up for sale. Mauchly bought a
lovely push-button desktop model secondhand, for seventy-five
dollars. "It never would have happened if we hadn't had that
nice depression," he recalled years later.

With his calculator, Mauchly set out to tackle what he called
big problems. One of the biggest was weather forecasting. Inspired by the emerging picture of the global weather machine,
Mauchly thought it might be possible to make fairly accurate

long-range weather forecasts, six months or even a year or two ahead. One might not be able to foretell how many inches of rain would fall on Topeka on a given day one year in the future, but one might be able to predict generally whether conditions would be hotter or cooler, wetter or dryer, or close to normal.

This kind of forecast would be more than a mere convenience. It would have profound economic importance if it could be done, for many sectors of the economy, such as agriculture, are heavily dependent on weather, and reliable long-range warnings might save a lot of money and distress. Joseph, in the Bible, performed this kind of forecast in a dream. Mauchly hoped to do it by numerical analysis of weather data. He also hoped to demonstrate that solar activity—that is, sunspots—had an important bearing on the weather here on earth.

Reams of weather data were available from the Carnegie Institution and the U.S. Weather Bureau. On visits to the Bureau's data warehouse in Washington, Mauchly and his student assistants copied much of the information by hand. Money-hungry students at Ursinus were glad to help Mauchly for payment of fifty cents an hour.

Soon Mauchly had assembled a team of about a dozen students and set them to work with calculators. The students were diligent and the data, good—the problem was with the calculating machines. They simply weren't up to the jobs Mauchly had in mind for them. There was too much opportunity for error when the students punched in the numbers they read from sheets of weather data.

Also, the machines had no way of storing the results of calculations, so the students had to write down the results of one calculation before going on to the next. That introduced another source of error. It was all too easy for the hand or mind to falter and write 5,672 instead of 5,627, and that seemingly small error could make a calculation useless.

Mauchly knew that to sell other scientists on his dream of long-range weather forecasting, he would first need machines that could handle much longer calculations in far less time. Even relatively minor problems in numerical weather forecasting required the reduction of millions of digits of data, and as the scale of the forecasts increased, so did the magnitude of the figuring involved. Moreover, the machines would have to eliminate human error from the calculating process. No more jumbled numbers on a note pad. The machines would have to get calculations right and keep them right, from beginning to end.

So around 1936, Mauchly began thinking of building his own calculating machines: not pokey mechanical devices like those currently in use ("slow, slow, slow!" Mauchly described them) but electronic devices based on the vacuum tubes that researchers in physics were using to count particles.

Mauchly and several of his students visited laboratories at Johns Hopkins and the Carnegie Institution to see vacuum-tube hardware at work. The tubes nestled in amidst dials and wiring like eggs in a nest. Vacuum tubes came in different shapes and sizes. Some were no bigger than cigarette butts and looked like unpainted Christmas tree lights; others were thumb-sized; still others were the size of small cucumbers. Their glassy shells glistened like soap bubbles, and when turned on in the dark, the tubes glowed with delicious warm colors—butter yellow, sunset red, citrus orange. They also gave off considerable heat. One good-sized vacuum tube could keep a cup of coffee warm.

The tubes were doing more than merely glowing and warming the air. They were also counting, splitting time into infinitesimally small parts. The tubes could mark the time it would take a beam of light to travel across the street. Vacuum-tube particle counters, like the one devised in 1929 by Wynn-Williams of the Bletchley Park team, could count a million particles per second. Why, Mauchly wondered, couldn't they count a million bits of weather data per second just as well? A machine using vacuum tubes might carry out an addition in a tiny fraction of a second instead of the ten seconds required with a desktop calculator. Just take vacuum tubes, plug them into a circuit, and let 'em rip. That was how Mauchly saw it.

Mauchly also was familiar with the calculating machinery being used at the Watson Scientific Laboratory at Columbia. Originally know as the Thomas J. Watson Astronomical Computing Bureau, the laboratory was housed in a remodeled fraternity house near the university. It was headed by a Yale man and astronomer named Wallace Eckert.

Eckert had set up his computing establishment in 1929 with help from the university, of which the elder Watson was a trustee, and IBM. Eckert was interested in calculating the ever-changing position of the moon. The mathematical theory of the moon's motion had been worked out already by an American astronomer named George Hill, who published his lunar theory in 1878. So accurate were Hill's equations that his lunar theory was used to fix the momentary positions of the moon until well into the age of space travel.

The moon's motion may sound like a highly academic and impractical pursuit for the 1930s, but it was a matter of life and death for mariners and air crews who needed extremely precise astronomical data for navigation. An error of half a degree might have sent an aircraft crashing into a mountain at night. Since the required calculations were too long and complicated to be done by hand, Eckert was using IBM calculators. He was getting extremely good results and produced an entire almanac without a single computational error. The success of the Watson Scientific Laboratory encouraged Mauchly to pursue his own plans for building electronic computing equipment.

Before getting under way, Mauchly did what any professional scientist and engineer would do. He performed a literature search, and his effort was greatly rewarded. Publications such as *Physical Review* and *Review of Scientific Instruments* turned out to be full of information on circuits for counting. For practical advice on building hardware, Mauchly turned to the journal *Electronics*. In these magazines he found diagrams of vacuum-tube-based counters that could be adapted for computing.

Mauchly was trained as a physicist rather than as an engineer, and he needed more background in electronics before he could start putting together the calculating machines of his dreams. So in the autumn of 1936 he enrolled in an evening graduate course in electronics at the University of Pennsylvania in Philadelphia. But Mauchly got little practical benefit out of that course, because it emphasized theory rather than the how-to aspect of electronics.

Mauchly returned to the journals and to tinkering with circuits and tubes. He soon learned that where electronic circuitry was concerned, faster was not necessarily better. There came a point where one had to weigh the advantage of increased speed against its added cost in hardware. Vacuum tubes were expensive, and Mauchly realized that "a thousand times faster doesn't mean a thing if you have to pay a thousand times as much for it."

To cut expenses, Mauchly learned to substitute little neon bulbs for vacuum tubes. They were not quite as good as vacuum tubes but cost much less and functioned essentially the same way: they worked electronically and lit up to show results. At first Mauchly got the bulbs by cracking fuses open and removing the indicator lights inside them. Then he discovered that he could buy the tiny bulbs from General Electric for eight cents each.

Mauchly used these bulbs to build circuits called flip-flops. A *flip-flop* is an electronic version of a seesaw, in that it flips over and flops back. A flip-flop is made up of two vacuum tubes (or neon lights, in the case of Mauchly's early machines) hooked together so that only one of them can be on at any given moment, just as only one end of a seesaw can be up in the air at any particular time.

Flip-flops are binary counters, since they can register only two states, which may be designated zero and one. They are similar to the lazy-man switches that Mauchly built as a child. The prototype flip-flop that Mauchly constructed sat on his office desk—it looked like a railway crossing signal with its two lights flashing on and off.

Mauchly wanted counters that could count beyond zero and one, so he joined ten of his flip-flops together in a ring to make a "decade counter" that could count to ten. He also had plans to build flip-flops using condensers instead of bulbs or tubes. A few years later Mauchly would use such a device to help build one of the most famous computers of all time.

The neon-bulb counters came in handy for another, more

modest project that Mauchly conceived in the thirties. Cryptanalysis was one of Mauchly's interests, and he used his flip-flops to build a digital codebreaking machine that was about the size of a phonograph and had a control panel covered with rotary switches.

This device operated in a base-3 number system and could put messages into code as well as decipher them. Mauchly's machine used a simple substitution method like that of the early Enigma, replacing one character in a message with another, at random. Punched cards were used to record messages, which were read by the light of neon bulbs shining through holes in the cards. Mechanical switches rearranged wiring in the machine to scramble and unscramble messages. According to Mauchly's wife and biographer, Kathleen Mauchly, he had wanted to use a standard keyboard like the one on Stibitz's Bell Labs Model 1 calculator but was unable to find a keyboard at the secondhand radio shop where he bought most of his equipment.

The Mauchly cryptanalytic machine would never have put Colossus out of business. Mauchly demonstrated the contraption once for William Friedman, the man who later cracked the Japanese code, at the Army Security Agency in Arlington, Virginia, in 1937. Uncle Sam was uninterested, however, and the Mauchly code machine dropped into obscurity. (Mauchly did not learn until after the war of the British codebreaking computers designed and built at Bletchley Park. When he did, he thought the Britons suffered from tunnel vision when designing their computers, for Colossus and Heath Robinson were highly specialized in their mission. They were not general-purpose machines like those Mauchly had in mind.)

Mauchly had more success with another of his machines, the *harmonic analyzer.* It was an electric-powered relative of Lord Kelvin's tidal harmonic analyzer of half a century earlier, and operated in much the same way. The Kelvin machine isolated cycles, or harmonics, in the tides. Mauchly's machine did the same for the atmosphere. At last Mauchly had a machine that could sift through large amounts of data quickly, and he used the analyzer to pick out two cycles in American weather: a two-week and a four-week fluctuation in rainfall over the United States.

Mauchly's harmonic analyzer was an analog device that used voltage to model operations on numbers. Results were read off a meter that was sensitive to a change of a millionth of an amp. To work properly, the machine needed a steady voltage input, which was sometimes hard to get. When someone was using the freight elevator in the physics building, voltage could rise or fall fifteen percent.

So Mauchly wired together some neons to form an early version of what a later generation of computer users would call a surge protector. It was about the size of a lunch box and reduced voltage variation to less than half of one percent. The results were excellent. With the voltage regulator turned on, Mauchly's analyzer was safe from the ravages of elevator users and delivered ninety-nine percent accuracy.

Mauchly's work was aided by a new component that RCA released in 1937. He described it as a "trigger tube" or a "cold cathode gas tube." It looked like a vacuum tube but had some advantages. The little gas-filled tube operated in much the same manner as the trigger on a gun: it used a small release of energy to set off a much more powerful outburst. It therefore could save electric power (only a little pulse of current was needed to accomplish a job) and, in so doing, would reduce heat buildup, one of the leading killers of vacuum-tube systems. Mauchly wired together several of these cold gas tubes into a ring and produced a simple base-2 counting device that could count up to ten. This counter further demonstrated what could be accomplished with electronic equipment.

Mauchly became even more committed to electronic hardware after he visited the New York World's Fair in 1939. There he saw what he called mechanical trash—punched-card machines and others that were being passed off as the computing technology of the future. Mauchly noticed that these huge machines took perhaps six seconds to carry out a multiplication. That was not appreciably faster than an ordinary desktop adding machine. Even the fleetest of the machines on display was no more than one order of magnitude swifter than a hand-operated calculator. "What had they gained?" Mauchly asked.

Clearly, not much. Mauchly thought he could do a hundred or even a thousand times better by using vacuum tubes in place of mechanical relays. Then he could carry out the weather data analyses of his dreams.

Better yet, an electronic calculator would not be confined to digesting weather data. It could do great things for finance and bookkeeping, too. Mauchly was sure his dream of electronic calculating machinery could become a successful—and profitable—reality, if such machines could be built and set working. "But nobody was really behind it then," he said.

When Mauchly recalled, in later years, his struggles during this period, he sometimes portrayed himself as a lone crusader against ignorance, stupidity, and benighted resistance to the new gospel of electronic equipment. He described how, with the exception of the rare soul who gave him encouragement, everyone he spoke with told him to forget about vacuum tubes. He remembered his academic colleagues saying, almost verbatim, what British electronics experts told Thomas Flowers just before the making of Heath Robinson. Mauchly was told, "Vacuum tubes are so poor, unreliable. They're always burning out."

Though Mauchly met resistance to his vacuum-tube suggestions, that resistance was not due simply to inertia or bone-headed conservatism on the part of other scientists. Vacuum tubes actually had some serious strikes against them. They did burn out fast. More importantly, no two vacuum tubes performed in exactly the same way. A mechanical relay would open and shut reliably, click-click. You couldn't tell what a vacuum tube would do beforehand.

Mauchly wanted to use vacuum tubes to demonstrate, as he told Wiener at the demonstration of Stibitz's complex calculator, the Model 1, that electronic technology was the way to go. There was a limit to what Mauchly could do at Ursinus, however, because of budget constraints. He could not afford much vacuum-tube work on the salary Ursinus paid him. As head of the physics department he received two thousand dollars a year. That was a comfortable income by depression-era standards, but after bills were paid, Mauchly had very little cash left for experimentation with calculating machines.

The college could offer Mauchly no financial help with his experiments, though the school placed no restrictions on what Mauchly could do with his own cash and on his own time. So Mauchly got smart, as he put it, and started looking for a job with higher pay, outside academe.

The most promising place to start looking for a new position was in the research department of a major company such as Du Pont. A research scientist there could make three times what a college professor did. But businesses had a prejudice against academics, and they told Mauchly no. They saw him as someone from an ivory tower, who had been spoiled by the soft life of a teacher and could no longer do research. The companies advised Mauchly to go back to school and relearn research methods before contacting them again. Then he would be ready for the cost-conscious confraternity of scientists in industry. "We have to work to a budget," they told Mauchly. He was frustrated. "They thought I was throwing money around, maybe?" he recalled later.

So Mauchly remained in academe and did the best he could on his professor's salary. By late 1940 he felt he was ready to build an inexpensive digital computer using only electronic components—"no moving parts," as he put it. He described his planned device in letters to colleagues. To one he wrote, "I expect to have, in a year or so ... an electronic computing machine, which will have the answer as fast as the buttons can be depressed."

In another letter Mauchly went into greater detail: "We ... are now considering the construction of an electrical computing machine to obtain sums ... as rapidly as the numbers can be punched into the machine. The machine would perform its operations in about 1/200 second, using vacuum tube relays and yielding mathematically exact, not approximate, results." (When Mauchly wrote of "vacuum tube relays," he meant utilizing vacuum tubes for jobs then performed by mechanical relays.)

Mauchly added that his machine's calculations "would not be

limited to the accuracy with which one can read a meter scale, but could be carried out to any number of places if one cared to construct the machine with that many parts."

Mauchly planned to give his machine a keyboard to input data and operations so that doing calculations would be a matter of pushing a few buttons. Mauchly's machine was little more than an electronic version of the familiar desktop calculator of that day, with electronic, nonmoving counters substituted for the calculator's clicking ten-toothed wheels.

As 1940 drew to a close, Mauchly prepared to report on his progress in computing machinery. At a meeting of the American Association for the Advancement of Science (AAAS) on December 28, 1940, in an extraordinarily dusty classroom in Philadelphia, he read a paper on data analysis in weather prediction and described how he had gotten his results with the help of his electronic analyzer. In the audience was John Atanasoff.

After Mauchly finished speaking, Atanasoff approached him and introduced himself. Atanasoff mentioned that he, too, had been using vacuum tubes to build computing machinery, and he spent a few minutes discussing with Mauchly the potential of electronic computers. Finally they shook hands and parted after promising to correspond.

Mauchly took notes about the conversation on the back of his program for the meeting. The notes mention the harmonic analyzer and the calculations it performed and indicate that the two men talked about binary counters using gas tubes.

Mauchly came away from the AAAS meeting thinking that Atanasoff's machine was entirely electronic. Mauchly also had the impression that Atanasoff had discovered some marvelous cost-cutting measure. On the back of Mauchly's program Atanasoff wrote, "J. V. Atanasoff. ISC [Iowa State College]," and the tantalizing figure, "$2 per digit." That meant, in terms of hardware, spending only two dollars to build each counter.

Two dollars per digit of storage—about the cost of a single phone relay—seemed a phenomenally low cost for a computer, considering the high price of vacuum tubes. Had Atanasoff found a better way to do the job electronically? Was there a new and fantastically cost-effective way to hook vacuum tubes together into counters? Or had Atanasoff found something that worked better than vacuum tubes, operated electronically, and cost only a fraction as much?

Mauchly was intensely curious and wrote to Atanasoff on January 19, 1941: "I am wondering how your plans with regard to computing devices are working out. Need I say that I await with some suspense the time when you will be able to let me have more information? How the recording end functions is the biggest puzzle, I guess. 450 digits at less than $2 per digit sounds next to impossible, and yet that is what I understood you to say, approximately." Mauchly then dropped heavy hints that he would appreciate an invitation to Ames to witness Atanasoff's work.

The invitation arrived several days later. "By all means arrange to pay us a visit in Ames during your Spring recess if this is possible," wrote Atanasoff in a letter dated January 23, 1941. Atanasoff added, "I can think of many things that I would like to talk to you about. This list includes statistical Fourier analysis [and] computing machines of all kinds, and I suspect there are plenty of other things. I will be glad to have you as my guest while you are in Ames."

Then came the clincher: "As an additional inducement I will explain the two dollars per digit business." Mauchly accepted the invitation and spent the next few months preparing for a trip to Iowa, while he puzzled over Atanasoff's two-dollar-per-digit business.

Atanasoff divulged nothing more about his methods while Mauchly was getting ready for his trip, but the two men continued to correspond. In one letter Mauchly complained about the quality of human computers. "My crew . . . has been augmented, but perhaps not for the better," he wrote to Atanasoff in February 1941. "The new members are fit only for adding machine work, and even then can't get the same total more than two out of three times (so it seems!)." Mauchly concluded, "Here's hoping that you have made progress in Iowa, and that I'll get to see it all."

Mauchly was making little progress trying to solve the two-dollars-per-digit riddle. Whatever kind of circuit he designed, however he juggled the vacuum tubes and wiring on paper, he could not design a counter for less than about thirteen dollars. Was Atanasoff, he wondered, somehow scrunching lots of data into individual circuits? Could one use a single tube to handle a great number of digits? That puzzler was reminiscent of the medieval debate over how many angels could dance on the head of a pin.

Mauchly looked for ways to pack lots of data into such a small container, and eventually had some success. He drew up circuits in which a digit such as the number one could be represented by the strength of voltage at a given place in the circuit. He also came up with an idea that would come to be known as *pulse-position coding*: a number is represented by its position in a series of ten pulse times (a pulse of current in the fifth position out of ten, for example, would stand for the number five). Yet he never came close to that astounding two-dollar figure.

The two-dollars-per-digit mystery continued to vex Mauchly all through the late winter and spring. Meanwhile he was working on his gas-tube devices and investigating ways to improve their performance. In late April of 1941, Mauchly wrote to his meteorologist friend H. Helm Clayton: "In June I am thinking of doing two things. One is to go to Ames, Iowa, to see an electric computing machine being developed there in the Physics Dept. by a friend of mine, and the other is to further the construction of my own devices."

About four weeks later Mauchly wrote to Atanasoff, told him that preparations for the trip to Ames were proceeding nicely, and mentioned cost figures for a new Bush-type differential analyzer being planned for defense work. Mauchly reported that a friend at the University of Pennsylvania had quoted an estimate of half a million dollars for an electronic machine. That was a staggering bill indeed at a time when $8,000 would pay for the construction of a new home (Atanasoff paid almost exactly that sum to build his home in Ames).

"Absolutely startling," Atanasoff called the $500,000 figure in a May 31, 1941, reply to Mauchly's letter. Atanasoff then tossed out another intriguing hint of what he was doing at Ames. "I . . . obtained an idea as to how the computing machine that we are building here can be converted into an integraph," he wrote. It would not, he revealed, be an analog machine like the Bush integraph but something different and capable of carrying out numerical integration in "arbitrarily small" steps. That is to say, one could then "slice up" the area under a curve as finely or coarsely as one liked while carrying out the integration.

"It should therefore equal the Bush machine in speed and excel it in accuracy," Atanasoff wrote, adding that "Progress on the construction of this machine is excellent . . . and I am in a high state of enthusiasm about its ultimate success. I hope to see you within two or three weeks."

About two weeks later, Mauchly was ready for his journey to Iowa. He did not hitchhike to Ames, as some historians have claimed, but instead drove to Iowa in the company of his young son and two neighbors, who had agreed to come along and split the cost of gasoline as far as their destination in Illinois. The trip was arduous. Mauchly drove long hours through the green Appalachians, across the Ohio Valley, over the great grain fields of the Midwest. He was heading for one of the most fateful appointments in the history of computing.

Mauchly and his son arrived at Atanasoff's home on the evening of Friday, June 13, or Saturday, June 14, 1941 (accounts differ on this detail). Atanasoff was interested in hearing Mauchly's news about computing in the East, and on Sunday Mauchly had an opportunity to see what Atanasoff and Berry had been doing.

Atanasoff and his family accompanied Mauchly and his son to the laboratory to see the ABC. For protection from dust, the computer was covered with a sheet, like a monument ready for unveiling. Atanasoff whipped off the cloth, and Mauchly had his first view of the two-dollar-per-digit computer.

Kathleen Mauchly reports that her husband was unimpressed. Apparently he had expected a general-purpose, all-electronic machine suitable for a wide variety of uses, and what he found—"a mechanical gadget that uses some electronic tubes," as Mauchly described the ABC later—was a surprise.

Mauchly remembered, "It was a disappointment because there had been nothing said in my meeting with him at the University of Pennsylvania which indicated that this machine was not a fully electronic machine." He added, "I thought his machine was very ingenious, but since it was in part mechanical, involving rotating commutators for switching, it was not by any means what I had in mind."

At least Mauchly now had the answer to the two-dollar-per-digit riddle that had so perplexed him. Atanasoff had not used vacuum tubes for all the electronic components. Instead he had opted for an arrangement of tiny condensers arranged on rotating drums—a semi-mechanical, semi-electronic hybrid. Because the ABC was not entirely electronic, Mauchly observed, "it became perfectly clear without much examination or talking that . . . it was sacrificing too much of the electrical end." The limited capabilities of the ABC were also clear. It was obvious, said Mauchly, that the ABC had been built to solve "a special class of problems rather than a general class."

Part of Mauchly's disappointment was due to the fact that the ABC was not yet complete. "At Dr. Mauchly's visit," said Atanasoff afterward, "the machine was in no condition to carry out a full demonstration. . . . Quite a number of the things necessary for these steps had not been worked out. Only the function was described to Dr. Mauchly, not the details of the structure."

Mauchly's introduction to the ABC made the two-dollar-per-digit issue "unimportant," because, as Kathleen Mauchly remembered, the cost made no difference "if the tremendous speed and versatility that vacuum tubes offered were not being realized."

On Monday Mauchly went back to the lab and looked at the ABC again. He met Berry at that time. Atanasoff asked Berry to get the computer up and running while Mauchly was in town, so he could see the machine put through its paces. Berry prepared the machine for a run. Mauchly may have assisted him, because a graduate student in Atanasoff's lab recalled later seeing Mauchly working, with his coat off, on or around the computer. The demonstration was less than spectacular, because many components of the ABC had not been installed or even designed. Only one drum was in place on the shaft. The card reader was not working, so data had to be entered on the condensers by touching them with an electric probe. There was no timing control device on the computer as yet, so it was limited to making only one cycle at a time.

Many things about Atanasoff's computer puzzled Mauchly. Among them was the use of the vacuum tubes. Atanasoff had used the fast-working tubes to build the add-subtract unit, yet the swift operation of the tubes was nullified by the slow motion of the drum, which spun around only once per second. Under those circumstances, Mauchly thought, there was no advantage in using vacuum tubes at all. It was rather like putting racing tires on a tractor.

Yet Mauchly was impressed by Atanasoff's use of condensers in the memory. Mauchly thought jogging the memory was a marvelous concept. He himself had been thinking of using condensers as memory elements and was delighted to see how Atanasoff had dealt with that problem.

While at Ames, Mauchly had an opportunity to read Atanasoff's written description of the ABC and its operation. Memories of what Mauchly did while reading the manuscript differ: Kathleen Mauchly reports her husband read the paper but was warned by Atanasoff against copying it or making notes about its contents; Atanasoff, however, claims Mauchly did take notes, using paper that Atanasoff had given him.

Atanasoff arranged for Mauchly to give a talk about his work in data analysis, and his harmonic analyzer in particular, while he was visiting ISC. The two men spent most of their time together talking about the computing art, and Atanasoff recalls their relationship as cordial in the several days Mauchly was Atanasoff's guest. On Tuesday, June 17, Mauchly received welcome news from the East: he had been accepted in a defense-related electronics course at the Moore School of Engineering at the University of Pennsylvania in Philadelphia. Here would be his opportunity to pick up the electronic know-how he needed for building more advanced machines.

After promising to keep in touch with Atanasoff by mail, Mauchly said goodbye, and he and his son departed Ames early the following morning. On the way back to Pennsylvania he picked up his two other passengers, and they arrived back at Ursinus on the night of June 19, 1941.

Like Atanasoff on his midnight ride a few months earlier, Mauchly was thinking intensely about computers as he drove. "On the way back East," Mauchly wrote to Atanasoff shortly after arriving home, "a lot of ideas came barging into my consciousness. . . . They were on the subject of computing devices, of course. If any look promising, you may hear from me later."

Atanasoff did hear from Mauchly again, repeatedly, over the course of many years. The ideas that passed back and forth between the two men, by mail and in conversation, eventually would become issues in a federal court trial. That fierce controversy continues to this day, and late in life Mauchly felt he received nothing from his visit to Ames except "the royal shaft."

This mechanical computer was built at the University of
Pennsylvania in the 1870s and later thrown away because
no one remembered what it was. (*MOORE SCHOOL OF ELECTRICAL ENGINEERING*)

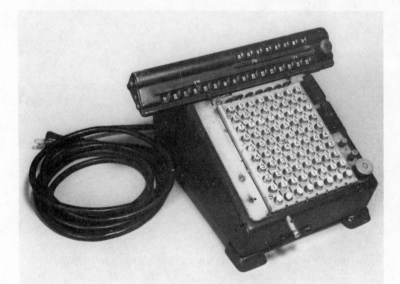

Desktop calculators like this Monroe were the workhorses
of data processing in the first third of the twentieth century.
(*SMITHSONIAN INSTITUTION PHOTO NO. 77-9543*)

Norbert Wiener, the absent-minded MIT mathematician who laid down guidelines in the 1930s for the development of later computers. (*MIT MUSEUM*)

Vannevar Bush contemplates his differential analyzer, or "integraph." (*MIT MUSEUM*)

Another view of the Bush integraph, showing the disc-and-wheel integrators in the cases at far right. (*SMITHSONIAN INSTITUTION PHOTO NO. 53201*)

D.H. Lehmer, whose number sieves were among the first high-speed computers.

(*GEORGE M. BERGMAN*)

George Stibitz, who turned telephone relays into computers. (*DARTMOUTH COLLEGE NEWS*)

An array of relays like those in Stibitz's Model 1. The best tool for cleaning them was said to be a dollar bill slipped in between the contacts. (*DARTMOUTH COLLEGE NEWS*)

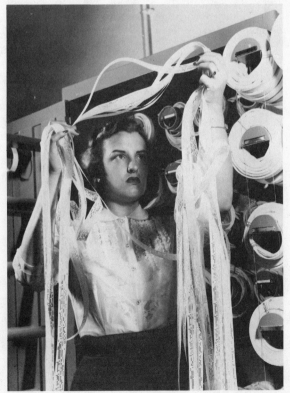

A
diagram of
the relay-operated
Model 5 computer
in its air-conditioned suite
at Langley Field, Virginia. (NASA)

Some of
the paper
tapes
used to
run the
Model 5 at
Langley
Field.
(NASA)

The nineteen-foot tunnel building at Langley Field, where the Model 5 was housed. This photo was taken near the bus stop where the Model 5's operators watched its "beehive lights" glowing through the windows. (NASA)

Evan Snyder of the Ursinus College physics department displays a reconstruction of John Mauchly's early skateboard. Mauchly's original skateboard left the grooves on the table during one of his demonstrations. (ART WILKINSON)

I.J. Good in his office at Virginia Tech. (VIRGINIA POLYTECHNIC INSTITUTE AND STATE UNIVERSITY)

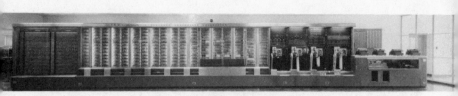

"Bessie," the Mark I Automatic Sequence Controlled Calculator (ASCC) built by Howard Aiken, Harvard University, and IBM during World War II. (*SMITHSONIAN INSTITUTION PHOTO NO.*

John Mauchly built this "railroad signal" flip-flop, or binary counting circuit, at Ursinus College and kept it on his desk. (*HOLCOMBE PHOTO SERVICE*)

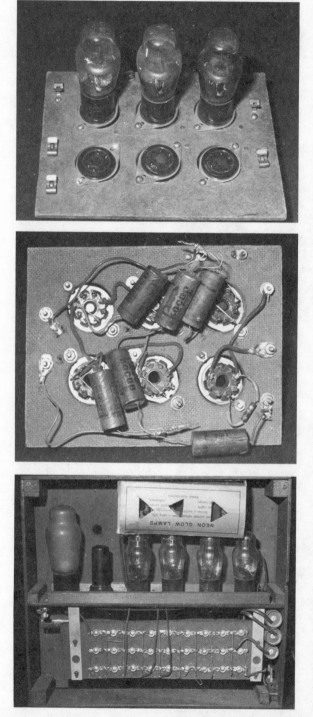

Vacuum tubes like those in this Mauchly-built counting circuit would replace relays in computer technology during World War II. (HOLCOMBE PHOTO SERVICE)

Each vacuum tube in a computer required lots of wiring and other components to back it up, as this bottom view of a Mauchly counting device shows. (HOLCOMBE PHOTO SERVICE)

A rear view of the voltage regulator Mauchly built at Ursinus to defend his computers against the effects of an elevator. Mauchly sometimes used the neon glow lamps as substitutes for more expensive vacuum tubes. (HOLCOMBE PHOTO SERVICE)

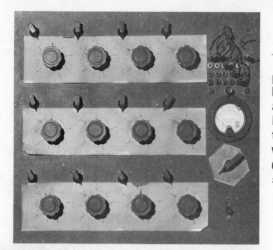

The control panel of the harmonic analyzer that Mauchly built to analyze weather data. (*HOLCOMBE PHOTO SERVICE*)

Mauchly built this code-making device and tried unsuccessfully to sell it to the U.S. Army. (*HOLCOMBE PHOTO SERVICE*)

A close-up view of the Atanasoff-Berry Computer. One of the memory drums is visible at upper center, and at lower right are a few of the vacuum tubes in the add-subtract mechanisms. (*IOWA STATE UNIVERSITY*)

The old and the new: a memory drum from the Atanasoff-Berry Computer in front of a modern digital electronic computer. (*IOWA STATE UNIVERSITY*)

Clifford Berry, co-inventor of the Atanasoff-Berry Computer. (*IOWA STATE UNIVERSITY*)

The ENIAC team poses for a picture with the computer. J. Presper Eckert Jr. stands at center left adjusting a switch, John Mauchly leans against the column at center right, and Herman Goldstine stands second from right, in Army uniform. (*MOORE SCHOOL OF ELECTRICAL ENGINEERING*)

Inside ENIAC. This forest of
vacuum tubes filled two of the
computer's 36 panels. No
vacuum-tube computer of this
size and complexity had ever
been built before. (*MOORE SCHOOL
OF ELECTRICAL ENGINEERING*)

John Grist
Brainerd in
1981. (*MOORE
SCHOOL OF ELECTRICAL
ENGINEERING*)

The IAS Computer. The cylinders along the base of the machine housed the troublesome wire memory units. (SMITHSONIAN INSTITUTION PHOTO NO. 64771)

John von Neumann poses with the IAS Computer. (THE INSTITUTE FOR ADVANCED STUDY, PRINCETON, N.J.)

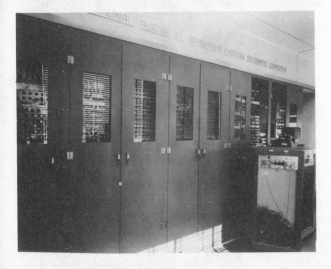

The National Bureau of Standards Eastern Automatic Computer, or SEAC. It went into operation in 1950. SEAC's users sometimes checked it for bugs by jumping up and down on the floor to see if anything shook loose. (NATIONAL BUREAU OF STANDARDS)

Ralph J. Slutz (left) examines SEAC's paper tape input. Once he had to crawl into the computer's access tunnel to save his young son from electrocution.
(*NATIONAL BUREAU OF STANDARDS*)

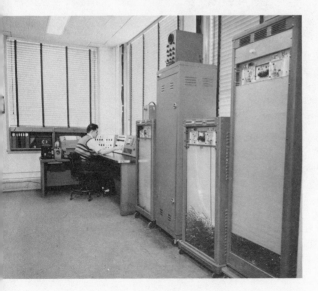

The Standards Western Automatic Computer, or SWAC. It and SEAC were the first two stored-program computers built and operated in the United States.
(*NATIONAL BUREAU OF STANDARDS*)

SEAC exposed. In this photo the outer panels have been removed, and the computer's internal circuitry is visible. In the foreground is the teletype machine used for input and output. (NATIONAL BUREAU OF STANDARDS)

A view of SWAC showing the control console and, at far right, the input typewriter. (NATIONAL BUREAU OF STANDARDS)

Computer memory, circa 1950: one of the cathode-ray tubes from SWAC's Williams-tube memory. (NATIONAL BUREAU OF STANDARDS)

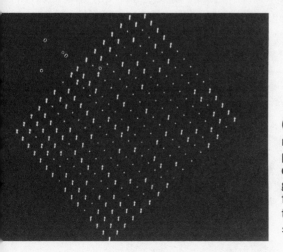

Computer memory made visible. This pattern of dots and dashes was photographed from the face of a cathode-ray tube. (NATIONAL BUREAU OF STANDARDS)

A portion of MIT's Whirlwind computer on display. In the background is the IAS Computer. (*SMITHSONIAN INSTITUTION PHOTO NO. 78-3920*)

Jay Forrester of MIT.
(*THE MIT MUSEUM*)

# 8
# ENIAC

America's war effort gave all research and development work an imperative: everything must be subordinated to defense needs. And so the computer pioneers found their work and their lives abruptly rearranged to suit Uncle Sam.

Among the scientists' priorities was to keep out of the draft if possible. Clifford Berry was young and stood to be sent off to the foxholes unless he could find war-related work at home. Fortunately he soon found a position with Consolidated Engineering Corporation of Pasadena, California, and he moved there in 1942 after marrying Atanasoff's secretary, Jean Reed. Berry's departure effectively put an end to work on the ABC.

Atanasoff was to old to be drafted, so he went into military research and development and wound up, in September 1942, in what he describes as a "noisy, dirty" office at the U.S. Naval Ordnance Laboratory (NOL) in Maryland. The site of the Navy's gun factory, NOL was experimenting with improved mines and depth charges, and Atanasoff began work on acoustic mines, which were designed to be set off by the sound of a passing ship's propellers.

Meanwhile John Mauchly was at the Moore School of Engineering—an institution that is to computing roughly what Kitty Hawk, North Carolina, is to aviation. The Moore School was endowed in 1923, and though not everyone there realized it, the University of Pennsylvania already had a tradition of pioneering the development of computing machinery.

Around 1870, one faculty member had financed the building of a mechanical calculator fashioned on the model of Charles Babbage's Difference Engine. He had stipulated only that the machine's maker leave it with the university after the device was exhibited at the Philadelphia World's Fair in 1876. The calculator was built, put on show, and eventually stored in the attic of the physics building. That machine then met the same fate as Atanasoff's ABC: when the physics department moved, the calculator was thrown out because no one could recall what it was for.

The engineering school started out with a young and dynamic faculty determined to get things done. Among their achievements in the early thirties was to get a differential analyzer like the one at MIT; and they got it by what was then an unusual approach. They asked the government for a grant to build it.

Just how radical a tactic that was at the time is hard for us to appreciate today. In our time the federal government hands out millions and even hundreds of millions of dollars for research and development on a single project; half a century ago federal largesse had not begun to approach that level. So, the Moore School was forced to approach the government very cautiously, in the manner a student approaches a rich but tightfisted uncle for a loan.

To get government backing in the early thirties, during the depths of the Great Depression, the Moore School required an endorsement by a reasonably powerful government agency. Fortunately, the school had an alumnus in the Ballistic Research Laboratory at Aberdeen and through him was able to get an endorsement from the Army.

The Army and the Moore School together went to Vannevar Bush at MIT and asked if he would help them build copies of his differential analyzer. Bush agreed, and in 1933 MIT undertook a joint program with the Moore School and the Army to build two duplicates of the Bush machine, one in Philadelphia and the other at Aberdeen. For this project the Moore School recruited a team of skilled draftsmen and machinists, and they assembled a fine machine in about two years. The depression had put thousands of highly skilled workers out of their jobs, so people jumped at a chance for employment on the differential analyzer.

When completed, the Moore School differential analyzer contained a dozen Bush-type integrators and was, for a short time, one of the two biggest computing machines in the world. (The other was the giant Westinghouse Network Analyzer, which was used to determine the stability of electric power networks. In other words, it determined what was likely to fail and cause a blackout, and how often.)

There was a string attached to the Army's sponsorship of the differential-analyzer project. In return for its backing, the Army Ballistic Research Laboratory at Aberdeen wanted the use of the Moore School's differential analyzer for ballistic research. The Philadelphians agreed, whereupon the Army had access to the Moore School's computer in addition to its own differential analyzer at Aberdeen. The University of Pennsylvania engineers used their machine to run problems that the Aberdeen analyzer was unable to handle.

Soon the Moore School analyzer was also working on problems sent down from MIT. John Grist Brainerd, a Moore School faculty member whose name would become famous in the history of computing, went up to Cambridge to take a course in ultra-high-frequency techniques. While there he was told some of the problems that the MIT Radiation Laboratory, better know as the Rad Lab, was facing. They seemed to be difficulties the Moore School machine could solve. The Rad Lab was intrigued and gave Brainerd a list of ten problems for the machine in Philadelphia to work on. For that assignment, Brainerd assembled a group which included J. Presper Eckert, Jr., a brilliant graduate student who would change both Mauchly's career and the history of technology.

A striking-looking young man with patrician features and a high forehead, Eckert came from a prosperous family and attended Penn Charter, a private high school in Philadelphia. He was skilled in electronics, and in his youth he earned pocket money by rigging up sound systems to play chimes in cemeteries. While still in school he held a patent on an early TV component.

Eckert's dedication to his work was awe-inspiring. Bernard Gordon, who worked for a computer firm that Eckert headed after the war and later became president of Analogic Corporation, recalls that Eckert once advised him: "When you go home tonight, your wife is going to want you to cut the grass. Don't do it. Hire somebody else to cut the grass for you, and design for the company." Gordon confesses he never did cut the grass. Once he described Eckert's philosophy of engineering as one of "great attention to detail," knowing everything about components, their weaknesses and tolerances.

Eckert liked generalities. He wrote in a memoir, "One of the things that has always interested me very much is trying to get as much generality as I can in the things that I do." That included computers. Eckert's inclination toward general principles and broad applications set him apart from previous computer pioneers who designed and built machines for narrowly defined tasks. His yen for generality would play an important part in the shaping of both ENIAC and the whole category of general-purpose computers. He was looking for "good generality," as he called it, that would make a computer problem-independent, as opposed to "bad generality" that forced one to waste time and effort on needless tasks.

Eckert was twelve years younger than Mauchly when the latter arrived at the Moore School in the summer of 1941. Mauchly was delighted to find someone who shared his interest in computing and the possibility of doing it both automatically and electronically. Mauchly recalled later how Eckert "gave me considerable encouragement. If it hadn't been for J. Presper Eckert, I don't know what would have happened next."

When he came to the Moore School, Mauchly had no way of getting his hands on the electronic parts needed for building a computer, much less starting work on the machine, for he was on the very lowest rung of the school's hierarchy. In later years Mauchly would claim he joined the Moore School as a staff member, but in fact he was only a student in the Emergency Science and Defense Management Training Course when he joined the Moore School, and he did not rise to the status of instructor until the autumn of 1941.

Taking the defense course was a step down for Mauchly as far as his career was concerned. He had quit his post as head of the physics department at Ursinus, because he thought the opportunity to pick up more knowledge about electronics made the move worthwhile. He explained in a letter: "I had a chance to teach for the summer in a defense course given to high school graduates, but turned that down in order to become a student myself."

About the time he started in the summer 1941 course, Mauchly mentioned Atanasoff in a letter to a friend: "Immediately after commencement here, I went out to Iowa to see the computing device which a friend of mine is constructing there. His machine, now nearing completion, is electronic in operation, and will solve within a very few minutes any system of linear equations involving no more than thirty variables. It can be adapted to do the job of the Bush differential analyzer more rapidly than the Bush machine does, and it costs a lot less."

Mauchly added that his own computing devices used "a different principle, more likely to fit small computing jobs." Within a few months Mauchly would be preparing for huge computing jobs, for which he would help design and build an equally huge computer similar in some ways to Atanasoff's. Mauchly expressed his intellectual debt to Atanasoff in notes he wrote in his personal diary in August 1941, on the subject of computing. The notes began:

Notes on Electrical Calculating Devices
August 15, 1941                          JWM personal diary notes
   1. Analog versus impulse types. Computing machines may be con-

veniently classified as either "analog" or "impulse" types.* ... Impulse devices comprise all those which "count" or operate on discrete units corresponding to the integers [that is, whole counting numbers] of some number system.

Mauchly explained in a footnote, "I am indebted to Dr. J. V. Atanasoff of Iowa State College for the classification and terminology here explained."

Mauchly went on to describe the virtues of impulse computers: "There is no theoretical limit to the accuracy to which such systems will work; practical limitations on the bulk or cost or convenience of operation provide the only restrictions." Therefore, Mauchly continued, "it is in the impulse machines that major improvements in speed and accuracy are to be expected and sought for."

To improve speed and accuracy, Mauchly advocated the use of vacuum tubes. "For speedy (and noiseless) operation, vacuum tubes and associated circuits are the obvious answer," he wrote. He admitted that "after taking care of stability, freedom from error, ease of servicing, etc., one might conceivably wind up with a design too costly to build. But economically feasible designs are possible. It may not be possible to build a commercial competitor for the mechanical desk computer, but larger machines for more involved, more lengthy, or more specialized jobs are practical."

In a memo written that same month, Mauchly listed his specifications for a desirable general-purpose computer:

A. Considerable number of registers (add to these readily).
B. Ability to transfer numbers from one register to another at will.
C. Ability to operate with number in one register on another register without losing number in original register—so that it may be used again, or checked.
D. Provision for a certain number of constant factors in machine. . . .
E. Possible automatic sequence of operations with subtotals printed (for numerical integration).
F. Ten-key operation?

Mauchly kept in touch with Atanasoff and wrote to him, in a letter dated September 30, 1941:

As time goes on, I expect to get a first-hand knowledge of the operation of the differential analyzer—I have already spent a bit of time
watching the process of setting up and operating the thing—and with
this background I hope I can outdo the analyzer electronically.

A number of different ideas have come to me recently anent computing circuits—some of which are more or less hybrids, combining
your methods with other things, and some of which are nothing like
your machine.

Then Mauchly mentioned the possibility of building a machine like Atanasoff's at the Moore School. Mauchly asked: "Is
there any objection, from your point of view, to my building
some sort of computer which incorporates some of the features
of your machine? . . . would the way be open for us to build an
'Atanasoff calculator' (à la Bush analyzer) here?" Atanasoff replied that he would be glad to get in touch with Mauchly and
discuss calculators with him the next time he was in the East.

In September 1941 Mauchly finally joined the Moore School
as an instructor. He had great plans for inventions in the computing field. They would of course have to be patented, and in a
letter Mauchly noted with pleasure what he thought to be the
Moore School's policy on publications and patents: "The school
doesn't restrict your publication in any way, and although it has
rights to patents, it always releases engineering patents to the individuals anyway, so that's that." That, as it turned out, was def-
initely not the case. After the war Mauchly and Eckert would
have a fight with the Moore School over patent rights—a fight
that would have important effects on the postwar computer industry.

In September of 1941, most "computers" were still human,
and a platoon of young women was pressed into service to help
out the differential analyzers by doing calculations on desktop
machines. The women labored in groups of a hundred or more.
Lieutenant (later Captain) Herman Goldstine supervised their
calculations. The president of the American Mathematical Society helped, too. He had an office in a neighboring building, one
faculty member recalls, so the Moore School prevailed on him
"to send us . . . girls if they were math majors or even if they had
gone through some reasonable amount of mathematics." Yet

even their tireless assistance was not enough. More powerful computing machines were needed. That much was certain. The question was how to design and build them.

What about ganging up teams of desktop calculators as proposed in 1938 at Bell Labs? The Moore School faculty looked into it but concluded that it wasn't worthwhile. When the Moore School engineers asked themselves what would be worthwhile, the same answer kept coming up. Electronic computers were the thing.

Mauchly discussed the possibilities for electronic computing machinery in a memo he wrote in 1941. The opening lines of his memorandum went directly to the core of the matter:

There are many sorts of mathematical problems that require calculation by formulas which can readily be put in the form of iterative equations.

Purely mechanical calculating devices can be devised to expedite the work. However, a great gain in the speed of the calculation can be obtained if the devices which are used employ electronic means for the performance of the calculation, because the speed of such devices can be made very much higher than that of any mechanical device.

Later he described how to use a high-speed electronic calculator: "Since a sufficiently approximate solution of many differential equations can be had simply by solving an associated difference equation [the "broken-down" version of a differential equation], it is to be expected that one of the chief fields of usefulness for an electronic computor [sic] would be found in the solution of differential equations."

Mauchly was following the same trail Atanasoff had taken and getting ever closer to his dream of building an "Atanasoff calculator" at the Moore School. Apparently Atanasoff's work was never far from Mauchly's thoughts. In a paper he wrote about computing circuits in September 1941, Mauchly discussed the possibility of using "JVA's binary condenser system adapted to decimal system (like Stibitz's use of relays for decimal calculation)." Mauchly also proposed building a pulse generator that would help to synchronize all the various parts of a computer in much the same manner as a metronome gives pianists a steady beat to follow.

All this while Mauchly, in his own words, "was continuing to actively think about and talk to others about the possibility of using entirely electronic circuits to try to accomplish calculations, computing, for any kind of scientific or engineering job." Recalling this period many years later, Mauchly liked to portray himself as something of a scientific Saint Paul preaching to the heathen about the coming age of electronic computing. But "everyone was saying no," Mauchly said, "except one graduate student [Eckert] who was saying yes." Mauchly described how faculty members first expressed no interest and then justified their lack of enthusiasm by pointing out that the war would probably be over before the machine Mauchly envisioned could be built and set to work.

Mauchly was exaggerating when he said that everyone was saying no to his ideas. There was skepticism among the faculty, to be sure, but Mauchly's idea was so persuasive that it won some influential friends. Mauchly himself admitted, in a postwar letter, that Brainerd considered the Mauchly proposal for an electronic calculator a "good idea."

As Mauchly talked and thought about electronic computers, the Moore School's mechanical differential analyzer was clattering away. Its output seemed to satisfy Aberdeen and the Rad Lab, and work kept coming in. Mathematical problems were not the only things that Brainerd and his group received from Cambridge. They got an attractive proposition as well. In March 1943 one of the Rad Lab faculty paid Brainerd a visit in Philadelphia and made it known that the Rad Lab would like Brainerd to join MIT and bring his team of young co-workers with him.

The offer was tempting, but Brainerd declined the invitation. After reading Mauchly's memo, Brainerd had a feeling that what he called big things—perhaps as important as radar research—were just ahead for him and his associates at the Moore School.

Brainerd's hunch was right. A few weeks later he, Mauchly,

and Eckert would start work on a big thing indeed: a general-purpose electronic calculating machine the size of a one-bedroom house.

Mauchly thought an electronic calculating device would have several advantages over a Bush-style differential analyzer. The electronic machine could be made faster, more accurate, and simpler to maintain because of its relative lack of moving parts. It could also be made easier to program, because it would not require the extensive tinkering that was needed to set up a problem on a mechanical differential analyzer. (Eckert once pointed out that Vannevar Bush's analyzer "took days to set up with screwdrivers and lead hammers and so on.") On an electronic machine, one could use a control panel like a telephone switchboard to set up problems, as was done with Colossus.

Mauchly imagined a big electronic calculator with perhaps two dozen components, each component being an electronic version of a desktop machine. The whole contraption would act as a parallel processor and would be able to handle multiplications (Mauchly indicated) at the astonishing rate of 100,000 per second. That speed promised big advances in ballistics. The calculation of an artillery shell's trajectory involved an estimated 100,000 multiplications, so the machine Mauchly envisioned could, in theory, come up with the trajectory in only a second. That was miraculous compared to perhaps half an hour on a mechanical differential analyzer and much longer on a desktop calculator.

In fact, that estimate was overly optimistic. It should have been only 1,000 multiplications per second. Even so, that was as good as any mechanical integraph could do, and the electronic machine that Mauchly conceived would have an edge in accuracy and reliability over a purely mechanical device. (Later Mauchly found that the number of multiplications needed per trajectory could be reduced from 100,000 to about 10,000.) So on all grounds, the large high-speed electronic calculator described by Mauchly in his memo appeared to be the improvement that computer technology had been waiting for.

Early in 1943, Mauchly began visiting Atanasoff at the Naval Ordnance Laboratory. Mauchly also was working with NOL at the time, and Atanasoff recalls Mauchly stopping by the office for a chat "every time he came in."

On one visit Mauchly told Atanasoff that he and Eckert had come up with a fresh approach to computing. Atanasoff was intrigued and asked for details. Mauchly declined, saying the information was classified. "I really believed him pretty much," said Atanasoff years later. He wondered why Mauchly was such a frequent caller. Atanasoff's boss at NOL thought the reason was plain. "He was watching you," he told Atanasoff.

Eckert and Mauchly talked over their ideas with Brainerd, and in April 1943 the three men developed a proposal for a high-speed electronic calculator that could solve differential equations much faster than any mechanical analyzer could. This document was the initial sketch for ENIAC. Its title was "Report on an Electronic Diff. Analyzer, Submitted to the Ballistic Research Laboratory, Aberdeen Proving Ground, by the Moore School of Engineering, University of Pennsylvania." A footnote explained the vague but intentional abbreviation *Diff.*:

The word "Diff." is deliberately abbreviated. Present differential analyzers operate on the basis of integrating continuously, i.e., by differential increments; the electronic analyzer, although it is believed that it would be both speedier and more accurate, would operate using extremely small but finite differences. The abbreviation "Diff." may thus be considered to represent "difference" rather than "differential" in the case of the electronic device.

Writing proposals for an electronic supercalculator was one thing, but finding the money to build one was something else again. Where could the Moore School obtain the backing for this project?

As before, the Ballistic Research Laboratory at Aberdeen seemed the most promising place to start looking, and so, later in April 1943, Eckert and Mauchly accompanied Brainerd and Herman Goldstine (who served as liaison officer between Aberdeen and the Moore School) to Aberdeen to put their case for a high-speed electronic computer to the Army. Brainerd and Goldstine made a presentation while Eckert and Mauchly polished the report.

Brainerd was impressed by the collection of minds he encountered at Aberdeen. Among them were Oswald Veblen of Princeton, and Marsten Morse, then president of the American Mathematical Society. Also present were Colonel (later Major General) Leslie E. Simon, head of the Ballistic Research Laboratory, and Colonel Hermann Zornig, its founder.

After making his speech, Brainerd stepped outside the room while the mathematicians and military men deliberated. Finally Veblen emerged. "You look like the cat that swallowed the canary," he told Brainerd. Brainerd was unsure what Veblen meant and asked him to explain. "You are going to get the contract," said Veblen.

"And that," said Brainerd later, "was that."

The University of Pennsylvania agreed to the terms of the contract with the Army, and Brainerd and company were on their way. The university gave its approval, however, only on the condition that Brainerd take full responsibility for the project. That meant, in effect, that Brainerd would have to resign if the computer turned out to be a failure. Brainerd called that situation "an interesting challenge."

The Moore School group, then, had the contract and the Mauchly-Eckert proposal for the computer. That machine would be dubbed ENIAC—Electronic Numerical Integrator, Analyzer, and Computer—and as its name indicates, its principal job was integration, the process used to analyze shell trajectories.

Before building their machine, the computer makers at the Moore School required a set of guidelines to direct their work. ENIAC was designed and built with the following principles in mind:

• *Flexibility of Control.* This was the major problem, according to Eckert. Though ENIAC was designated a numerical integrator, Eckert and Mauchly wanted the machine to go as far beyond that narrow mission as possible; they wanted a much more flexible computer. The key to this was the subroutine. Eckert and Mauchly knew that subroutines would make the computer more versatile and flexible by permitting it to do lots of little jobs on the side, in addition to the main program. Therefore switches and other components were rigged for subroutines, and the results made ENIAC far more flexible than, say, the Harvard ASCC, or Mark I. Aiken's machine, Eckert pointed out, originally "had no facility for proper use of subroutines." Eckert added that he and Mauchly were "proud of the fact that we did provide this flexibility."

• *Simplicity.* ENIAC would have hundreds of thousands of separate parts and several dozen major components, so simplicity was essential if the machine was to stay manageable. As Arthur Burks, who helped to design large sections of ENIAC, put it, the goal here "was to achieve, in a highly complex system, the greatest possible simplicity of design, construction, operation, and maintenance, in order to hold down both human and mechanical error."

• *Worst-case design.* By figuring what the worst disaster that could happen to a component was, they could plan to survive it. The object was to prepare for voltages gone haywire and assume that everything would happen twice as slowly as it should. Then, when catastrophe struck, they would be ready.

The computer makers had few precedents to guide them in the building of a high-speed electronic calculating machine. They had not heard of Charles Babbage, nor were they aware of his work until ENIAC was already built and running. They had no knowledge of what was happening across the Atlantic at Bletchley Park; neither did they have any idea what Konrad Zuse was doing in Germany, since the Nazis were not supplying classified military information to the Allies. The Philadelphians were familiar with the ASCC at Harvard, the Bell Labs computers, and the Bush analyzer, but those were mechanical and electromechanical devices. Mauchly had built little electronic counting devices, but nothing had approached the scale of the machine they now had in mind. (Brainerd described Mauchly's work in electronics at Ursinus as "an interesting illustration, not much more.")

Yet Brainerd's team was now committed to building one of the largest, most complicated and advanced machines of its kind. Herman Goldstine's arithmetic gives an idea of the magnitude of the challenge facing the Moore School team: ENIAC was to have some 17,000 tubes operating at a rate of thousands of pulses per second, so in any given second ENIAC would have millions of opportunities to miss a pulse and go wrong. That, according to Goldstine, was "why the undertaking was so risky."

"Risky" was a mild word for it. The Moore School group needed all the guidance it could get. For advice they sent copies of the ENIAC proposal to electronics experts at Aberdeen. They dismissed the idea of an electronic computer as impractical, because a tube or two seemed bound to blow, and so shut down the machine, before a calculation could be finished.

Aberdeen mathematicians, on the other hand, went wild with enthusiasm. They had no idea how such a machine might be built, but they knew it would be able to carry out marvelous feats of calculation, and they wanted to see the machine built and put in service. The mathematicians were a large and influential bloc at Aberdeen, so the Army stuck by Brainerd and his team in spite of the odds against success.

As work got under way on ENIAC, Brainerd found that his job as project boss was full of those interesting challenges he mentioned. Among them was secrecy. Much of the work on ENIAC was sensitive information, and Brainerd had in his office a rubber stamp for marking documents "CONFIDENTIAL." Posters all around warned, "The enemy may be listening."

The hush-hush nature of their work caused the ENIAC team great inconvenience and worry. They were scientists, not spies; they had heretofore worked in a research community where ideas were debated in the open, not whispered in closed-door meetings and then buried in confidential documents. It was difficult for the ENIAC group to adjust to the precautions of wartime.

Yet those precautions had to be observed. The scientists were forbidden to talk about what they were doing, except in small work areas specifically set up for particular jobs. They were not even allowed to discuss their work over lunch at a restaurant: the ears of the foe were everywhere. In this suspicious and oppressive environment, the ENIAC builders feared that they might slip and let loose sensitive information and then get punished for it. Mauchly complained that the engineers weren't certain they knew all the rules, "nor what penalties might be visited on us for violating rules."

Though there was no shortage of rules, parts shortages were a problem. The Moore School team had a hard time getting good commercial resistors for the machine, and ENIAC required some 70,000 of them. So ENIAC's makers went to the same source that provided the relays for George Stibitz's K-Model. They visited a junk pile.

Brainerd had heard from a Moore School graduate that one manufacturer of electronic parts had a big bin full of resistors that had failed rigorous tests, but not by much: they were maybe four or five percent outside the accepted limits for resistance. Heaped in the bin were oodles of resistors just for the taking. They were banded in colors to indicate their capabilities and were adequate for the Moore School's purposes, and so junk resistors kept ENIAC in business.

The quality of components remained a problem. Not all the resistors, tubes, and other parts performed identically. Arthur Burks mentions how their behavior showed considerable variation—which, multiplied by the huge number of components, made ENIAC, in Eckert's words, a scary project. In smaller systems, Burks points out, circuit designers could compensate for these variations by fine tuning. But in a gigantic system like ENIAC such detailed adjustments were impossible. One just had to plow ahead and hope for the best.

To make matters worse, Aberdeen kept escalating its demands. No longer satisfied with the original proposal, the Army asked for a bigger and more complex ENIAC. Originally the machine was to have only about 5,000 tubes, but Army requirements eventually inflated ENIAC to more than three times its original size and almost three times its initial budget. The preliminary cost estimate of $140,000 swelled to a final figure of some $400,000 or almost $10 million in today's dollars.

Eckert gets much of the credit for simplifying and speeding up this gargantuan job, for he saw how all the parts of the machine could be pulled together and made to work as a team. Such teamwork was vital, for ENIAC, like Colossus, was a parallel machine.

Yet ENIAC was more than a parallel-processing computer; it was very close to the modern multiprocessor. Eckert once described ENIAC as a machine that could carry out several different independent processes at once, so it was "a multiprocessing device as well as a parallel device." ENIAC technically was not a multiprocessor as we define it today, however, because no single unit of ENIAC could calculate on its own.

In its final form ENIAC was made up of some thirty different units (for input and output, computing, and other functions) that had to be synchronized with one another and kept running simultaneously. ENIAC handled this tricky job of timing, as Colossus did, with the aid of a sophisticated internal electronic clock called the central timing unit or cycling unit.

The cycling unit was the descendant of the pulse generator that Mauchly had envisioned earlier, but it was more complicated than a mere electronic metronome. Rather than synchronizing all the units to the beat of a single drum, as the inventions of Atanasoff and Berry literally did, the cycling unit generated ten different signal frequencies to communicate the beat to all the many different parts of the machine. The process was like a coxswain in a boat race calling out "Stroke! Stroke! Stroke!" to his crew in ten different tempos at once and at the same time making sure they didn't get their oars tangled. Burks describes the cycling unit as "one of ENIAC's important contributions to electronic computing."

The other components of the computer included:

• *Accumulators.* There were twenty of these in the finished machine, and they handled both arithmetic and storage. Each accumulator could hold a ten-digit decimal number (say, 1,234,-567,890) and had a device in it called a binary counter for storing the sign of the number, either positive or negative. The binary counters used Boole's one-and-zero reckoning system. Zero meant the number was positive, and one signified that it was negative. The accumulators in the ENIAC were equivalent in a way to the dials equipped with carry-over mechanisms in the early Pascal calculator.

• *Multiplier.* This one simply carried out multiplications. Eckert and Mauchly described it in their report as an "electronic switching device which . . . [will] form in the accumulator the product of . . . two numbers . . . "

• *Divider.* Its job was just the opposite of that of the multiplier.

• *Function generator.* Here we see some of the "good generality" that Eckert loved to build into machinery. The function generator allowed the programmers to slip in an *arbitrary function*, meaning one that the machine was not originally programmed to accomplish. An arbitrary function might be one too complicated to be generated by a simple difference equation. One might say the function generator made ENIAC a little "smarter" than special purpose computers by increasing ENIAC's versatility and generality.

• *Recorder.* Eckert and Mauchly defined it as "a device for making a permanent record of the results of calculation at any determined stage of the work." They suggested using a card-punch machine. ENIAC in its final form used punched cards for both input and output.

• *Program control unit.* This component was in a sense the brain of the mechanism, for it was supposed to tell the computer what to do and when. It was described in the Eckert-Mauchly proposal as "a unit which contains the necessary control circuits for initiating the various steps of the calculation in their proper order." Programs were set up by plugging in cables and setting switches, in much the same way as on Colossus.

ENIAC prefigured many features that would later become standard in electronic computer technology. For example, Eckert and Mauchly were designing modularity into their machine several decades before the microcomputer age began. ENIAC's circuits were built into plug-in modules that could be taken out for repairs as needed without having to shut down the whole computer. Replacing a defective module was merely a matter of slipping another, functional module into its place. ENIAC had only a few types of plug-in modules, and the variety of all its other components was kept to a minimum, in line with the design principle of simplicity.

Simplicity and reliability were also the reasons ENIAC worked in the decimal number system rather than in binary. (One of the most persistent misconceptions about ENIAC is that it was a binary machine. Eckert spoke for both himself and Mauchly when he said, in 1976, "We cringe a little when we hear ENIAC described as a binary machine; it was not.") ENIAC might have been able to get away with using fewer vacuum tubes in a binary arrangement, but the savings would have been small. The machine would have been forced to convert from decimal to binary and then back again at input and output respectively, as in Zuse's Z3 and the ABC. For ENIAC's purposes it was safer and easier to go decimal. This is a good example of the trade-offs computer designers often have to make between cost and efficiency. What seems a nice cost-cutting measure may actually make a machine less efficient and therefore less cost-effective in the long run.

The design philosophy behind ENIAC—simplicity, flexibility, and worst-case scenarios—paid off. Contrary to the predictions of doomsayers who warned that electronic technology would never do the job, ENIAC turned out to be not only versatile, fast, and reliable, but rugged, as well. The mammoth machine survived even after being taken apart at the Moore School and reassembled at Aberdeen. ENIAC was still in good working order when it was finally dismantled after ten years of almost trouble-free performance.

The Moore School greatly surpassed Mauchly's original dream of building an "Atanasoff calculator (à la Bush analyzer)." They produced what one visitor described as "a damn big machine," large enough to fill a fair-sized gymnasium. When fully grown, ENIAC was a far cry from the desk-sized ABC. ENIAC stood almost two stories tall, weighed thirty tons, had approximately the same volume as a railway boxcar, and was equipped with big ducted fans on top to carry off heat from the thousands of tubes.

The computer's cabinets were arranged in a U-shape, inside the curve of which three *function table matrices*, arrays of switches mounted on frames about the size of garment racks, stood on wheels, connected by fat cables to the main body of the computer. The function table matrices were used to set up programs by turning the switches—hundreds of them on each matrix—back and forth.

A long arrangement of cables snaked across the inside face of the curving line of cabinets. These cables made up the *digit trunk,* which served much the same function in ENIAC as the spinal cord does in a human. It kept the "brain" of the computer in touch with all the other parts of the machine's "nervous system." Other cables were strung between jackplugs, much as on the Enigma plugboard, to supplement the switches in setting up programs.

It was among the first general-purpose electronic digital computers, if not the very first one. ENIAC was not limited, as the Atanasoff-Berry Computer was, to solving sets of differential equations. Though ENIAC's stated purpose was integration, it was capable of handling anything from complex integrations to the figuring done in banks. Other machines with general-purpose capability had been built, including the Harvard Mark I, but ENIAC was the first such electronic machine.

ENIAC went into operation in 1945. It was too late for the war effort but just in time for postwar weapons design. ENIAC's first assignment was to carry out a long and involved calculation having to do with nuclear bombs. The problem and its outcome are still classified.

It is fitting that ENIAC's first problem should have to do with atomic weapons, for the A-bomb, as mentioned earlier, ranks along with the general-purpose electronic digital computer as one of the most important inventions to emerge from World War II. Nuclear weapons determined the global strategies of the superpowers during the postwar years, while ENIAC set the fashion for data-processing machinery during that same period. ENIAC demonstrated beyond reasonable doubt that one could use electronics successfully to design and build large general-purpose computing machines. That was quite an achievement for a computer built with junk resistors.

ENIAC performed splendidly in Philadelphia, but at Aberdeen it got off to a shaky start. At one point the computer performed so poorly there that its up-time for some months was less than fifty percent. Most of the time the computer was just sitting around doing nothing. Apparently the difficulty was something at Aberdeen, for in Philadelphia its up-time had been closer to ninety percent, and the engineers who tested ENIAC before it was moved to Aberdeen had concluded the machine was in good working order. What was the matter?

Mauchly discovered the trouble in a conversation later with one of the people from Aberdeen, who called ENIAC's performance very bad and said, "We were lucky to get anything done at the end of the day, after spending most of our time trouble-shooting. When we turned the machine on in the morning, all sorts of things seemed to go wrong."

That last remark startled Mauchly. "Why did you turn it off?" he asked.

"Those were the rules," he was told.

Regulations at Aberdeen required the computer to be turned off at night, to save electricity and to spare a guard from having to keep an eye on the hot equipment all night for fire prevention (18,000 vacuum tubes, the number finally installed in ENIAC, can put out a tremendous amount of heat). Even Colossus, which had only a small fraction that number of tubes, had made its environs so warm that operators were uncomfortable working in shirtsleeves.

The Aberdeen rules clearly were made by someone who had no idea what ENIAC was like and how it operated. Turning the machine off and powering it up again saved a little electricity but destroyed tubes as effectively as a bullet, for the expansion and contraction caused by heating up and cooling off wore them out in short order. (Aiken had faced this same problem with his first electronic computer, Mark III, but had avoided the trouble by keeping it powered up all the time.) Mauchly dismissed the Aberdeen difficulties as a case of "stupid rules, stupidly applied."

When it was working, and that was most of the time when proper precautions had been observed, ENIAC was faster than any other calculating machine of its kind. Two women using desk calculators spent a year working out a test problem that was used to find out if ENIAC gave the right answers. ENIAC solved the problem in an hour.

When ENIAC was dedicated, it showed off its powers by computing an artillery shell's trajectory in twenty seconds. That, Burks reports, was "faster than the shell itself, which took thirty seconds to reach its target!" Brainerd and a graduate student once used ENIAC for a weekend at Aberdeen to solve an outlandishly difficult equation, simply to demonstrate what the machine could do. That weekend, ENIAC carried out fifteen million multiplications—roughly forty years' labor for a person using a desktop machine.

Nearly all the computers that surround us today, from handheld calculators to giant supercomputers capable of 250 million multiplications per second, can be traced to ENIAC. A triumph of generality, simplicity, and planning, ENIAC did more than any other individual machine to make the modern computer a reality; and ENIAC's success is a monument to the genius of a handful of men and their perseverance in the face of myriad problems, from senseless rules to official secrecy.

# 9
# EDVAC AND THE STORED PROGRAM CONCEPT

ENIAC was virtually the only large electronic computer working just after World War II. ENIAC stood alone, but its makers did not stand still: Eckert and Mauchly and their Moore School colleagues were pondering ideas that would later become familiar parts of home computer technology.

Goldstine was thinking of ways to accelerate data storage. In a memorandum at Aberdeen, Goldstine bemoaned the shortage of high-speed storage devices in ENIAC. He suggested the Moore School be commissioned to keep up research on ENIAC with the aim of eventually building "a new ENIAC of improved design." Goldstine thought the new ENIAC ought to be smaller, less expensive, easier to program, and faster than the original—and should contain "many fewer tubes." How the Moore School team achieved all these goals is a fascinating story, made all the more absorbing by the contributions of John von Neumann, who came to work with ENIAC's creators at the end of World War II.

Today there is no one in the scientific fraternity comparable to von Neumann. His invention of game theory, which in an ideologized version provided much of the theoretical foundation for U.S. postwar strategy against the Soviet Union, would mark him as one of the most gifted and productive mathematicians of all time. Yet his other achievements in both pure and applied mathematics were so numerous that an entire book would be needed to discuss them all.

A portly man with thinning hair and a mischievous gleam in his eyes, von Neumann belonged, some of his more worshipful biographers have said, to a race of intellectual giants the like of whom our world had never seen before and may never see again: "a species greater than man," one of his disciples called him.

Von Neumann was no demigod; rather, he was an exceptionally brilliant man who had unprecedented opportunities to turn his ideas into reality. He made his share of mistakes and could be wilfully ignorant as well as supremely enlightened. It is also a matter of debate whether some of his achievements were victories or disasters. But these facts detract nothing from his stature as a scientist and inventor. For more than two decades John von Neumann dominated the scientific fraternity in America and did much to shape our modern global society. In a world where so many great accomplishments are team efforts, von Neumann was a rare and splendid example of the individual who makes a difference.

Because of his vivid personality, anecdotes about von Neumann are legion. He was a workaholic. His wife Karla, a distinguished programmer, said, "His capacity for work was practically unlimited." He brought paperwork home, labored late into the night, and then resumed at dawn. So meticulous was he that when asked to write an abstract 250 words long, he would go through and count every last word before sending the paper in. Von Neumann also had incredible powers of concentration and seemed capable of doing creative work anywhere, at any time. One colleague recalls him reeling off a complicated and abstruse mathematical proof while standing in the middle of a room full of partygoers.

Von Neumann feared no equation. Other mathematicians might hesitate before plowing into an infinite series—a frightening lineup of calculations full of exponents—but von Neumann actually seeemed to enjoy it. For him it was the mental equivalent of pumping iron. He prided himself on his reputation as the fastest brain in mathematics and could solve in his head math problems that took his colleagues all night with pencil and adding machine.

When giving lectures, he sometimes would play games with his audience. One computer specialist who attend a von Neumann talk recalls:

He was lecturing on a method of generating random numbers—or rather, pseudorandom numbers, which are almost the same but not quite. Truly random numbers are the kind you get from a roulette wheel; pseudorandom numbers are created by some other process. His method involved taking parts of numbers, squaring them, then taking parts of the squares and squaring those, and so on. He told us this would result in virtually random numbers. Then he looked at the board and said, "Or would it?"—and proceeded to disprove everything he had just said. It was like an O. Henry story. There was that unexpected twist at the end.

Though an inspiring lecturer, von Neumann wrote in a maddeningly detailed style. Like Isaac Newton, he made no effort to clean up and simplify his work for the benefit of readers less gifted than himself. His colleague P. R. Halmos recalls how von Neumann once wrote a paper expanding on a function that was written $\emptyset (x)$. The next step he denoted as $\emptyset ((x))$, the next as $\emptyset (((x)))$, and so forth. Finally he came up with the following equation:

$$(\Psi (((((a))))))^2 = \emptyset (((((a)))))$$

Equations like that one, Halmos writes, "have to be peeled before they can be digested." Students referred to it as von Neumann's onion.

Much of von Neumann's influence was due to his personal charm as well as his genius. He was a master storyteller and carried in his head a vast collection of amusing stories, limericks, and puns. Often humor helped him put colleagues at ease. Accordng to one story, he was once approached by a graduate student who confessed his inability to understand a certain topic in higher math. "Young man," said von Neumann affably, "one never really understands mathematics. One just gets used to it."

Von Neumann had a quip ready for all occasions. Once, following a car accident (he was a notoriously reckless driver and cracked up cars on a regular basis), von Neumann described the wreck in terms of relativity theory. "The trees on my right were passing in orderly fashion at fifty miles per hour," he said. "Suddenly one of them stepped out in my path!"

His reputation for infallibility awed many of his colleagues. Tongue in cheek, it was once proposed that members of a race of superbeings had come to earth from Mars in ages past and settled in Hungary. To avoid being attacked and killed by the primitives on Earth, the Martians had adopted terrestrial form and mannerisms but had been unable to conceal their towering intelligence. That scenario sounded almost plausible, for von Neumann was one of several world-caliber mathematicians and physicists who had emigrated from Hungary to the United States; another was Edward Teller, "father" of the hydrogen bomb.

Not everyone, however, joined in the hymn of praise for von Neumann. Some of his fellow mathematicians were put off by the cult that surrounded him. When told of a marvelous new development and asked who he thought was responsible for it, one of von Neumann's co-workers reportedly said, "It must have been Saint Johnny."

Though he helped produce the world he lived in, von Neumann was also very much a product of his times and society. He was born John Louis Neumann in Budapest in 1903. (The prefix *von* came when the Neumann family was elevated to the nobility of his native Hungary—he translated his father's newly acquired title of Margittai into the German equivalent.)

He was the firstborn child in his family and was known as Jansci, or "Johnny." His father was a banker and could afford to give Jansci the best education available. It paid off splendidly. Jansci showed a genius for mathematics at an early age. One possibly apocryphal story has it that at age three he noticed his mother staring abstractedly out into space and asked her, "What are you calculating?' He was speaking with his father in classical Greek by age five, and at eighteen he published his first scientific paper in collaboration with his tutor.

Von Neumann studied at Göttingen but, fond as he was of German intellectual life in the years before World War II, felt compelled to leave Germany in 1930 as the Nazis rose to power and made Göttingen an increasingly unpleasant place for scholars of Jewish descent such as himself.

Before World War II broke out, von Neumann came to the United States at the invitation of Oswald Veblen and joined the mathematics faculty of Princeton's Institute for Advanced Studies (which despite its name has no direct affiliation with Princeton University itself). Sometimes von Neumann is mentioned in the same breath as his colleague Albert Einstein, who lived near him in Princeton. The two men did have some traits in common: both were products of the German university system, both moved to America to escape the Nazi madness, both were among the most brilliant mathematicians of all time. Furthermore, both contributed to the most important new technologies of the twentieth century—the nuclear bomb and the electronic computer.

But there the resemblance ends. Indeed in many ways no two scientists had less in common than von Neumann and Einstein did, and their differences reveal much about their outlooks on life.

Einstein was a pacifist and regretted his contribution to the development of nuclear weapons. Von Neumann embraced the technology of the atom enthusiastically and enjoyed attending bomb tests in the southwestern desert. Once he even argued that a few thousand additional deaths per year from  radiation-induced disease was an acceptable price to pay for maintaining America's technological lead over the rest of the world. (There was a tragic irony in this argument, for von Neumann died of bone cancer which may very well have been induced by radiation picked up when he attended those postwar bomb tests.)

Einstein prized his privacy and was forever declining invitations to sup with the famous and the mighty; von Neumann enjoyed being the center of attention and delighted in rubbing elbows with the influential. Einstein's friends were poets and philosophers; von Neumann's, admirals and generals. Einstein condoned Stalin's purges; von Neumann hated the Russians and their communist ideology and saw the nuclear bomb as imperative to contain Soviet aggression. Einstein was a slovenly dresser who cared little for material possessions; von Neumann wore expensive, well-tailored suits and enjoyed an elegant lifestyle. Einstein ended his days as little more than a figurehead, a totem for public veneration; von Neumann remained at the forefront of mathematics research to the very close of his life.

Perhaps the most fundamental difference between the two mathematicians, however, lay in their views on the moral and social dimensions of science and technology. Einstein thought scientists were obligated to consider the social implications and morals of their work and suppress research, if need be, to spare the world more horrors. Those considerations apparently meant little to von Neumann, who was prepared to follow mathematics—especially applied mathematics—to wherever it might lead, regardless of its impact on the world. Einstein was an ethical philosopher, as well as a mathematician—a rare combination in his time, or in any other time. Von Neumann, on the other hand, was the model technocrat—a type that would soon become all too familiar.

During World War II, von Neumann applied his interest in hydrodynamics—which in a broad sense means the mathematics of fluid motion—to the design of the first atomic bombs at Los Alamos, New Mexico. He taught the Los Alamos group how to model explosions mathematically so as to improve the design of the bomb's trigger mechanism. Those mathematical models involved long and arduous calculations, which would have been much simpler had they had access to a high-speed general-purpose computer. But von Neumann's involvement with computers would not begin until 1945, after a fateful encounter on the train platform at Aberdeen.

Herman Goldstine was waiting for the train to Philadelphia when he looked up and saw von Neumann. Goldstine was understandably nervous at meeting the great mathematician, but von Neumann's charm and friendly manner soon put him at ease, and the two men started talking about their work. Goldstine revealed that he and his colleagues in Philadelphia were working on an electronic machine that could carry out more than three hundred calculations per second.

All at once, Goldstine wrote later, "the whole atmosphere of the conversation changed from one of relaxed good humor to one more like the oral examination for the doctor's degree in mathematics." Von Neumann pressed Goldstine for details of the machine and was invited to the Moore School for a look.

Von Neumann visited Philadelphia later in 1945 to inspect ENIAC. Tests were under way on the accumulators. According to Goldstine, Eckert had in mind another kind of test, to see whether or not von Neumann really was the genius he was said to be. If von Neumann's first question about ENIAC concerned the logical structure of the computer, then that would prove he actually was a mastermind. "Of course," writes Goldstine, "this was von Neumann's first query."

Von Neumann started thinking of a more advanced computer than ENIAC. Despite its spectacular achievements, ENIAC still had many shortcomings. It was too big and was based on all-too-fallible technologies, such as those thousands and thousands of vacuum tubes. Von Neumann and the Moore School group imagined a computer that could be put together with fewer materials, have a larger and highly reliable memory, and depend on fewer tubes.

The most important consideration here was the memory. A computer is only as good as its powers of data recall, and up to this point it had been difficult to design and build a truly reliable and capacious memory. Tubes were bulky, while cards and tapes were clumsy and took a long time to prepare. Was there some other mechanism that could store data compactly, provide quick recall, and be easy to record on?

Thanks to Eckert and Mauchly, there was: the mercury delay storage line. It had orginally been used in radar sets, but Eckert and Mauchly saw its potential as a computer memory device and adapted it for use with data processing machinery. Like the Hollerith tabulator many years before, the delay line made clever use of the properties of mercury. Hollerith had used mercury to carry data as electrical signals. The Moore School engineers used it to carry data in the form of acoustic shock waves.

The mercury delay storage line consisted of a long metal tube, roughly the dimensions of a broom handle, filled with mercury and sealed at either end with round plugs of quartz. The quartz had a property called *piezoelectricity*. A piezoelectric material responds to an electric current by changing its shape slightly and then snapping back to its original form when the current is shut off. One might say it goes "ouch" when subjected to an electric shock.

Piezoelectric materials are handy for many uses, such as generating sonar pulses to guide ships and submarines around obstacles in the sea. Piezoelectricity let the computer makers at the Moore School turn data-bearing electrical signals into data-bearing waves in the mercury.

Here is how it worked. Data would be sent along wires to the quartz crystals as electrical impulses. Those impulses would make the crystals vibrate and transfer their mechanical energy, the vibrations, to the mercury in the tube. Because mercury is so dense, it conducts vibrations very well. Just set the liquid in motion, and waves will ripple back and forth.

The memory had to be jogged now and then to prevent the waves from dying out altogether, but this was easily done. Removing data was also easy, thanks to the piezoelectric properties of the quartz plugs. Not only could they deform themselves in response to electric current, but they could also turn that process around and generate an electric current. When jiggled by the waves in the mercury, they would produce little jolts of power that could be picked up and sent back into the computer as data. The mercury delay storage line has been compared to a jungle tom-tom, only the drumbeats in this case will keep resounding long after sound waves in the air would have died away.

A rack of mercury delay storage lines could hold huge amounts of data by the standards of the late 1940s. It became possible to store more information inside a computer than ever before. The mercury-delay-storage-line arrangement had dollar savings in its favor too. ENIAC had used a very wasteful procedure for storing data. It required a pair of vacuum tubes, joined together in a flip-flop, to hold a single bit of data. Tubes were expensive, and one had to buy one or two of them for every single bit of data. The bill for vacuum tubes added up fast, especially in an ENIAC-like computer with thousands upon thousands of them.

One mercury delay line could replace dozens of vacuum tubes. Goldstine figured that a mercury-filled tank roughly six feet long could handle 1,000 binary digits—the contents of a thousand flip-flops—at the cost of ten vacuum tubes. So the delay lines meant a ninety-nine percent saving in the cost of tubes, not to mention the saving in space. The vast arrays of vacuum tubes could now be replaced by relatively tiny racks of mercury-filled delay lines; one could practically fit a computer's memory in the back seat of a car. That was a miracle of miniaturization, and it helped to make possible the single greatest advance in programming since computers got program control: the stored program concept, which was embodied in ENIAC's successor, the Electronic Discrete Variable Computer (EDVAC).

Soon after von Neumann's arrival in Philadelphia, he began work on a report that would become one of the most renowned documents in the history of technology and a center of sometimes bitter controversy for many years to come. It was a 101-page paper entitled *First Draft of a Report on the EDVAC*. Apparently von Neumann had intended it merely as a rough draft, a guide to future studies, but without his approval or knowledge the report was typed up and issued.

The principles embodied in the *First Draft* were worked out by von Neumann and the Moore School engineers during extensive conversations there. Von Neumann conceived of a hypothetical computer that was everything he thought a computer ought to be. Hardware did not figure prominently in his thinking. He was more concerned with the logical structure of computers, how they operated in principle rather than how they could be put together. Let us look briefly at his model for computer structure and operation, for it provided the theoretical underpinnings for the modern digital electronic computer.

Von Neumann divided his hypothetical model computer into six parts:

1. A central arithmetical unit (CA, in von Neumann's abbreviation) that would carry out addition, subtraction, multiplication, and division.

2. A central control unit (CC) that would tell the computer which arithmetical operations to carry out in which sequence.

3. A memory unit (M).

4. An input device (I).

5. An output device (O).

6. A recording device (R).

Once again, Charles Babbage's concepts of "mill" and "store" had resurfaced in the design of a computer. Here the store had the label M on it, and CA and CC together made up the mill where data would be processed.

How much von Neumann knew about Babbage is uncertain. Von Neumann's published works contain no references to Babbage or his Analytical Engine, and while von Neumann's scholarship was vast, it was not all-encompassing. In fact, von Neumann seemed ignorant of much widely known information in his own field. A story is told that von Neumann once saw a group of graduate students working out a problem on the blackboard, and he asked what they were doing. "Oh, you know," they told him, "the usual identification convention." In fact he did not know. Although the subject was so elementary that most graduate students knew about it, von Neumann did not. Yet von Neumann's associates at Princeton report hearing him mention Babbage in conversation on at least two occasions, so it seems likely that von Neumann was familiar with Babbage's work and

drew on the thought of his great British predecessor while for-
mulating his criteria for a computer.

The size of the memory was perhaps the most important consideration. Von Neumann used his experience with hydrody-
namical calculations and decided the machine called for a
memory of 2,000 to 8,000 numbers of thirty-two binary digits
apiece. With mercury delay lines to help, this memory could be
built using perhaps only a few hundred vacuum tubes, as opposed to the 18,000 tubes in ENIAC.

Sometimes von Neumann underestimated the number of
tubes he could get away with. Arthur Burks tells of the time von
Neumann presented a plan for an adding device and claimed
that only five tubes would be needed to handle the logical operations involved. Eckert and Burks were present and were aston-
ished.

"No," Eckert told him, "it takes at least ten tubes."

"I'll prove it to you," von Neumann replied, and sketched his
design for the circuit on a nearby blackboard.

Eckert and Burks were unconvinced. They pointed out that
the adder von Neumann had drawn could not operate quite as
quickly and simply as he imagined. A second set of five tubes
would be needed to keep the initial five tubes from running haywire. Finally von Neumann had to admit defeat. The problem
wasn't quite as easy to solve as he had thought. But he conceded
his error in a face-saving way: "You're right," he said, "it takes
ten tubes to add—five tubes for logic, and five for electronics!"

The EDVAC had some 3,500 tubes when completed in 1951,
but its electronic specifications are of only minor concern here.
Much more important are two historical concepts it embodied,
the stored program and the "von Neumann machine."

A stored program, as noted earlier, is a program that can be
stored in a computer and can modify itself while in the computer. The stored-program computer uses a set of commands fed
in with the data to be analyzed. Combining data with instructions saves time and effort. Remember that earlier computers
such as the Bell Labs Model 5 and Heath Robinson had to have
separate tapes prepared for data and instructions. Those awk-

ward and inflexible arrangements became obsolete with the advent of the stored-program concept.

Eckert's and Mauchly's mercury delay storage line helped make the stored program possible by expanding memory. Even a very short and simple program contains a lot of information—too much, in fact, for pre-EDVAC computers to store. Storing programs in those machines was like trying to pack *War and Peace* into a fortune cookie. The storage lines solved this problem by replacing the bulky arrays of tubes and wires with a much more compact device that substituted waves in fluid metal for impulses in flip-flops.

If the delay storage lines were Eckert's and Mauchly's great contributions to the stored-program computer, then another important part of it—the variable-address code—was von Neumann's. The variable-address system may be visualized as a juggling act. Just as a juggler must keep his clubs constantly in motion to sustain his act, the computer must keep shifting data from one spot in memory to another if the program is to modify itself as needed. Von Neumann worked out a coding system that allowed the computer to "juggle" data inside itself.

The stored program soon became an integral element of computers, partly because von Neumann was its champion. Maurice Wilkes, who had found Aiken's company bluff but delightful, said in a postwar lecture: "That von Neumann should bring his great prestige and influence to bear was important, since the new ideas were too revolutionary for some, and powerful voices were being raised to say that . . . to mix instructions and numbers in the same memory was to go against nature."

The stored-program concept became the focus of a bitter controversy involving von Neumann and his Moore School colleagues. Von Neumann is widely credited with originating the stored-program concept and did outline it in his *First Draft*. But ENIAC's makers say they worked out the concept in discussions among themselves. According to Mauchly, the ENIAC group was planning stored programs "long before von Neumann had heard of the EDVAC project." Mauchly and Eckert asserted that von Neumann picked up the stored-program idea from them in conversations about the ENIAC and EDVAC and then wrote it down in the *First Draft* without giving credit where credit was due.

Eckert also complains that von Neumann gave lectures on the work that Eckert, Mauchly, and their Moore School colleagues had done on the Moore School ENIAC and EDVAC projects, but he "rarely if ever" gave credit to the University of Pennsylvania or to the people "who had actually produced the ideas." As for the assertion, attributed to von Neumann, that no one can assign authorship to ideas when they are discussed within a group, Eckert replies: "Really!"

A document from the Moore School makes it clear that Eckert and Mauchly were thinking about stored-program computers before von Neumann joined them. A progress report on the ENIAC written by Eckert and Mauchly in September 1945 states that "in January 1944 a 'magnetic calculating machine' was disclosed" and that an "important feature of this device was that operating instructions and function tables would be stored in exactly the same sort of memory device as that used for numbers." The report goes on to credit von Neumann for his contributions but makes the priority of Eckert and Mauchly quite plain.

Did von Neumann purloin his colleagues' work? After the *First Draft* was released, von Neumann was quoted as saying he never intended it for publication in that early form, because he had included no acknowledgments and had not put in the references that he wished to include.

Brainerd's testimony supports this account of what von Neumann had intended to do. Brainerd says the *First Draft* contained sixty-seven points in which von Neumann had made provision for references but had put nothing there except a *(cf.)* to indicate a reference would follow. Then, according to Brainerd, the incomplete report was "printed by one of [von Neumann's] enthusiasts." Burks also takes a charitable view of von Neumann's motives. At a 1976 symposium Burks pointed out that von Neumann "undoubtedly . . . would have given credit to others," specifically Eckert, Mauchly, Goldstine, and Burks himself.

So it may be an exercise in futility to argue over who came up first with the stored-program idea. One might just as well charge von Neumann with lifting it from Turing, who visited him at Princeton before the war and, as mentioned in chapter five, had his own vision of the stored-program concept. (It is interesting to note that Turing was opposed to using the mercury delay storage lines—which made stored-program computers possible—as memory units. Goldstine mentions that Turing visited him and von Neumann at Princeton shortly after the war and argued that the mercury delay lines would never work for that application. Turing's reasoning seemed convincing at the time, Goldstine writes, but "fortunately experiment and experience proved him wrong.")

The fight over the origin of the stored-program concept is an example of jockeying for priority among computer pioneers. Academics jealously guard priority to their ideas as Scrooge guarded his gold. Unfortunately for academics, ideas themselves may not be copyrighted or patented; only the expression of those ideas, in writing or in the form of inventions, can be legally protected.

The debate over the stored-program concept aside, no one seriously questions that von Neumann originated—for better or worse—the concept of the von Neumann machine. Generally speaking, a von Neumann machine is an electronic digital computer that operates rigidly in serial mode. It starts at the beginning of a program and goes straight to the end, one step at a time, without doing any parallel operations, as ENIAC did, along the way. A von Neumann machine has been compared to a bucket brigade, passing along parcels of information.

That was the approach used in EDVAC, and Burks explained the rationale behind it. EDVAC was so much faster, smaller, and simpler than ENIAC that it was unnecessary to use parallel processing for added speed. Therefore it was decided to store numbers serially and process them the same way. Burks summed up the guiding principle of EDVAC design as "One thing at a time, down to the last bit!"

What the von Neumann machine gained in speed and simplicity of operation, however, it sacrificed in flexibility. No longer was it possible to program a computer to do several different things at once, as was the case with ENIAC and, before it, the Lehmer number sieves. This change from parallel processing to serial mode was what D. H. Lehmer had in mind when he spoke of computers being ruined.

Today many computer experts would say that Lehmer was right. The von Neumann machine has severe limitations that we are only now starting to overcome, and programmers and designers are looking forward to the day when, after some forty years in the grip of serial processing, computers finally break out of the "von Neumann mold." Artificial intelligence specialists are especially keen to make that break, because high-speed parallel-processing computers will come much closer than von Neumann machines ever could to the functioning of that superb parallel processor, the brain. So, we may soon see computers "thinking" in much the same fashion as humans.

Ironically, EDVAC—the report on which helped start the row over the stored-program concept—was neither the earliest computer to employ stored programs nor the first to use the mercury-delay-storage-line memory which made stored programs possible. Those honors belong to a computing machine developed at Cambridge University in England.

The Cambridge machine was called EDSAC (Electronic Delay Storage Automatic Computer) and was among the machines to emerge, directly or indirectly, from the cradle at Aberdeen. One of the men behind EDSAC was Maurice Wilkes, who attended a 1946 course of lectures at the Moore School on the design and building of ENIAC; he went back to Britain full of enthusiasm for building such a computer there. (Britain's wartime pioneer computers—the Bombe, Heath Robinson, and Colossus—were still official secrets.)

Wilkes set up the Computation Laboratory at Cambridge and began using the ideas in von Neumann's *First Draft* to design and build a British version of the EDVAC. "The EDSAC is based on principles first enunciated in an unpublished report . . . in which ideas for a machine known as the EDVAC were set out," wrote Wilkes in an article for the *Journal of Scientific Instruments* in 1949.

Like EDVAC, EDSAC was an electronic digital machine equipped with mercury delay storage lines. The British group used the mercury delay line because it was "really the only thing you could count on at the time," said Wilkes. EDSAC's makers at Cambridge wanted only technology they could rely on, because their goal was to get a machine built and running fast, using only the technologies at hand. There were no quantum breakthroughs in hardware on EDSAC, because, in the Turing tradition, it was not a "hardware machine" meant to push the frontiers of computer hardware; rather, it was a "software machine" aimed at improving programming. Wilkes explained, "building the machine was only the start of the project." Much remained to be learned about "how to use the machine for numerical analysis, numerical calculation, and all the rest of it."

Some of the rest came as a revelation, especially the problem of debugging software. EDSAC showed the Britons that writing workable programs wasn't as easy as they had expected. Debugging techniques had to be  invented, and Wilkes said he recalls "the exact instant when I realized that a large part of my life from then on was going to be spent in finding mistakes in my own programs."

The Aberdeen machines made their mark on IBM projects, too, and an IBM computer would be among the first to embody the stored-program concept.

While ENIAC was under development, Thomas Watson, Sr., and IBM had little interest in computers beyond the firm's ill-fated alliance with Howard Aiken at Harvard. IBM's principal products were items like adding machines and time clocks. The elder Watson simply did not see the need for large numbers of very big and powerful computing machines like the one Aiken had built. It was a widely held attitude at that time that large numbers of computers would not be needed in the foreseeable future. It seemed a relative handful of computer "powerhouses" would be adequate for the nation's needs.

Soon after the nuclear explosions over Japan signaled the end of World War II, however, another explosion shook IBM. It was ENIAC. Here was something completely new, and for which IBM had been unprepared.

IBM felt it had to do something in the face of the Moore School success. But keeping up with the Moores was not IBM's only motive. The top management also wanted revenge on Howard Aiken. They had never forgiven him for snubbing IBM at the dedication of the Mark I and were itching to get back at the man who, they believed, had grabbed IBM's money and then betrayed the firm. So IBM, partly to match ENIAC's achievement but also to even the score with Aiken, started work on a huge new machine of its own, the Selective Sequence Electronic Calculator (SSEC).

Watson and Wallace Eckert (whose work at the Thomas J. Watson Astronomical Computing Bureau had so inspired John Mauchly in the thirties) called together a team to work on the computer. The SSEC team labored twenty-four hours a day, seven days a week, at the IBM engineering laboratory, and in a few months their labor brought forth a computer.

Like ENIAC, the IBM SSEC was a room-sized monster containing more than 12,000 tubes. The SSEC also fixed the image of computers in the public's mind for the next generation. The machine was adorned with flashing lights and proved a bonanza to cartoonists and filmmakers, who used it as a model of big data-processing machines. So when one sees a cartoon or motion picture showing a giant computer bedecked with lights in the manner of a Christmas tree, one is looking at a caricature of Watson's SSEC.

The SSEC was quickly profitable. It handled calculations for the government, private businesses, and universities at a rate of $300 per hour. As if to make victory complete, IBM even hired one of Aiken's people from Harvard to come down to New York and serve as the computer's keeper.

Completed in 1948, the SSEC was installed at IBM headquarters on the corner of 57th Street and Madison Avenue. The machine was set up on the ground floor, but the space there was insufficient to house the giant power supply and air-conditioning plant it required, as well. So IBM bought out a shoe store just around the corner and stuck SSEC's support equipment in there.

The SSEC itself was enthroned in the showroom—a "glass and stainless steel palace," one observer called it—and was standing there resplendently when Watson came by to inspect it, several days before the dedication ceremony. Watson was upset to find that several large columns ran along the midline of the room. He found them aesthetically unpleasing, and worse, they blocked the public's view of his masterpiece.

"Everything is lovely," Watson said. "You gentlemen have done a beautiful job. But I think we should remove those columns." That was impossible to do without bringing down the building. So IBM simply recalled the illustrated brochure that had been prepared for the dedication and inserted a centerfold illustration depicting the computer room without the columns. An artist's hand accomplished what structural engineers could not.

The ceremony went off fine, and afterward Watson spoke gratefully of the dedication his employees had brought to the SSEC project. "They have been diligent and successful," Watson said. "We will celebrate by having a weekend at the Waldorf." Senior IBM employees who had worked on the SSEC were invited along with their families to the celebration. The crowd was large. At the festivities, Watson stood up and told the assemblage how much he loved them and how IBM was one big happy family.

But the merrymakers were celebrating the birth of a dinosaur, for the SSEC was obsolete even before it was completed. Its vast complement of vacuum tubes was supplemented by more than 21,000 old-fashioned electromechanical relays. Their antique presence made the SSEC a machine of the past, not the future. Watson's triumph over Aiken turned out to be hollow. Watson had won, but at a game no one was playing any more.

# 10
# FROM
# IAS
# TO
# WHIRLWIND

After getting acquainted with ENIAC, von Neumann had planned to work with the Moore School group on a computer of his own design, but he changed his mind and decided instead to work at Princeton's Institute for Advanced Study (IAS). Goldstine and Burks were with him, and von Neumann wanted another gifted individual to add to the team. He turned to Norbert Wiener for recommendations.

Wiener and von Neuman were not always friends. Late in their careers they developed an animosity toward each other, partly because Wiener's pacifism was so strongly opposed to von Neumann's hawkish views (he once proposed a preemptive nuclear strike against the Soviet Union). During one conference they both attended, Wiener went to sleep in the middle of von Neumann's address and snored loudly through the rest of the talk. Von Neumann retaliated later by sitting in the front row during Wiener's speech and loudly rattling the pages of the newspaper he pretended to read.

In the late forties, however, Wiener was on good terms with von Neumann and was an occasional guest at the von Neumann home in Princeton. Von Neumann's house was located near an intersection known as von Neumann's corner, because he had had so many automobile mishaps there. That Wiener ever found the von Neumann home is something of an achievement, for von Neumann's directions to it were sometimes vague in the extreme. Once von Neumann told a colleague who was coming over for dinner, "You can't miss it. It's the one with the pigeon out front." But find it Wiener did, and he was pleased that Karla von Neumann, knowing his aversion to meat, prepared him vegetarian meals.

During one conversation with Wiener, von Neumann asked him to recommend a co-worker for the computer project the IAS was planning. Weiner recommended Julian Bigelow, and so von Neumann invited Bigelow to participate in the project. Bigelow accepted and was soon collaborating on what would be known as the IAS computer.

At its outset, Bigelow reports, the IAS computer project had "few tangible assets" other than von Neumann and Goldstine. But soon von Neumann convinced the Atomic Energy Commission (AEC) to back the project, and the IAS computer was under way.

Much of the IAS group's attention was focused on speeding up *memory I/O*, or the input (I) and output (O) of data to and from memory. At first the Princeton team conceived an interesting I/O mechanism based on pulley-driven wires. This arrangement resembled the bedsteads on Heath Robinson and worked reasonably well on a model built of wire and motor-driven bicycle wheels. The model's success led von Neumann's group to think the setup could be transferred in a more sophisticated form to the IAS computer.

The wires were tried but failed. They had a habit of snapping, and when they were reknotted, the repair upset the operating characteristics of the computer. Moreover, friction from the wires wore deep grooves in the pulleys and generated dust that affected the machine's operation.

It was time to find something else for memory I/O, and the Princeton team found what they were looking for across the ocean, in Britain, where Manchester University researchers were using early television technology to improve computer memory.

Memory, as mentioned earlier, was going through a step-by-step process of adding dimensions. At first computers had to make do with storage in essentially zero dimensions by vacuum tubes. Later memories became much more powerful and capacious when Eckert and Mauchly realized the potential of the mercury delay storage line as a data-storage mechanism; that added a linear dimension to computer memory.

Now why not add still another dimension: make it possible to "write" out data on a flat surface, as words are written on a printed page? That was the next logical step in computer memory development, and the page on which data would be written was a cathode ray tube (CRT) like those in modern television sets and computer monitors, only smaller.

The CRT used in computer memories during the late 1940s had the dimensions of a medium fireplace log or a large loaf of bread. It used an electron beam to write out data on the screen.

The electron beam produced glowing dots that lasted only a few moments before they faded away, which meant that the dots had to be written and then read and then rewritten very quickly. But that was no great problem, for the "electron gun" used to write out the information could inscribe it and then refresh it as fast as desired. (This was a different way of jogging memory than Atanasoff had used with his ABC. Whereas Atanasoff had used brushes to restore electrical charges to the condenser as soon as they were read, the CRT used the electron beam. But the principle involved was the same.)

The originators of this memory device, F. C. Williams and Thomas Kilburn of Manchester University in England, wrote, "Looking back, it is amazing how long it took to realize that if one can read a record once, then that is entirely sufficient for storage, provided that what is read can be immediately rewritten in its original position."

The CRT system was used in Manchester University's Mark I computer, which was built in 1948. The Mark I was an untidy-looking machine that looked like an abandoned hardware store in which a flock of starlings had built nests of scrap wiring. At about neck level, a CRT screen stared out from the wiring like a great cataracted eye.

Sloppy as it looked, the Mark I was a great advance in computer technology because of its CRT storage. The Manchester computer's storage consisted of two parts, the "fast" Williams tube and a slower-paced magnetic drum somewhat like the one used by Atanasoff and Berry.

Each part of the Mark I storage was housed on a different floor of the building. This situation caused inconvenience when switch settings had to be coordinated. To load information, someone would have to go to the foot of the stairs and shout up, "We are ready to receive!" and then specify the track and tube. The people upstairs had to shout orders down in order to withdraw information.

At Manchester the Williams tube was used in serial mode. It was also suitable for parallel use, however, and that possibility intrigued Bigelow and his co-workers in America, where computers had not yet settled into a rigid serial arrangement.

Bigelow was impressed with Williams and described him as a good example of "the British 'string and sealing wax' inventive genius," meaning one who does the best possible job with the tools at hand. Bigelow had an unexpected opportunity to see Williams's tinkering skills at work. Williams was showing Bigelow the machine one day when suddenly there was a flash of light, a puff of smoke, and (Bigelow reported) "everything went dead." Unruffled, Williams merely turned off the power, went to work with a soldering iron, and soon had the computer back in working order.

The Williams tube seemed ideal for what the IAS team had in mind. No more wires, no more dust, no more fuss. So the IAS computer makers adapted the Williams tube for use in parallel mode, and the Princeton computer was on its way with CRTs.

The Williams tube made memory operations much faster and made the computer as a whole both speedy and reliable. Once a team of scientists from Los Alamos used the IAS computer for a daunting calculation in the making of the hydrogen bomb. The computer ran twenty-four hours a day for two months and made only about half a dozen errors, according to Bigelow.

That was an almost incredible performance in the late forties, when the mean free time between failures—MFTBF, computer users called it—was usually measured in minutes rather than hours or days. So successful was the IAS computer that von Neumann's wife, Karla, celebrated her husband's triumph by presenting him, at a party, with a sculpture of the computer carved in ice.

Von Neumann enjoyed matching wits with the IAS computer. When the arithmetic unit for the machine was being tested, von Neumann stood beside it, carried out assigned calculations in his head, and announced the answers at the same time as the computer. Most times he was correct, but once the machine bettered him. Its answer turned out to be right. Von Neumann accepted defeat cheerfully, Bigelow said later, as a minor victory of "matter over mind."

One of the IAS machine's "offspring" was a computer named, in von Neumann's honor, the JOHNNIAC. It was assembled at the Rand Corporation in California and incorporated some features that later would become standard equipment on home microcomputers.

JOHNNIAC was an Air Force effort to increase the MFTBF of computers. If it succeeded in doing so, then users would no longer have to sit around waiting until the computer, so to speak, felt like working. As ENIAC did, JOHNNIAC used punched-card I/O for reliability; and as happened with Atanasoff's work at Iowa State, it created a conflict with IBM. The IBM people were outraged when they learned that JOHN-NIAC's makers planned to add one little toggle switch on one piece of IBM card-punching equipment. It took months to convince IBM to agree to this tiny modification.

Piece by piece, JOHNNIAC arose in a wire-enclosed work

area known as the zoo. JOHNNIAC had what a Rand newsletter called a human-engineered console that kept controls as simple as possible. The computer also was superbly protected from harm. In the tradition of Eckert's worst-case scenarios, built-in systems safeguarded JOHNNIAC against damage from blown fuses, voltage failure, and just about anything else that could befall it. When something went seriously wrong, the computer would shut down, an alarm would go off, and lights would flash on to reveal what was responsible for the malfunction.

JOHNNIAC went into operation in 1953 and lived up to its makers' expectations. Except for minor trouble with the punch-card equipment, JOHNNIAC was one of the most reliable computers in existence. Its MFTBF was greater than one hundred hours, in which time the machine's arithmetic unit could carry out billions of calculations.

JOHNNIAC was programmed with a set of binary operation codes that included several *halts* and a *hoot*. A halt stopped operation, while a hoot signaled trouble. Often JOHNNIAC hooted audibly, for the computer had a loudspeaker system designed to let users hear the machine's operation.

The loudspeaker was installed to remedy one of the drawbacks of electronic computers: their silence. Noise had been one great advantage of mechanical and electromechanical computers, because one could tell if they were running well just by listening to the sounds they made. Electronic computers had few or no moving parts, however, and diagnosis by ear was more difficult with them. So JOHNNIAC was given a voice.

JOHNNIAC's loudspeaker made it perhaps the first musical computer. Certain combinations of computer orders, which made no sense in terms of computation, would produce tunes on the loudspeaker when run. So in their spare time the JOHNNIAC team "orchestrated" their computer. One member of the group wrote in a memoir of the project, "A lot of extra-curricular programming effort went into the construction of card decks that would cause the computer to 'play' things like 'Jingle Bells' and 'Hail to the Chief' (in case the President dropped in)."

George Stibitz had prophesied that one day computers would be used to compose music, and JOHNNIAC showed how right he was. A few years after JOHNNIAC made its musical debut, composers would be writing programs similar to JOHNNIAC's "scores" to produce electronic symphonies. Modern home computers that have sound synthesis capabilities and play little melodies can all trace their musical skills back to JOHNNIAC.

Sometimes JOHNNIAC seemed phobic as well as musical. Its makers jokingly said it was scared of the dark, because JOHNNIAC worked fine during the day but tended to develop trouble at night, when lighting in the room was dim.

The source of that trouble was a mystery until someone checked the card-reading I/O apparatus and found that the neon bulbs used in it had become so "fatigued" with age that they only operated when they had energy input from an external source—in this case, daylight. JOHNNIAC was given a set of night lights to see it through till morning, and never was afraid of the dark again.

In the late forties, many practical questions about the building of computers remained to be answered. For example, how fast could a computer be built? How quickly could one put together a high-speed electronic computer using only stuff off the shelf?

The National Bureau of Standards in Washington, D.C., decided to find out, and in 1950 commissioned the building of two machines, the Standards Eastern Automatic Computer (SEAC) in Washington and the Standards Western Automatic Computer (SWAC) at the Institute for Numerical Analysis in Los Angeles. These were the first two stored-program computers built in the United States. They went into service a few months before EDVAC and helped confirm the feasibility of the stored-program concept pioneered at the Moore School.

The SWAC project boss was Harry D. Huskey, the American who had helped Turing's group with the Pilot ACE at the National Physical Laboratory. In England he had lived amid what he called fairy-tale surroundings, in a rented house in Bushey Park, a former royal hunting preserve next to Hampton Court Palace. The house had allegedly been the home of, as Huskey delicately put it, a girlfriend of the eighteenth-century Duke of Clarence.

Back in the more plebeian environment of the United States, Huskey made SWAC a parallel computer, using the CRT technology pioneered by the Britons. The CRTs had to be protected from the broadcast-saturated U.S. airwaves, because the tubes— which were, in effect, little television sets—tended to intercept whatever was on the air. Huskey writes, "This required careful shielding of the input, or all the local radio stations would appear on the computer full blast!"

Across the continent, Ralph Slutz was helping the SEAC group put together its computer and was doing something never before attempted: building a computer with all-diode logic. (A diode restricts the flow of current primarily to one direction. In the vacuum tube era, a diode was a tube housing one positive and one negative electrode. In the early 1950s the tubes were being replaced with semiconducting "solid-state" diodes.) This was an important leap forward in computer construction, because the all-diode setup was a forerunner of what would later be called solid state technology. There were no tubes to burn out and be replaced—a situation the engineers at Aberdeen, struggling with their ENIAC, would have envied.

The diodes performed fine. So did almost everything else about SEAC and SWAC. When completed, SEAC looked like an electronic ziggurat, tapering up in steps to a narrow pinnacle. SWAC was more bulky and looked somewhat like a squashed skyscraper. The screens of two Williams tubes glowed on its control console.

Sometimes the SEAC and SWAC teams used unorthodox tests. One was called the stir-with-a-wooden-spoon technique. While a test program was running, someone would take a wooden kitchen spoon and go around rapping gently on every part of the computer to see if anything was in danger of coming loose. If the program suddenly quit running, the tester had found a problem.

Then there was the Bureau of Standards' Standard Jump. This was used to check out the SEAC. The computer was housed in a building with wooden floors that shook when anyone walked on them. The Standard Jump was a matter of jumping six inches in the air and landing on the floor with maximum force. If the computer survived the resultant shaking, it was considered free of mechanical bugs. SEAC's keepers also started running computational test programs on it, and, according to Slutz, "even more interesting bugs" would appear.

SEAC taught computer designers that computers had to be not only fast, reliable, and efficient, but childproof as well. One day at an open house in 1951, Slutz's wife, then pregnant, hurried up to him and told him to come into the next room, where SEAC was located. When he arrived Slutz found his two-year-old son crawling through a narrow walkway that ran through the middle of the computer to provide access to its innards. The youngster was making his way straight toward the computer's uninsulated power supply—and possible electrocution.

Slutz's wife was too big at that time to fit into the narrow opening, so Slutz had to rescue his child from the maw of the machine. After that experience he described the perilous walkway as "a real hardware flaw."

While SEAC and SWAC were being assembled, MIT engineers in a baroque two-story building near Kendall Square in Cambridge were working on a monster computer for the cold war against Russia: the famous Whirlwind. Like many other computers, Whirlwind started out as something quite different from what it became. Initially Whirlwind was intended to be an analog computer that would serve the Navy as an aircraft flight simulator and trainer. The trainer was, in effect, an earthbound plane that used a computer to model the aircraft's flight characteristics mathematically and made the controls respond as if the plane were actually built and flying.

It owed its operation to *real-time control*, the engineer's expression for keeping in touch with what is happening here and now. Real-time control was needed to simulate an airborne plane's behavior under various conditions (airspeed, altitude, et cetera). Change airspeed, and the trainer had to respond appropriately and immediately. That is real-time control.

The MIT engineers knew real-time control was possible for a computer. To be sure, the computer would have to be big and powerful, but ENIAC in Philadelphia and Howard Aiken's Mark I at Harvard had demonstrated that mighty machines could be constructed.

With that issue settled, the MIT people then faced the same choice John Atanasoff had confronted when planning his ABC. Should they go the analog or the digital route? One of the MIT engineers, Jay Forrester, recalls that the analog idea was soon dropped because of the inherent inaccuracy of analog machines—the same reason Atanasoff had decided against building an analog computer at Iowa State. In Whirlwind's case the designers felt that an analog computer would present the user with a solution of the machine's own "idiosyncrasies," not of the problem being considered. Digital machines promised better results.

So Whirlwind would be digital. It also would need a big memory, because great amounts of information were required to provide real-time control for an aircraft trainer. In the words of a 1952 project report, memory was "the most important factor affecting reliability of the Whirlwind . . . system."

Unfortunately, the demands of Whirlwind's memory outstripped the technology at hand. Whirlwind was going to require something more than the delay lines of EDVAC and EDSAC and the glowing CRTs of the Williams memory system. The Whirlwind team did its best with the Williams tubes, but the screen-written memory was simply inadequate. What could be done?

Forrester thought of adding one more dimension to the Williams storage concept. He imagined converting the two-dimensional Williams memory into something three-dimensional, in much the same way that pages stacked atop one another make a book.

But the Williams tubes could not accommodate that extra dimension. A whole new technology was called for, and at first no one knew what that would be.

Then Forrester, like Atanasoff in the Illinois tavern, was enlightened in a flash. While glancing through the journal *Electrical Engineering* one evening and looking at the advertisements,

Forrester spotted an ad for a material which, he explains, had "a very rectangular hysteresis loop."

A hysteresis loop sounds like a physical object but is not. It exists only on paper and in the mind. *Hysteresis* is the five-dollar word for the time lag between the passage of a magnetizing force through a ferromagnetic material (iron-bearing substance that can be magnetized) and the actual magnetization of the material.

Hysteresis is like the delay when soldiers on a drill field are called to attention. There is a slight interval between the instant the sergeant shouts "Ten-HUT!" and the moment the soldiers actually snap to attention. Here the sergeant's command is the magnetizing force, the state of attention is a state of magnetization, and hysteresis is the instant in between.

Turn the magnetizing force on and off, and one can plot a diagram of the hysteresis of a material. The diagram is a closed curve called a hysteresis loop. Many materials have S-shaped hysteresis loops, but the material referred to in the ad was more nearly a rectangle. For various reasons, that rectangular loop promised big advances in computer memory by improving the flow of electric current into and out of a memory unit.

Forrester studied the magnetic material and its block-shaped loop. "Can we use it as a computer memory?" he asked himself. "Is there some way to fit it into a three-dimensional array for information storage?" He thought about those questions for the next two days and nights. Both evenings he went out after dinner and roamed the nighttime streets, weighing prospects for a three-dimensional computer memory.

Forrester looked at several configurations before finally settling on a boxlike memory arrangement. One could slip data into and out of its three-dimensional lattice of memory elements by controlling voltage on the $x$-axis (width), $y$-axis (length), and $z$-axis (height).

In theory the lattice was feasible, but the engineers had to find just the right material for building the memory elements. At first they tried rolled-up bits of magnetic tape. They worked. Next the engineers tried iron-bearing, or ferrite, ceramics. They worked much better. The ceramics were cast in the shape of tiny rings and mounted on lattices, and when magnified looked like doughnuts strung up on a chain-link fence.

These *magnetic-core-memory elements*, as they were dubbed, gave Whirlwind the powerful, reliable memory it needed, and the giant computer went into service in 1951. It did not serve as part of a flight trainer, as originally planned, but as an important element of U.S. air defense. Whirlwind helped coordinate New England military radar units which scanned the skies for Soviet planes.

Before Whirlwind officially started work, Howard Aiken, who only ten years before had presented his mechanical Mark I to Harvard, stopped by the MIT laboratory near Kendall Square for a look at Whirlwind. The Whirlwind team showed him the multiplier unit of the computer and pointed out how it had run for a month and a half, carrying out 10,000,000,000 multiplications without a single error. "Not bad," said Aiken, and off he went.

Even in their "most brazen moments," Forrester said, Whirlwind's makers never imagined some of the uses to which computers would be put in the postwar years. "Our . . . crystal ball wasn't all that good," he admitted. Only two decades after Forrester helped build Whirlwind, a computer selected one of his acquaintances to become the Episcopal bishop of Delaware.

By that time Whirlwind seemed almost ancient history. A few years after the computer picked the bishop, Forrester delivered a speech to a meeting of economists in Washington, D.C. A dinner preceded the address, and during the meal Forrester was seated at the same table with a retired economist for a major computer company. At one point the economist turned to Forrester and asked, "Was it your father who invented the magnetic core memory?"

Times had changed. When Aiken built the Mark I, the fraternity of computer makers was so small and tightly knit that everyone in it knew almost everyone else. But that was no longer the case after Whirlwind. The new technology of computers had given rise to a huge and growing society of computer experts. By

1960 there were enough people in the computer field to populate a major city, and the pioneer computers and the old guard of computer pioneers seemed almost forgotten.

Forrester once attended a single meeting of 30,000 computer specialists. "I didn't meet a single person that I knew, and there wasn't anyone who had heard of me," he said later. "I decided I shouldn't ever go again."

# 11
# WHO DID IT, REALLY?

While SSEC whirred and clicked away in its "palace," and Whirlwind and all the various -AC computers were taking shape in their laboratories, Eckert and Mauchly were running their own computer company and facing rough times.

They submitted a patent application for ENIAC in 1946, claiming for themselves the invention of "the automatic electronic digital computer," and received the patent in 1964. (Note the use of the definite article here: not *a*, but *the* automatic electronic digital computer.) Also in 1946—only six weeks after ENIAC's dedication ceremony—Mauchly and Eckert left the University of Pennsylvania following a dispute with the university over patent rights.

Contrary to what Mauchly had imagined when he first arrived at the Moore School, the university wanted patent rights to ENIAC and thought Eckert and Mauchly ought to relinquish them. When Eckert and Mauchly refused, the school, in effect, told them to get lost. It was a foolish and short-sighted decision on the university's part, for with the departure of ENIAC's makers, the Moore School lost its preeminent status in the field of computing.

Cast out from the Moore School, the two colleagues founded the Electronic Controls Corporation, later renamed the Eckert Mauchly Computer Company. There Eckert and Mauchly set about building a new generation of computing machines. Mauchly served as president and handled the firm's contacts with the government and with private businesses, while Eckert became vice-president and had charge of engineering.

Bernard Gordon, whom Eckert once advised against cutting the grass when he could be designing, has provided some interesting glimpses of what life was like at the Eckert Mauchly Computer Company. Gordon reported for work at the company's wooden building on Wissahickon Drive in Philadelphia one sweltering day in the summer of 1948. His first exposure to the company was disconcertingly literal: he went inside and met another employee who was stripped to his underwear while working on circuitry. Gordon wondered at the time if that was the company uniform.

The Eckert Mauchly Computer Company was a youthful organization. Gordon was fresh out of school, and Eckert himself was not much older. Some of the other employees were still students. Eckert was impressed with Gordon's work on memory units and put him in charge of several other employees, with instructions to fire any student worker caught repeatedly studying on the job.

For Eckert, people worked. Hard. He wanted every engineer to turn out one tube's worth of circuitry every thirty minutes, every day. That was a considerable output in the late forties, when a tube's worth of circuitry might weigh several pounds and occupy as much volume as a box of breakfast cereal.

To discourage sloppy work, the company had its soft-drink rule: anyone who inserted a screwdriver in the wrong place at the wrong time and blew up a dial was expected to buy everyone at the company a soda, perhaps forty sodas in all. One day someone blew up 18,000 dials at once. History does not tell whether he was required to buy three-quarters of a million drinks.

Soon after their business was organized, Mauchly and Eckert signed an agreement with the National Bureau of Standards in Washington, D.C., to build an EDVAC-like computer to help in computing the U.S. national census—the task for which Hollerith had built his tabulator three-quarters of a century before. Troubles began almost immediately. The government tried to get its machine on the cheap and allocated only $75,000 for its development and construction. That sum was insufficient to design and build the computer, so Eckert and Mauchly looked for more contracts to tide them over while the NBS machine was in the works.

Soon they found another client in the Northrop Aircraft Company. Northrop was working on a secret project for the Air Force, a guided missile called the Snark. A sleek red craft with swept-back wings and a jet engine slung under its fuselage, the Snark was a pilotless aircraft like the V-1 "buzz bombs" that the Germans used against England in World War II. Snarks would fly toward a target low and slow, to avoid detection by radar, and deliver either conventional or nuclear warheads. The Snark was the forerunner of the modern cruise missile.

The Snark needed an on-board computer to guide its flight. Could Eckert and Mauchly, Northrop asked, squeeze one of their computers into the cramped inside of the hull? The Philadelphians said yes, and Northrop was persuaded to back the building of a guidance computer for the missile. Northrop provided $80,000 up front, with an additional $20,000 to be paid when the machine was delivered.

Eckert and Mauchly dubbed the machine the Binary Automatic Computer, or BINAC. It seemed their financial troubles were over, but in fact they were just beginning.

BINAC exceeded its budget, partly because Eckert and Mauchly underestimated the cost of building the computer. According to company folklore, Gordon related, Eckert estimated design costs by counting the number of solder joints that a machine was likely to require; then he allowed so many pennies per solder joint to design the computer. If that was what he actually did, the method was unsuccessful. The eventual cost of developing BINAC came to almost $300,000.

Eckert and Mauchly tried to get more money out of Northrop but failed. The Air Force, which ultimately was paying for the Snark's development, pointed out that government regulations required them to stay within a budget, and they advised Northrop against bailing out the BINAC effort. At the same time Northrop was having financial trouble of its own; the aircraft firm had contracted to build a set of experimental aircraft at a fixed price and wound up taking a bath on that contract.

Far over budget and pressed for time, BINAC fell behind schedule. Originally Eckert and Mauchly thought they could build the machine in eight months, but they took eighteen, prompting Northrop to say that the Eckert Mauchly Computer Company was "sadly in default" of their agreement.

When BINAC finally was delivered, Northrop was dissatisfied. Northrop described the memory as very unsatisfactory and complained of poor workmanship, referring particularly to the use of cheap parts in an apparent effort to control cost. One Northrop memo described the BINAC's condition as deplorable and faulted it for unreliability. Northrop reported the BINAC ran only "about one hour per week, but very poorly." Nonetheless Northrop finally pronounced the job satisfactory.

It would be unfair to lay all the blame for this fiasco on the Eckert Mauchly Computer Company, for Northrop, too, appears to have underestimated the time it would take to complete the computer, and the BINAC, a fragile system employing mercury delay storage lines, was handled roughly during shipment. Regardless, Northrop demanded alterations in the machine—a further big expense at a time when the computer company had already spent the entire budget for the BINAC.

All this labor eventually turned out to be in vain, for BINAC was never installed in the Snark. The guided missile was a washout. Its early tests were disastrous; Snarks launched from Cape Canaveral, Florida, had a distressing tendency to fall into the Atlantic Ocean, and jokes started circulating about the "Snark-infested waters" off the cape. Only a few Snarks were built and deployed before the missile went out of production.

The Eckert Mauchly Computer Company had the same basic trouble that bedevils many high-tech businesses. It was unsure whether to emphasize business or technology. Striking a balance between those two goals can be difficult, and in this case it was exceedingly so. To make matters worse for Eckert and Mauchly, the census-counting computer—which would come to be known as UNIVAC (Universal Variable Computer)—ran far over budget. On top of everything else, the company was tarred at one point by the red-baiting senator from Wisconsin, Joseph McCarthy.

"Holy Joe," as McCarthy's critics called him, whipped up anti-communist fever to a point where even the slightest hint of subversive affiliations was enough to doom a career or a company. Suspicion fell on the Eckert Mauchly Computer Company when it was discovered that a secretary there had once dated a man who had attended a few communist party meetings years before. Trivial as that incident may have been, it was sufficient to make the government leery of dealing with Eckert and Mauchly, and the firm lost two million dollars in government contracts.

Eckert and Mauchly were only two of the many scientists wounded by the McCarthy crusade. George Stibitz recalls how national paranoia about communism "worked to destroy patriotic and useful people . . . who had built up the Bureau of Standards into a world-famous scientific organization." Stibitz points out, "McCarthy was using the big-lie technique exploited by Hitler: make outrageously false and damaging assertions about someone, and when confronted by the truth, dash off to malign someone else. . . . as Joe well knew, the press would carrry his accusations on the front page but the forced retraction on page 20."

Finally Remington Rand, later to merge with Sperry Corporation and become Sperry Rand, rescued the Eckert Mauchly Computer Company, and the bad times were over . . . for a while. Then Mauchly's 1941 visit with Atanasoff came back to haunt him in a lawsuit over the patent rights to ENIAC.

The suit involved the legitimacy of Eckert's and Mauchly's claim to have invented the automatic electronic digital computer. That claim was called into question when Honeywell, which Sperry Rand was then suing for patent infringement over the use of equipment supposedly covered by the ENIAC patent, sued Sperry Rand right back for violating antitrust laws by trying to enforce a fraudulently obtained patent.

What gave Honeywell the idea that the patent might have been acquired by fraud? Honeywell knew of Mauchly's 1941 visit to Iowa and suspected that much of ENIAC's technology might have been derived from the work of Atanasoff. If ENIAC had in fact used technology that Atanasoff and Berry invented, then the ENIAC patent might be overturned.

The road to court began for Atanasoff in late April of 1967, when he received a visit at his Maryland farm from a patent attorney named Allen Kirkpatrick. Atanasoff was being sought in connection with another lawsuit that Sperry Rand was bringing against Control Data Corporation over the ENIAC patent and another patent governing computer memory. According to Atanasoff, it soon became clear that "these lawsuits would become monumental" in the history of computer technology.

A few months later, on November 10, 1967, Atanasoff received a telephone call from John Mauchly. The conversation was friendly, Atanasoff reports, and in it he learned that a patent attorney named Dodds had asked Mauchly to arrange a meeting with him and Atanasoff to discuss the pending case against Control Data. Mauchly described the preparations for the trial as "very cloak and dagger" and said that Kirkpatrick had already questioned him closely. Mauchly complained to Atanasoff that Kirkpatrick "practically accused me of plagiarizing everything I've done."

Atanasoff met with Mauchly and Dodds on December 16. Mauchly and the attorney arrived at Atanasoff's home in Frederick, Maryland, in the late morning. Dodds and Atanasoff discussed the latter's work and its possible bearing on the ENIAC patent. According to Atanasoff's notes on the meeting, Mauchly was silent for most of the time but spoke up occasionally to tell an irrelevant story.

Soon it was lunchtime, and over a light meal Atanasoff asked Dodds how he expected to win the case. Atanasoff recalls Dodds saying, "You don't know anything about how federal judges are likely to act. They may decide that question upon their own impulse instead of on fact, law, or reason."

That answer startled Atanasoff into silence. While Atanasoff mulled over that comment, Dodds added, however, that the judge slated to hear the case was "very learned and able" and unlikely to make a decision impulsively.

After lunch, Mauchly and Atanasoff spent part of the early afternoon discussing Mauchly's work for the Naval Ordnance Laboratory between 1943 and 1946. Then Atanasoff gave his guests a tour of his home, and Dodds left at three o'clock to catch a plane at the Baltimore airport.

Mauchly lingered with Atanasoff and continued their friendly conversation for the rest of the afternoon. Before dinner they walked to a nearby lake and back to the house. The sixty-year-old Mauchly was in poor health, and Atanasoff recalled that Mauchly "suffered . . . severely" from this brief excursion and had to stop and rest several times along the way. (In addition to being a heavy smoker, Mauchly had a condition that occasionally caused him to bleed internally.) After having dinner with Atanasoff and his wife, Mauchly finally said goodbye and departed.

Clifford Berry was not around to help prepare for the trial. In 1963 Atanasoff had received a letter from Jean Berry, Clifford's wife and Atanasoff's former secretary, informing him that Berry was dead. Later Atanasoff learned that Berry had been found in bed with a plastic bag over his head; his death was ruled a suicide.

The patent case went to trial in federal court several years later. In the meantime Atanasoff had helped to reconstruct his prototype computer, and the machine was hauled into court to show off its capabilities. It carried out additions and subtractions. Lights flashed on and off. The court was fascinated. Pictures of some of Mauchly's early electronic devices were also introduced as evidence, but curiously, nothing more about them was produced in court.

Eventually, after the trial records had accumulated to more than 100,000 pages (a stack of paper taller than ENIAC itself), the judge tossed out the ENIAC patent. Under other circumstances his judgment would probably have made headlines, but it attracted little publicity because it was announced on October 19, 1973, the day of the Watergate Saturday Night Massacre, in which President Richard Nixon fired Special Prosecutor Archibald Cox.

The court decision alone was more than 200 pages long. The essence of it was, "the subject matter of one or more claims of the ENIAC was derived from Atanasoff, and the invention claimed in the ENIAC was derived from Atanasoff." The decision went on to say, "Eckert and Mauchly did not themselves first invent the automatic electronic digital computer, but instead derived that subject matter from one Dr. John Vincent Atanasoff."

There was no finding of deliberate fraud. The judge remarked that Mauchly "may in good faith have believed that the monstrous machine he helped create had no relationship to the ABC or to Atanasoff." The court also cited a statement by Mauchly in 1944 that the ABC was "ingenious" but "not by any means what I had in mind." Since there was no determination of fraud, the court merely ruled that the patent was invalid, and neither corporation involved in the suit had to pay the other anything.

Mauchly and Eckert were of course displeased. Mauchly complained that written material concerning his work on vacuum-tube computers at Ursinus College was not introduced as evidence, although photos of his flip-flops and other inventions were. He also wondered bitterly why he was judged to have lifted his ideas from Atanasoff in particular, when he had met with other computer pioneers and discussed their work with them prior to starting work on ENIAC. Thinking back to the night he saw Stibitz operate the Model 1 by long-distance telegraph at Dartmouth, Mauchly said sarcastically, "Maybe I got [my ideas] by remote control from Stibitz."

In the last analysis, what probably determined the outcome of the case was the sweeping claim of Eckert and Mauchly to have invented "the automatic electronic digital computer." Their use of the definite article here, *the*, left them wide open to the charge that, since other inventors had come up with comparable machines about the same time, Eckert and Mauchly had only invented *a* computer, not *the* computer; therefore the ENIAC patent must be invalid.

So who did invent the electronic computer? The court handed that award, in effect, to Atanasoff. In the years since that decision was handed down no conclusive new evidence has been unearthed to show that the judge ruled incorrectly.

On the other hand, Eckert and Mauchly went far beyond the achievement of Atanasoff. The finished ENIAC was much advanced over the little ABC, which indeed was never completed. Atanasoff had built a partially finished mechanism for doing one particular job, whereas ENIAC was a fully finished, general-purpose computer.

As Eckert himself said, "What's important is usually the person who gets a system going. What Mauchly and I did was to get a system going. What Atanasoff did was build some little hunk of a system and then talk about a system."

Eckert cited another case in point: the invention of the electric light bulb. The idea behind the light bulb had been written down in the mid-1800s, but Thomas Edison was the inventor who actually sat down and built the bulb, so Edison deserves the credit for inventing. Eckert argued that the same principle is involved in the origin of ENIAC and digital electronic computing.

The origin of the digital electronic computer is one case that historians, not jurists, will ultimately have to decide. As Mauchly pointed out in a 1976 memoir of ENIAC, "legal decisions are not scholarly judgments," and it might be a mistake to accept the federal court's ruling in this case as the final word. Brainerd remarked after the trial that the judge, though an "earnest man," had merely been tutored in computer science and technology for a month before the case came to trial, and therefore there was some "question about his judgment in these matters."

Henry Tropp, a leading historian of computers, has taken a similarly dim view of the legal trappings that surround and confuse the issue of how digital electronic computing began. He sees similarities between the ABC-ENIAC dispute and the case of Samuel Langley, the early aeronautical researcher for whom Langley Field was named. Langley has been called "The Great

Almost" because he achieved the first powered flight of a man-carrying aircraft several days before the Wright Brothers' famous flight at Kitty Hawk. Yet the Wright Brothers usually get the credit for being the first to fly.

Tropp imagines the Wright Brothers submitting a flawed patent application two years after their flight at Kitty Hawk. In that case, Tropp asks, "what would have been the judicial outcome of patent litigation by Samuel Langley? I don't know the answer to this question, but I do know who flew first."

The computer, however, is too great an achievement ever to be assigned to one individual, or even a small group. J. Presper Eckert, Wallace Eckert, Mauchly, Brainerd, Atanasoff, Berry, Zuse, Stibitz, von Neumann, Newman, Flowers, Coombs, Good, Turing, Aiken, Bush, Hopper, Wiener, Veblen, Lehmer—these are only a few of the people who helped to lift computing out of the mechanical age and into the era of electronics. The epic of the modern computer truly has a cast of thousands. Let us therefore celebrate the computer as the greatest group invention the world has seen.

# APPENDIX

## The Machines

### Atanasoff-Berry Computer (ABC)

When Built: Late 1930s.
Where: Iowa State College (now Iowa State University).
Designed By: John V. Atanasoff and Clifford Berry.
Character: Electronic.
Purpose: To solve sets of linear differential equations.
Description and Accomplishments: Approximately the size of an office desk and based on condensers and vacuum tubes, the ABC is widely considered to be the forerunner of modern electronic digital computers, despite the fact that it was a special-purpose and not a general-purpose computer. The ABC proved that electronic computers operating in the binary mode could be made fast and reliable.

### Babbage Analytical Engine

When Built: Designed in mid-1800s but never constructed.
Where: Great Britain.
Designed By: Charles Babbage.
Character: Mechanical.
Purpose: General.
Description and Accomplishments: The Babbage Analytical Engine was conceived as a general-purpose calculating machine to be powered by steam. Had it been completed, it would have had many of the capabilities of modern electronic computers; but the technology of Babbage's day was inadequate for the project, and Babbage never completed even a working model of it.

### Bell Laboratories Model 1

When Built: Late 1930s.
Where: Bell Telephone Laboratories.
Designed By: George Stibitz and colleagues.
Character: Electromechanical.
Purpose: General, but intended originally to help with calcu-

lations involving complex numbers (those including the imaginary number $i$, the square root of negative one).

Description and Accomplishments: The Model 1 was based on electromechanical relays like those used in telephone switching systems, and it incorporated binary arithmetic in its design. The Model 1 demonstrated that binary systems could be used successfully to carry out long and complex calculations both quickly and with great reliability. It was the first computer ever to be controlled by long distance and led to the construction of several larger and more powerful computers in this series.

### Binary Automatic Computer (BINAC)

When Built: Late 1940s.

Where: Philadelphia, Pennsylvania.

Designed By: J. Presper Eckert, John Mauchly, the Eckert Mauchly Computer Company.

Character: Electronic.

Purpose: In-flight navigation.

Description and Accomplishments: BINAC was intended as a compact airborne computer for military use. It utilized mercury delay storage lines and had approximately the dimensions of a file cabinet. Numerous setbacks plagued the project, and BINAC was never put to its intended use. It served as valuable experience, however, for the construction of later electronic machines.

### Bombe

When Built: Early 1940s.

Where: Bletchley Park, England.

Designed By: Alan Turing and other employees of the Government Code and Cypher School.

Character: Electromechanical.

Purpose: Decryption of German ENIGMA ciphers.

Description and Accomplishments: Bombe was built to help crack the German military codes prepared by the ENIGMA code machine. Similar in principle to other electromechanical devices built about the same time, Bombe was extremely special in its purpose and was the forerunner of more advanced code-breaking computers built later at Bletchley Park.

### Bush Differential Analyzer (Integraph)

When Built: Middle 1930s.

Where: Massachusetts Institute of Technology, Cambridge, Massachusetts.

Designed By: Vannevar Bush.

Character: Mechanical.

Purpose: To solve sets of differential equations.

Description and Accomplishments: Based on technology provided decades earlier by Charles Babbage and Lord Kelvin, the Bush integraph was in a certain sense a modern version of Babbage's Analytical Engine, using electricity instead of steam to drive its moving parts. The Bush integraph was large and clumsy compared to later electronic devices but could solve large sets of differential equations and later helped to inspire the building of even bigger and more sophisticated computing machines.

### Colossus

When Built: Early 1940s.

Where: Bletchley Park, England.

Designed By: Thomas H. Flowers and other employees of the Government Code and Cypher School, the Telecommunications Research Establishment, and the Dollis Hill Research Station of the British Post Office.

Character: Electronic.

Purpose: Decryption of ciphers.

Description and Accomplishments: Colossus was a special-purpose computer built to assist in the decryption of German military codes in World War II. It contained more than one thousand vacuum tubes and proved that electronic technology was reliable enough for use in large and complex data-processing systems. Colossus enabled the Allies to decode intercepted German radio messages and obtain intelligence vital to the Allied victory. Because of security requirements no detailed information was released about Colossus until thirty years after the war.

### Electronic Delay Storage Automatic Computer (EDSAC)

When Built: Late 1940s.

Where: Computation Laboratory, Cambridge University, Great Britain.

Designed By: Maurice Wilkes and others.

Character: Electronic.

Purpose: General.

Description and Accomplishments: EDSAC was a British version of the American EDVAC and used much of the same technology, including mercury delay storage lines. It contributed greatly to the development of programming in Britain.

### Electronic Discrete Variable Computer (EDVAC)

When Built: Late 1940s.

Where: Moore School of Engineering, University of Pennsylvania.

Designed By: John Brainerd, J. Presper Eckert, Jr., John Mauchly, and others.

Character: Electronic.

Purpose: General.

Description and Accomplishments: EDVAC moved well beyond the technology of ENIAC, especially in the use of mercury delay storage lines—a technique adapted from radar technology—in computer memories. The EDVAC project also witnessed the application of the stored-program concept.

### Electronic Numerical Integrator And Calculator (ENIAC)

When Built: Early 1940s.

Where: Moore School.

Designed By: Brainerd, Eckert, Mauchly, and others.

Character: Electronic.

Purpose: General, though initially intended as a high-speed electronic integrator for ballistics research.

Description and Accomplishments: ENIAC is often cited as the first general-purpose digital electronic computer. It was built to help with calculations in preparing firing tables for the Army's Ballistics Research Laboratory at Aberdeen, Maryland, during World War II, but was not finished until the close of the war. ENIAC was technically an electronic integrator but actually had capabilities far beyond integration alone. It was the largest electronic device built to that date and incorporated high-speed multiplication circuitry. ENIAC demonstrated, as Colossus also did, that electronic components were suitable for use in fast, reliable, and versatile calculating machinery. ENIAC functioned without serious problems for a decade after its installation and was still in good working order when dismantled in 1955.

## Heath Robinson

When Built: Early 1940s.
Where Built: Bletchley Park, England.
Designed By: Thomas H. Flowers et al.
Character: Electronic.
Purpose: Decryption of ciphers.
Description and Accomplishments: A forerunner of Colossus, Heath Robinson was a high-speed electronic computer designed for analysis of German ciphers during World War II. Heath Robinson used coded tapes in a process similar to that used in D. H. Lehmer's number sieves. Among its other achievements, Heath Robinson helped to demonstrate the feasibility of all-electronic binary computing machines.

## Hollerith Tabulator

When Built: 1880s.
Where Built: United States.
Designed By: Herman Hollerith.
Character: Electromechanical.
Purpose: Automatic tabulation of census data.
Description and Accomplishments: Herman Hollerith created his automatic tabulating machine to assist in processing data from the U.S. national census. He used electrical circuitry to record and tabulate numerical data fed into the machine on punched cards. Hollerith's machine was so successful that he founded a company to manufacture it for commercial uses. That company later grew to become International Business Machines (IBM). The "IBM card" of today is essentially the same as those Hollerith used in his machine. Hollerith's punched-card system

was used for data storage and entry until well into the twentieth century.

### Institute for Advanced Studies (IAS) Computer

When Built: Late 1940s.

Where: Institute for Advanced Studies, Princeton, New Jersey.

Designed By: John von Neumann, Arthur Burks, Herman Goldstine.

Character: Electronic.

Purpose: General.

Description and Accomplishments: An outgrowth of ENIAC and EDVAC, the IAS computer was only partly successful due to problems with a memory mechanism based on wire wound around pulleys. The principal contribution of the IAS computer was the establishment of a pattern, including methods of funding, for other, subsequent computer projects.

### Kelvin Differential Analyzer

When Built: Conceived in the late 1800s but never constructed.

Where: Great Britain.

Designed By: Lord Kelvin.

Character: Mechanical.

Purpose: To solve differential equations.

Description and Accomplishments: The Kelvin differential analyzer was a precursor of the Bush integraph and was intended for the same purposes, but it could not be built because of a technical problem with one of its components. Bush corrected that problem half a century later and used Kelvin's ideas to build a successful differential analyzer.

### Pilot Automatic Computing Engine (ACE)

When Built: Late 1940s.

Where: National Physical Laboratory, Great Britain.

Designed By: Alan Turing and others.

Character: Electronic.

Purpose: General.

Description and Accomplishments: The Pilot ACE was a prototype for an ENIAC-like electronic computer that Alan Turing had been planning since before World War II. One of the goals of the Pilot ACE was to use programming to accomplish what previous machines had done through the use of new hardware. Thus the Pilot ACE placed an unprecedented emphasis on the quality of software. Turing left the project in 1947, before it was completed.

### Standards Eastern Automatic Computer (SEAC) and Standards Western Automatic Computer (SWAC)

When Built: Late 1940s.

Where: Washington, D.C., and Los Angeles, California.

Designed By: National Bureau of Standards.

Character: Electronic.

Purpose: To determine how quickly computers could be built uising only existing technology.

Description and Accomplishments: SEAC was the first stored-program computer to be completed in the United States; SWAC was the second. SEAC was also the first computer to use all-diode logic, and the two computers demonstrated the feasibility of systems much like the solid state computers of the 1950s and 1960s.

### Zuse Z-Series

When Built: Late 1930s, early 1940s.

Where: Germany.

Designed By: Konrad Zuse.

Character: Mechanical and electromechanical.

Purpose: General.

Description and Accomplishments: Zuse's Z-computers were originally designed to help with calculations in aeronautical engineering. They were remarkable in that Zuse developed the machines in virtual ignorance of other, similar projects under way abroad, as well as of the work of Charles Babbage.

# GLOSSARY

**Abacus.** Ancient Chinese calculating device using beads moved along metal rods to represent numbers and operations; in more modern machines, an electronic apparatus built of condensers or other electronic parts.

**Accumulator.** A component of early computers that held numbers to be operated upon.

**Algorithm.** An approach to solving a problem or calculation; in general terms, a calculating technique.

**Amplifier.** A circuit or other apparatus for increasing the strength of an electronic signal.

**Analog Computer.** A computing device that substitutes a mechanism, such as the opening and shutting of switches or the rotation of mechanical rods, for operations on numbers. Analog computers are easy to build but given to inaccuracy.

**Ballistics.** The science and mathematics of bodies in unpowered flight. Ballistics played an important role in the development of electronic computers, because fast and powerful calculating machines were needed to carry out ballistic analysis required for preparing firing tables for artillery.

**Binary Arithmetic.** The base-2 counting system in which the decimal number 1 is 1, 2 is 10, 3 is 11, et cetera.

**Capacitors.** Electronic components that store electrical charges somewhat in the manner of a jar filled with water.

**Coefficient.** A number used to multiply some variable or other quantity; the coefficient of $10x$, for instance, is 10.

**Condenser.** A small electronic component used to receive and store an electrical charge.

**Correlation.** A statistical link between two variables. Height, for instance, is correlated with weight; the taller a person is, the more he or she is likely to weigh.

**Cryptanalysis.** Codebreaking. Many of the early British electronic computers were designed to crack Nazi military codes during World War II.

**Cybernetics.** In a broad sense, the science of information control;

the word was derived from the Greek *Kybernetes*, "Steersman," by Norbert Wiener, the originator of cybernetic theory.

**Decimal System.** The familiar base-10 counting system (1,2,3,-4,5 . . .).

**Delay Storage Line.** A device first used in radar systems but later adapted for use in computer memories. The delay storage line consisted of a tube that was filled with mercury and stored data in the form of acoustical vibrations rippling back and forth through the liquid metal. Data were entered into the tube through piezoelectric quartz crystal plugs at either end. *See Piezoelectric Materials.*

**Difference Equations.** A simplified version of differential equations. *See Differential Equations.*

**Differential Equations.** A branch of mathematics used to describe changes in variables over time.

**Digital Computer.** A kind of computer that performs operations on numbers without substituting anything (as analog computers do) for the numbers and the operations. Most modern electronic computers are digital, because digital machines are inherently much more accurate than analog computers.

**Electrode.** One of the two terminals, positive or negative, of an electric source.

**Fourier Analysis.** A branch of mathematics used to break down complex wave patterns into their component parts, or harmonics. *See Harmonics.*

**Function.** In mathematics, a variable quantity whose value depends on and changes with the value of another quantity. In plain language, a function is a direct connection between two changing factors. Auto accidents are a function of alcohol consumption, for example.

**General-Purpose Computer.** A computing device suitable for a wide range of applications, not merely for one specific job, such as isolating prime numbers or breaking codes.

**Harmonics.** In Fourier analysis, harmonics are the individual components of a wave pattern—the little individual waves that are added together to make up the patterns as a whole. Isolating harmonics was a concern of computer designers in the late nineteenth and early twentieth centuries. *See Fourier Analysis.*

**Hydrodynamics.** Very generally speaking, the mathematics of fluid motion. The solution of complex equations in hydrodynamics was one of the requirements that led to the development of the first electronic computers.

**Input.** Information going into a system. If you ask a computer to solve the equation $2 + 2 = ?$, the input is $2 + 2$. *See Output.*

**Integraph.** A computer used to carry out integration. *See Integration.*

**Integration.** The mathematical technique used to find the area underneath a curve. Integration is an important part of the calculus and the mathematics of motion in general.

**Integrator.** In a general sense, any device that performs integration; more specifically, an arrangement of glass discs that was used for this purpose in certain preelectronic computers.

**Iterative.** Repetitive. Complex equations such as those involved in differential analysis can be converted into a form suitable for computers by breaking down the equations into longer iterative equations where the more sophisticated mathematical processes are reduced to long strings of additions, subtractions, or whatever.

**Jogging.** A term coined by John V. Atanasoff to describe the continual refreshment of computer memory as one draws on it.

**Logarithms.** Expressions of numbers as decimal fractions of powers of 10, or of some other given base number. Logarithms simplify calculations by eliminating the need to juggle large numbers in their entirety; instead the numbers may be represented by logarithms, so that the calculation goes much faster and more smoothly. The logarithm to the base 10 of 1984, for example, is 3.297541668. That means that 1984 equals 10 multiplied by itself approximately three and a third times.

**Matrix.** In mathematics, an array of coefficients with a given whole number of elements on a side; in electronics, a crisscross arrangement of wires or other components in a circuit. A mathematical matrix of the dimensions 3 × 3, for example, might look like this:

$$
\begin{matrix}
1 & 2 & 3 \\
4 & 5 & 6 \\
7 & 8 & 9
\end{matrix}
$$

**Modules.** In computers, ready-made "plug-in" components that can be inserted or withdrawn easily for repair or replacement without having to shut down the whole computer.

**Multiplicand.** The number being multiplied by something else in a multiplication problem. *See Multiplier.*

**Multiplier.** The number doing the multiplying in a multiplication problem. *See Multiplicand.*

**Multiprocessor.** A computer or computer component capable of doing several different operations at once.

**Number Sieve.** A device designed to isolate prime numbers. Number sieves were the first machines to use much of the technology that would later go into the making of more sophisticated, general-purpose computers. *See General-Purpose Computer, Prime Numbers.*

Output. Information that comes out of a system, usually in the form of solutions to equations. In the case of the equation $2 + 2 = 4$, the number 4 is the output. *See Input.*

Parallel Processor. A computer that can handle more than one operation at one time, all in a coordinated fashion. Parallel processing was used on many early electronic computers as a time-saving measure but was largely abandoned when high-speed electronic computers became available. *See Serial Processor, Von Neumann Machine.*

Photocells. Light-sensing devices used in number sieves and early electronic codebreaking computers. *See Number Sieve.*

Piezoelectric materials. Certain kinds of quartz, ceramics, and other materials that deform spontaneously when subjected to an electric current, and/or generate an electric current when deformed.

Prime Numbers. Whole numbers divisible only by themselves and one. The total number of prime numbers is theoretically infinite. They have many uses, including the making and breaking of codes.

Program. A set of instructions and data to be entered into a computer.

Rectifier. An electronic device, such as a vacuum tube, that converts alternating current into direct current.

Relays. Electromechanical or mechanical devices that flip open or shut to control circuits and transmit information.

Resistor. An electronic component that puts up resistance to electrical current and changes that current into heat.

Serial Processor. A computing device that carries out operations one at a time, in rigid sequence, all the way to the end of the program. Unlike the parallel processor, a serial processor can do only one thing at a time. *See Parallel Processor.*

Stored Program. A program in which instructions are fed into a computer along with data to be analyzed. The instructions are, in a sense, indistinguishable from the data. This arrangement allows the computer to modify the program as needed. The stored-program concept was pioneered at the Moore School of Engineering at the University of Philadelphia during and after the Second World War.

Subroutine. A subdivision of a computer program in which the computer temporarily halts what it is doing, performs another task for a while, then returns to its previous task at the point where it left off. The "GOSUB ... RETURN" loop in BASIC programming for home computers is a familiar example of a subroutine.

**Summation.** In mathematics, a total or aggregate of many different individual quantities or terms.

**Thermionic.** Using heat to produce electrons, as in a thermionic vacuum tube.

**Thyratron.** A device much like a vacuum tube but slower in operation. *See Vacuum Tube.*

**Torque.** A twisting or rotating motion.

**Vacuum Tube.** A sealed glass or metal tube containing a near-vacuum and three electronic components: a cathode (filament), an anode (plate), and a grid to channel the flow of electrons between cathode and anode. The vacuum tube has many uses and may serve, for example, as a rectifier or amplifier. *See Amplifier, Rectifier.*

**Valve.** A British expression for vacuum tube. *See Vacuum Tube.*

**Von Neumann Machine.** Very generally speaking, an electronic digital computer that operates exclusively in serial mode. The design of the von Neumann machine originated with the Hungarian-born American mathematician John von Neumann.

# A
# NOTE
# ON
# SOURCES

As Robert Caro wrote in his biography of Lyndon Johnson, bibliographies tend to be exercises in pedantry. Therefore a brief summary of information sources will suffice here.

The overall outline of computer history has been told many times, and among the best introductions to the subject are Herman Goldstine's *The Computer from Pascal to Von Neumann;* Brian Randell's *The Origins of Digital Computers;* and *A History of Computing in the Twentieth Century,* edited by Metropolis et al. The Goldstine and Metropolis works provide much helpful information on early mechanical computer technology, as well as some interesting anecdotes about von Neumann and his working methods.

## Pre-Electronic Computers

An excellent source of material on the evolution of mechanical computers is M. R. Williams's article, "From Napier to Lucas: The Use of Napier's Bones," in the July 1983 issue of *Annals of the History of Computing.* Williams's article contains a colorful story about a mystery surrounding a famous seventeeth-century calculating device.

The Pascaline, the Schickard calculator, the Leibniz wheel, and the Kelvin machines are described in detail in Goldstine's book and in the Williams article. Vannevar Bush's popular writings seldom touch on the subject of computers (he preferred not to burden his readers with exhaustive discussions of hardware), but he refers briefly to his Rapid Selector in his book *Pieces of the Action*. For an example of Bush's prescient views on the future—and the social cost—of technology, see his thoughts on the Apollo moonflight project, in Erik Bergaust's book *Murder on Pad 34*. Bush and his colleague Samuel Caldwell describe the structure and operation of the MIT differential analyzer in a May 1931 article for the *Journal of the Franklin Institute:* "The Differential Analyzer, a New Machine for Solving Differential Equations."

### Norbert Wiener

Wiener was one of the most colorful figures in the history of computing in the early twentieth century, and many memoirs of him exist. He wrote many works that are easily accessible to the non-mathematician, including a two-volume autobiography, *Ex-Prodigy* and *I Am a Mathematician*, and a still relevant warning about the misuse of automation, *The Human Use of Human Beings*. His book *Cybernetics* is rewarding for readers with the requisite background in higher mathematics. Perhaps the best biography of Wiener is Steve Heims's *John von Neumann and Norbert Wiener: From Mathematics to the Technologies of Life and Death*, a huge and painstakingly researched study of the two great mathematicians and their work. See also Dirk Struik's memoir, "Norbert Wiener, Colleague and Friend," in the March/April 1966 issue of *American Dialog*, and Norman Levinson's article, "Wiener's Life," in *Bulletin of the American Mathematical Society*, January 1966.

### Stibitz and the Bell Computers

Historians owe a debt of gratitude to George Stibitz for making himself so readily available for interviews and for taking so much trouble to provide written recollections of his work on the Bell computers. A two-part interview with Stibitz, conducted by Evelyn Loveday, was published in the April and May 1967 issues of *Datamation*, and is full of juicy anecdotes about the machines and their making. Stibitz also has a short but entertaining essay in the Metropolis anthology. Much of the material in this book concerning Stibitz's work came from Stibitz's own memoir, "I Remember," and from his address at the Computer Museum in Boston. A complete catalogue of

Stibitz's papers is available from Dartmouth College under the title *An Inventory of the Papers of George Robert Stibitz Concerning the Invention and Development of the Digital Computer.*

## Aiken and Zuse

Most of Aiken's works are highly technical and therefore unlikely to appeal to the average reader, but his memorandum, "Proposed Automatic Calculating Machine," is well worth reading and is available in the August 1964 issue of *IEEE Spectrum.* Not so easy to find, but rewarding, is *A Manual of Operation for the Automatic Sequence Controlled Calculator,* published in 1946 and still available from Harvard University.

Garrett Birkhoff's brief paper in the Metropolis anthology contains an interesting, though rather unflattering, portrayal of Aiken the man; and Henry Tropp's recollections, in the same book, throw light on Aiken's decision to stay with electromechanical technology for what might have seemed an unreasonably long time. The Tropp piece should be read in combination with Cuthbert C. Herd's article "Aiken Observed," in the April 1984 *Annals,* and M. R. Williams's article "Howard Aiken and the Harvard Computation Laboratory," in the same issue.

Aiken's connection with Thomas Watson, Sr., and IBM is outlined in Goldstine's book, and there is an interesting verbal portrait of Watson as an executive in Peter Drucker's article "Thomas Watson's Principles of Modern Management," in the December 1983 *Esquire.* Thomas Watson, Jr.'s slighting reference to Aiken and the ASCC may be found in his memoir of IBM, *A Business and Its Beliefs.*

Captain Grace Hopper has written several entertaining accounts of her work with Aiken on the ASCC project; she explains in the Fall 1983 *Computer Museum Report* how Aiken visualized the ASCC (and how he put her on the spot by telling her she was going to write a book about the computer!). In the July 1981 *Annals* she tells the story of how the word *debugging* originated, in her short article "The First Bug."

## ENIAC

Much of Goldstine's book describes—sometimes in mind-numbing detail—the design and building of the ENIAC. Mauchly and Eckert contributed two pieces of primary source material in their essays on the ENIAC in the Metropolis anthology. Arthur Burks is also represented in the Metropolis collection with a splendid essay on ENIAC, its descendants, and the origin of the stored-program concept.

The October 1981 *Annals* contains what is probably the best single short account of the making of ENIAC: Arthur and Alice Burks's essay on the ENIAC and its genesis, with commentary by many of the scientists and engineers involved with the project and the subsequent patent trial. Interesting secondary sources on the ENIAC's history include M. H. Weik's article "The ENIAC Story" in the *Journal of the American Ordnance Association*, January and Feburary 1961. "J. G. Brainerd on the ENIAC," in the January 1982 *Annals* is also an interesting and concise introduction to the ENIAC project.

## Colossus and Heath Robinson

Colossus and Heath Robinson are described in exhaustive detail in a set of essays in the July 1983 *Annals*, by Thomas Flowers, Allen Coombs, and W. W. Chandler. Also recommended are I. J. Good's memoir of his work at Bletchley, in the Metropolis anthology, and Ronald Lewin's absorbing history of the ULTRA project, "Ultra Goes to War." Other historians touch on the workings of Heath Robinson and Colossus in their writings about the Bletchley group, notably F. W. Winterbotham in *The Ultra Secret*, Cave Brown in *Bodyguard of Lies*, and R. V. Jones in *The Wizard War*. Brian Johnson's well-written and splendidly illustrated work *The Secret War*, based on the BBC-TV series, contains an excellent short history of the Heath Robinson and Colossus projects and a clear exposition of the ENIGMA's operation.

## The SSEC

Published only a few years ago and already a classic in its field, Katherine Davis Fishman's *The Computer Establishment* contains a few pages on the SSEC and its role as IBM's revenge on Howard Aiken. Fishman deals primarily with the rise of IBM and RCA as computer "superpowers"; however, she also devotes part of her book to the origin of the concept of the electronic digital computer, specifically the roles of Eckert, Mauchly, and Atanasoff in the making of the modern computer. See also Byron Phelps's article "Early Electronic Computer Developments at IBM," in the July 1980 *Annals*.

## Mauchly, Atanasoff, and the ABC

The best single source of information on the ABC and its genesis is Atanasoff's own article, "Advent of Electronic Digital Computing," in the July 1984 *Annals*. This article essentially recapitulates what Atanasoff had said in earlier speeches and in his court testimony during the ENIAC trial. There is also a short but informative discussion of the ABC and its importance to electronic digital computing in the Burks article on ENIAC, in the October 1981 *Annals*. For additional information on Atanasoff—and a markedly different viewpoint on his work—see Kathleen Mauchly's article, "John Mauchly's Early Years," in the September 1984 *Annals*, and Nancy Stern's obituary for Mauchly, "John William Mauchly: 1907–1980," in the April 1980 issue.

### Additional Material

The Computer Museum in Boston kindly provided some of the material that went into this book, and several issues of *The Computer Museum Report* were especially helpful. Maurice Wilkes, in the Fall 1983 issue, contributes a bright little curiosity in the form of a two-scene playlet about the life of Charles Babbage; the same issue contains a brief report by Captain Grace Hopper on her work with Howard Aiken on the ASCC at Harvard. The Winter 1983 issue is devoted to the Pioneer Computer Timeline exhibit at the Computer Museum and introduces about a dozen of the most important machines, from the Stibitz K-Model to Whirlwind, in chronological order, with abundant illustrations and quotations from the computers' makers.

Most valuable of all the material provided by the Computer Museum was a set of transcripts of lectures delivered by the computer pioneers themselves at the Museum over the past few years. These included Bernard Gordon's recollections of the Eckert Mauchly Computer Company (October 20, 1983), J. V. Atanasoff's lecture on the ABC (November 11, 1980), R. F. Clippinger's address on the ENIAC (September 26, 1982), Maurice Wilkes's account of the debugging problems on EDSAC (September 23, 1979), George Stibitz's description of the birth of the K-Model and the Bell Labs Model 1 (May 8, 1980), T. H. Flowers's speech on the design and use of Colossus (October 15, 1981), and John Grist Brainerd's address on the development of ENIAC (June 25, 1981).

# RECOMMENDED READINGS

There is a large literature on the history of computers, and interested readers may wish to consult some of the following works for additional information:

Austrian, G. *Herman Hollerith: Forgotten Giant of Information Processing.* New York: Columbia University Press, 1982. Hollerith is not exactly forgotten, but he deserves more attention than he usually gets in histories of the computer, and Austrian's book is a fine introduction to Hollerith, his work, and his place in the history of technology.

Bell, G. "A Companion to the Pioneer Computer Timeline." *The Computer Museum Report,* Winter 1983, pp. 1–15. A short, colorful, and lavishly illustrated guide to computers on exhibit at the Computer Museum in Boston.

Bernstein, J. *The Analytical Engine.* New York: Random House, 1964 (Newly rev: Morrow, 1981). An entertaining introduction to computers in general and to the work of Babbage and other computer pioneers in particular.

Bromley, A. "What Defines a 'General-Purpose' Computer?" *Annals of the History of Computing,* July 1983, pp. 303–305. Before we can say who invented the general-purpose electronic computer, we have to determine what constitutes such a computer, and Bromley's note shows how difficult that definition can be.

Burchard, H. "Reading Hitler's Mail." *The Washington Post*, March 27, 1981. Burchard has harsh words for a 1981 Smithsonian Institution exhibit of computing machinery that included a German ENIGMA machine. He discusses the long-neglected role of U.S. cryptanalysts during World War II and refutes a claim, made by the exhibition, that Turing's Bombe was originally developed in Poland. A fine, succinct piece of reporting.

Burks, A., and Burks, A. "The ENIAC: First General-Purpose Electronic Computer." *Annals of the History of Computing*, October 1981, pp. 310–400. One of the landmark papers in the history of computer literature, this survey describes the design and building of ENIAC as well as what it may or may not have owed to the earlier Atanasoff calculator. Included at the end of the paper are comments by Atanasoff, John Grist Brainerd, J. Presper Eckert, Kathleen Mauchly, Brian Randell, and Konrad Zuse.

Bush, V. *Pieces of the Action*. New York: Morrow, 1970. Vannevar Bush's semi-autobiographical memoir includes a description of his Rapid Selector.

Chandler, W. "The Installation and Maintenance of Colossus." *Annals of the History of Computing*, July 1983, pp. 260–262. Chandler describes what it took to keep the biggest computer in Europe running.

Coombs, A. "The Making of Colossus." *Annals of the History of Computing*, July 1983, pp. 253–259. Coombs provides a witty and engrossing account of how Colossus was built and set in operation.

Fishman, K. *The Computer Establishment*. New York: Harper and Row, 1981. Fishman deals primarily with the history of the computer industry (with special emphasis on IBM and RCA) after the closing of the Newton-Maxwell gap, but she includes some interesting sections on Atanasoff, Eckert, Mauchly, and the ENIAC trial.

Fleck, G., ed. *A Computer Perspective*. Cambridge, Mass.: Harvard University Press, 1973. An outstanding and well-illustrated book based on an IBM exhibition; highly recommended.

Flowers, T. "The Design of Colossus." *Annals of the History of Computing*, July 1983, pp. 239–252. One of the makers of Colossus describes how it evolved from the earlier Heath Robinson machine and what was involved in making a giant parallel processor run smoothly.

Forrester, J. "Conversation: Jay W. Forrester." *Annals of the History of Computing*, July 1983, pp. 297–301. In this interview with

Christopher Evans of the Smithsonian Computer Hisory Project, Forrester describes how he came upon the idea for the magnetic core memory. Forrester's comments are an enlightening adjunct to his remarks on Project Whirlwind in the Metropolis volume.

Goldstine, H. *The Computer from Pascal to Von Neumann*. Princeton, N.J.: Princeton University Press, 1972. A classic in the literature of computers, written from the viewpoint of one of von Neumann's disciples. It is interesting to compare and contrast Goldstine's views of von Neumann and his work with the opinions expressed by Eckert and Mauchly in the Metropolis anthology. Goldstine includes a brief but detailed account of computer development before 1900.

Heims, S. *John von Neumann and Norbert Wiener: From Mathematics to the Technologies of Life and Death*. Cambridge, Mass.: M.I.T. Press, 1980. Heims's book is one of the finest examples of scientific biography, neither too advanced for the average reader nor too simplistic for the professional historian. Heims says little about the genesis of computers here but provides valuable insights into the roles that Wiener, the pacifist academic, and von Neumann, the archetypical technocrat, played in the evolution of applied mathematics.

Holbrook, B. *Bell Laboratories and the Computer from the Late 30's to the Middle 60's*. Murray Hill, New Jersey: Bell Laboratories, 1975. The Bell Labs Model 1 through Model 5 are discussed along with the design and construction techniques used on them.

McCorduck, P. *Machines Who Think*. San Francisco: W. H. Freeman, 1979. A spicy, rambling, and entertaining study of computers and the debate over artificial intelligence, McCorduck's book opens with a short but useful discussion of the evolution of computing machinery from early mechanical devices to the microchip computers of today.

Metropolis, N., J. Howlett, and G.-C. Rota, eds. *A History of Computing in the Twentieth Century*. New York: Academic Press, 1980. A scholarly but revealing collection of papers originally presented at the International Research Conference on the History of Computing, held at Los Alamos in 1976, this volume includes accounts by Eckert, Mauchly, Stibitz, and others of their own work. Several essays deal in detail with the controversy over the origin of the stored-program concept and the outcome of the ENIAC patent trial. I. J. Good and Brian Randell describe the genesis of Heath Robinson and Colossus; Stanislaw Ulam contributes an interesting memoir of John von Neumann; J. H. Wilkinson discusses at length Turing's work on the Pilot ACE and other postwar computers; and Garrett Birkhoff reminisces about Howard Aiken's stormy career at Harvard.

Morrison, P., and Morrison, E., eds. *Charles Babbage and his Cal-*

*culating Engines.* New York: Dover, 1961. The Morrisons reveal in this biography of Babbage how painful it must be to have a great idea far in advance of its time.

Randell, B., ed. *The Origins of Digital Computers: Selected Papers.* Berlin: Springer-Verlag, 1975. Randell's book is one of the most important sources of historical information on the development of computers.

————. "The Colossus." In Metropolis et al., eds., *A History of Computing in the Twentieth Century.* Randell's list of references for this paper is impressive and invaluable.

Rochester, J., and Gantz, J. *The Naked Computer.* New York: Morrow, 1983. Lively and irreverent, this grab bag of computer fact and folklore is a pleasant antidote to more scholarly treatments of computer history and gives the reader a nice sense of the human side of computer development over the past half century.

Von Neumann, J. *The Computer and the Brain.* New Haven: Yale University Press, 1958. Based on the series of lectures von Neumann prepared shortly before his death, this work is fascinating for its analysis of the similarities and differences between the human brain and the computer.

Wiener, N. *Cybernetics.* Cambridge, Mass.: M.I.T. Press, 1961. Wiener's exposition of his theory of cybernetics; extremely heavy reading for the layman, but rewarding.

# INDEX